MACHINE LEARNING FOR DATA STREAMS
with Practical Examples in MOA

Adaptive Computation and Machine Learning

Francis Bach, Editor

Christopher Bishop, David Heckerman, Michael Jordan, and Michael Kearns, Associate Editors

A complete list of books published in The Adaptive Computation and Machine Learning series appears at the back of this book.

MACHINE LEARNING FOR DATA STREAMS
with Practical Examples in MOA

Albert Bifet
Ricard Gavaldà
Geoff Holmes
Bernhard Pfahringer

The MIT Press
Cambridge, Massachusetts
London, England

This book was set in Times Roman and Mathtime Pro 2 by the authors.

Library of Congress Cataloging-in-Publication Data is available

ISBN: 978-0-262-03779-2 (hardcover)
ISBN: 978-0-262-54783-3 (paperback)

Contents

List of Figures

List of Tables

Preface

Streaming data analysis in real time is becoming the standard to obtain useful knowledge from what is happening right now, allowing organizations to react quickly when problems appear, or to detect new trends, helping them to improve their performance. This book presents many of the algorithms and techniques that are currently used in the field of data stream mining. A software framework that implements many of the techniques explained in this book is available from the Web as the open-source project called MOA.

The goal of this book is to present the techniques in data stream mining to three specific groups of readers:

1. Readers who want to use stream mining as a tool, who do not have a strong background in algorithmics or programming, but do have a basic background in data mining. An example would be students or professionals in fields such as management, business intelligence, or marketing. We provide a hands-on introduction to MOA, in a task-oriented (not algorithm-oriented) way.

2. Readers who want to do research or innovation in data stream mining. They would like to know details of the algorithms, evaluation methods, and so on, in order to create new algorithms or use existing ones, evaluate their performance, and possibly include them in their applications. This group comprises advanced undergraduate, master's, and PhD students in computing or data science, as well as developers in innovative environments.

3. Readers who, in addition to the above, want to try including new algorithms in MOA, possibly contributing them to the project. They need to know the class structure of MOA and how to create, for instance, new learners for MOA.

To achieve this goal, the book is divided in three parts. Part I is a quick introduction to big data stream mining. It is structured in three chapters: two that introduce big data mining and basic methodologies for mining data streams, and a hands-on chapter on using MOA for readers who prefer to get started and explore on their own.

For a longer course on data stream mining, part II of the book presents a detailed explanation of the problems in data stream mining and the most important algorithms. Since this is a vast area, some priority has been given to the methods that have been implemented in MOA. It starts with a chapter covering sketching techniques, which in our opinion deserve to be better known (and used) by the stream mining community. Most of the chapters contain a set of exercises or an MOA-based lab session, or both.

Finally, part III is devoted to the MOA software. It covers its use via the graphical user interface and via the command line, and moves to using MOA via its API, and implementing new methods within MOA.

Readers of type 1 should read part I, possibly chapter 11 for a broad view of MOA's ecosystem, and then chapter 12 for other options available from the MOA GUI.

Readers of type 2 should read part I, at least sections 4.1 to 4.3 (and more of chapter 4 if they are interested in sketches), chapter 5, and chapter 6. After that, they can read chapters 7 to 10 pretty much independently according to their interests. Then they should continue to chapters 11 to 14 if they plan to call MOA from their applications.

Readers of type 3 should in addition read Chapter 15.

The accompanying website

`https://mitpress.mit.edu/books/data-stream-mining`

will contain updates and corrections to the book, slides, additional sets of exercises and lab sessions, and other course material. Contributions by readers are welcome.

Several books on data stream mining have emerged over the last decade. The books edited by Garofalakis, Gehrke, and Rastogi on data stream management [118], and by Aggarwal on data streams [4], cover some common topics with the material presented here, but the perspective of these books is more from the very-large-database community rather than from the data mining or machine learning communities.

The latter perspective is very much present in the book by Gama [110], who covers a similar territory but does not include a common framework for development and evaluation as provided by MOA. Rather, the book presents pseudo-code of algorithms, some of which are implemented in MOA and some not. As such, it is a very useful companion to this book.

To keep up with this rapidly developing field, we recommend regular reading of the proceedings of the following conferences: Knowledge Discovery in Databases (KDD), International Conference on Data Mining (ICDM), Symposium on Applied Computing (SAC) – has a track on data streams, European Conference on Machine Learning and Principles and Practice of Knowledge Discovery in Databases (ECML PKDD), SIAM Conference on Data Mining (SDM), and Data Science and Advanced Analytics (DSAA).

To date, there is no dedicated journal on data stream mining, so articles appear on the topic across a number of journals too numerous to list.

Acknowledgments. We would like to thank the following groups of people, who have contributed to this book and the software behind it. It is not possible to mention all by name, either because the names are unknown to us (e.g., the reviewers) or because the list is long and we may inadvertently miss someone (e.g., our coauthors or the many students and other people who have contributed to MOA by asking questions, pointing out bugs, and so forth, on the mailing list, or those who have directly contributed code).

We would like to thank the people at MIT Press, and in particular Marie Lufkin Lee, Christine Bridget Savage, and Kathleen Hensley, for their assistance.

It is worth acknowledging that the inspiration for this project and book came from the groundbreaking work of the WEKA project.

For those authors working in the area of stream mining, we would like to apologize in advance if your work is not mentioned in the book. Such a state of affairs will have arisen because of space limitations, ignorance, or the wrong choice on our part.

Work by Ricard Gavaldà has been partially supported by the MACDA project of Generalitat de Catalunya (SGR2014-0890) and by the APCOM project of MINECO (TIN2014-57226).

I INTRODUCTION

1 Introduction

Nowadays, we are creating a huge amount of data every day from all kinds of devices, in different formats, from independent or connected applications. This flood of big data has outpaced our capability to process, analyze, store, and understand these datasets. This rapid expansion is accelerated by the dramatic increase in acceptance of social networking applications, which allow users to create content freely and increase the already huge size of the Web.

Furthermore, with mobile phones becoming the sensory gateway to get real-time data on people from different aspects, the vast amount of data that mobile carriers can potentially process to improve our daily life has significantly outpaced our past call data record-based processing, which was designed only for billing purposes. We can foresee that Internet of Things applications will raise the scale of data to an unprecedented level. People and devices (from home coffee machines to cars, to buses, railway stations, and airports) are all loosely connected. Trillions of such connected components will generate a huge data ocean, and valuable information must be discovered from the data to help improve our quality of life and make our world a better place. For example, after we get up every morning, in order to optimize our commute time to work and complete the optimization before we arrive at the office, the system needs to process information from traffic, weather, construction, police activities, and our calendar schedules, and perform deep optimization under tight time constraints.

To deal with this staggeringly large quantity of data, we need fast and efficient methods that operate in real time using a reasonable amount of resources.

1.1 Big Data

It is not really useful to define *big data* in terms of a specific dataset size, for example, on the order of petabytes. A more useful definition is that the dataset is too large to be managed without using nonstandard algorithms or technologies, particularly if it is to be used for extracting knowledge.

While twenty years ago people were struggling with gigabytes, at the time of writing this book the corresponding memory unit in table 1.1 is between the terabyte and the petabyte. There is no question that in a further twenty years, we will be a few lines down from this point.

Big data was characterized by Laney in [154] by the three Vs of big data management:

Table 1.1
Memory units in multiples of bytes.

Memory unit	Decimal Size	Binary size
kilobyte (kB, KB)	10^3	2^{10}
megabyte (MB)	10^6	2^{20}
gigabyte (GB)	10^9	2^{30}
terabyte (TB)	10^{12}	2^{40}
petabyte (PB)	10^{15}	2^{50}
exabyte (EB)	10^{18}	2^{60}
zettabyte (ZB)	10^{21}	2^{70}
yottabyte (YB)	10^{24}	2^{80}

- Volume: There is more data than ever before, and its size continues to increase, but not the percentage of data that our tools can process.
- Variety: There are many different types of data, such as text, sensor data, audio, video, graph, and more, from which we would like to extract information.
- Velocity: Data is arriving continuously in streams, and we are interested in obtaining useful information from it in real time.

Other Vs have been added since then:

- Variability: The structure of the data, or the way users want to interpret the data, changes over time.
- Value: Data is valuable only to the extent that it leads to better decisions, and eventually to a competitive advantage.
- Validity and Veracity: Some of the data may not be completely reliable, and it is important to manage this uncertainty.

Gartner [200] summarizes this in his definition of big data in 2012 as "high volume, velocity and variety information assets that demand cost-effective, innovative forms of information processing for enhanced insight and decision making."

Applications of big data should allow people to have better services and better customer experiences, and also be healthier:

- Business: Customer personalization and churn detection (customers moving from one company to a rival one).

- Technology: Reducing processing time from hours to seconds.

- Health: Mining people's medical records and genomics data, to monitor and improve their health.

- Smart cities: Cities focused on sustainable economic development and high quality of life, with wise management of natural resources.

As an example of the usefulness of big data mining, we refer to the work by Global Pulse [236], which uses big data to improve life in developing countries. Global Pulse is a United Nations initiative, functioning as an innovative lab, whose strategy is to mine big data for:

1. Researching innovative methods and techniques for analyzing real-time digital data to detect early emerging vulnerabilities.

2. Assembling a free and open-source technology toolkit for analyzing real-time data and sharing hypotheses.

3. Establishing an integrated, global network of Pulse Labs, to pilot the approach at the country level.

The big data mining revolution is not restricted to the industrialized world, as mobile devices are spreading in developing countries as well. It is estimated that there are over five billion mobile phones, and that 80% are located in developing countries.

1.1.1 Tools: Open-Source Revolution

The big data phenomenon is intrinsically related to the open-source software revolution. Large companies such as Yahoo!, Twitter, LinkedIn, Google, and Facebook both benefitted from and contributed to open-source projects. Some examples are:

- Apache Hadoop [16], a platform for data-intensive distributed applications, based on the MapReduce programming model and the Hadoop Distributed File system (HDFS). Hadoop allows us to write applications that quickly process large amounts of data in parallel on clusters of computing nodes.

- Projects related to Apache Hadoop [260]: Apache Pig, Apache Hive, Apache HBase, Apache ZooKeeper, Apache Cassandra, Cascading, Scribe, and

Apache Mahout [17], which is a scalable machine learning and data mining open-source software based mainly on Hadoop.

- Apache Spark [253], a data processing engine for large-scale data, running on the Hadoop infrastructure. Spark powers a stack of libraries including SQL and DataFrames, MLlib for machine learning, GraphX, and Spark Streaming. These libraries can be combined easily in the same application.

- Apache Flink [62], a streaming dataflow engine that provides data distribution, communication, and fault tolerance for distributed computations over data streams. Flink includes several APIs for creating applications that use the Flink engine. If Apache Spark is a batch data processing engine that can emulate streaming data processing with Spark Streaming using micro-batches of data, Apache Flink is a streaming data processing engine that can perform batch data processing.

- Apache Storm [168], software for streaming data-intensive distributed applications, similar to Apache S4 and Apache Samza.

- TensorFlow [1], an open-source package for machine learning and deep neural networks.

1.1.2 Challenges in Big Data

There are many challenges for the future in big data management and analytics, arising from the very nature of data: large, diverse, and evolving [128]. Some of the challenges that researchers and practitioners will have to deal with in the years to come are:

- Analytics architecture. It is not clear yet how an optimal architecture of an analytics system should be built to deal with historical data and with real-time data at the same time. A first proposal was the Lambda architecture of Nathan Marz [169]. The Lambda architecture solves the problem of computing arbitrary functions on arbitrary data in real time by decomposing the problem into three layers: the batch layer, the serving layer, and the speed layer. It combines in the same system Hadoop for the batch layer and Storm for the speed layer. A more recent proposal is the Kappa architecture, proposed by Kreps from LinkedIn [152]. It simplifies the Lambda architecture, removing the batch processing system.

- Evaluation. It is important to achieve significant statistical results, and not be fooled by randomness. If the "multiple hypothesis problem" is not properly cared for, it is easy to go wrong with huge datasets and thousands of questions to answer at once, as Efron explains [95]. Also, it will be important to avoid the trap of focusing only on technical measures such as error or speed instead of on eventual real-world impact, as discussed by Wagstaff [242]: arguing against those who believe that big data is all hype is only possible by regularly publishing applications that meet reasonable criteria for a challenge-problem in the sense explained in that paper.

- Distributed mining. Many data mining techniques are not trivial to parallelize. To have distributed versions of some methods, substantial research is needed with both practical experiments and theoretical analysis.

- Time-evolving data. Data may be evolving over time, so it is important that the big data mining techniques are able to adapt to, and in some cases explicitly detect, change. Many data stream mining techniques in this book are motivated by exactly this requirement [110].

- Compression. When dealing with big data, the quantity of space needed to store it is very relevant. There are two main approaches: compression, where we lose no information; and sampling, where we choose data that we deem representative. Using compression, we will use more time and less space, so we can consider it as a transformation from time to space. Using sampling, we are losing information, but the gains in space may be in orders of magnitude. For example Feldman et al. [99] use coresets to reduce the complexity of big data problems; a coreset is a small subset of the data that provably approximates the original data for a given problem.

- Visualization. A main issue in big data analysis is how to visualize the results. Presenting information from large amounts of data in a way that is understandable to humans is quite a challenge. It requires new techniques and frameworks to tell stories, such as those covered in the beautiful book *The Human Face of Big Data* [228].

- Hidden big data. Large quantities of useful data are in fact useless because they are untagged, file-based, and unstructured. The 2012 IDC study on big data [117] explained that, in 2012, 23% (643 exabytes) of the digital universe would be useful for big data if tagged and analyzed. However, at that time only 3% of the potentially useful data was tagged, and even less was analyzed. The figures have probably gotten worse in recent years. The Open Data and Semantic Web movements have emerged, in part, to make us aware and improve on this situation.

1.2   Real-Time Analytics

One particular case of the big data scenario is real-time analytics. It is important for organizations not only to obtain answers to queries immediately, but to do so according to the data that has just arrived.

1.2.1   Data Streams

Data streams are an algorithmic abstraction to support real-time analytics. They are sequences of items, possibly infinite, each item having a timestamp, and so a temporal order. Data items arrive one by one, and we would like to build and maintain models, such as patterns or predictors, of these items in real time. There are two main algorithmic challenges when dealing with streaming data: the stream is large and fast, and we need to extract information in real time from it. That means that usually we need to accept approximate solutions in order to use less time and memory. Also, the data may be evolving, so our models have to adapt when there are changes in the data.

1.2.2   Time and Memory

Accuracy, time, and memory are the three main resource dimensions of the stream mining process: we are interested in methods that obtain the maximum accuracy with minimum time and low total memory. It is possible, as we will show later, to reduce evaluation to a two-dimensional task, by combining memory and time in a single cost measure. Note also that, since data arrives at high speed, it cannot be buffered, so time to process one item is as relevant as the total time, which is the one usually considered in conventional data mining.

1.2.3   Applications

There are many scenarios of streaming data. Here we offer a few example areas:

- Sensor data and the Internet of Things: Every day, more sensors are used in industry to monitor processes, and to improve their quality. Cities are starting to implement huge networks of sensors to monitor the mobility of people and to check the health of bridges and roads, traffic in cities, people's vital constants, and so on.

- Telecommunication data: Telecommunication companies have large quantities of phone call data. Nowadays, mobile calls and mobile phone locations are huge sources of data to be processed, often in real-time.

- Social media: The users of social websites such as Facebook, Twitter, LinkedIn, and Instagram continuously produce data about their interactions and contributions. Topic and community discovery and sentiment analysis are but two of the real-time analysis problems that arise.

- Marketing and e-commerce: Sales businesses are collecting in real time large quantities of transactions that can be analyzed for value. Detecting fraud in electronic transactions is essential.

- Health care: Hospitals collect large amounts of time-sensitive data when caring for patients, for example, monitoring patient vital signs such as blood pressure, heart rate, and temperature. Telemedicine will also monitor patients when they are home, perhaps including data about their daily activity with separate sensors. Also, the system could have results of lab tests, pathology reports, X-rays, and digital imaging. Some of this data could be used in real time to provide warnings of changes in patient conditions.

- Epidemics and disasters: Data from streams originating in the Internet can be used to detect epidemics and natural disasters, and can be combined with official statistics from official centers for disease and disaster control and prevention [63].

- Computer security: Computer systems have to be protected from theft and damage to their hardware, software and information, as well as from disruption or misdirection of the services they provide, in particular, insider threat detection [11, 229] and intrusion detection [194, 195].

- Electricity demand prediction: Providers need to know some time in advance how much power their customers will be requesting. The figures change with time of day, time of year, geography, weather, state of the economy, customer habits, and many other factors, making it a complex prediction problem on massive, distributed data.

1.3   What This Book Is About

Among the many aspects of big data, this book focuses on mining and learning from data streams, and therefore on the techniques for performing data analytics on data that arrives in sequence at high speed. Of the Vs that define big data, the one we address most is therefore Velocity.

The techniques are illustrated in a hands-on way using MOA–Massive Online Analysis. MOA is the most popular open-source framework for data stream mining, with a very active growing community. It includes a collection of machine learning (ML) algorithms (classification, regression, clustering, pattern mining, outlier detection, change detection, and recommender systems) and tools for evaluation. Related to the WEKA project, MOA is also written in Java, while designed to scale to more demanding problems.

Part I is an introduction to the field of big data, an overview of the main techniques, and a first hands-on introduction to MOA usage. Part II presents in detail a good number of algorithms for stream mining, prioritizing those that have been implemented in MOA, and provides pointers to the relevant literature for the reader who is interested in more. Part III delves into MOA in more depth. It presents some additional hands-on exercises and some of the internal structure of MOA, oriented to readers who would like to add algorithms to MOA or modify existing ones, or use MOA through its API in their applications.

Finally, we would like to mention that there are other data stream mining techniques that are very useful and important, but that could not be covered in the book, such as matching problems, motif discovery, ranking/learning to rank, recommender systems, recurrent concept mining, geospatial data, and mining of large streaming graphs. Also, in real projects, aspects such as missing data, feature extraction, outlier detection, and forming training instances, among others, will be important; we do not cover them explicitly here as they tend to be highly problem-dependent.

2 Big Data Stream Mining

In this chapter we give a gentle introduction to some basic methods for learning from data streams. In the next chapter, we show a practical example of how to use MOA with some of the methods briefly presented in this chapter. These and other methods are presented in more detail in part II of this book.

2.1 Algorithms

The main algorithms in data stream mining are classification, regression, clustering, and frequent pattern mining.

Suppose we have a stream of items, also called instances or examples, that are continuously arriving. We are in a classification setting when we need to assign a label from a set of nominal labels to each item, as a function of the other features of the item. A classifier can be trained as long as the correct label for (many of) the examples is available at a later time. An example of classification is to label incoming email messages as spam or not spam. Regression is a prediction task similar to classification, with the difference that the label to predict is a numeric value instead of a nominal one. An example of regression is predicting the value of a stock in the stock market tomorrow.

Classification and regression need a set of properly labeled examples to learn a model, so that we can use this model to predict the labels of unseen examples. They are the main examples of *supervised* learning tasks. When examples are not labeled, one interesting task is to group them in homogeneous clusters. Clustering can be used, for example, to obtain user profiles in a website. It is an example of an *unsupervised* learning task.

Frequent pattern mining looks for the most relevant patterns within the examples. For instance, in a sales supermarket dataset, it is possible to know what items are bought together and obtain association rules, as for example: *Most times customers buy cheese, they also buy wine*.

The most significant requirements for a stream mining algorithm are the same for predictors, clusterers, and frequent pattern miners:

Requirement 1: Process an instance at a time, and inspect it (at most) once.

Requirement 2: Use a limited amount of time to process each instance.

Requirement 3: Use a limited amount of memory.

Requirement 4: Be ready to give an answer (prediction, clustering, patterns) at any time.

Requirement 5: Adapt to temporal changes.

2.2   Classification

In batch or offline classification, a classifier-building algorithm is given a set of labeled examples. The algorithm creates a model, a classifier in this case. The model is then deployed, that is, used to predict the label for unlabeled instances that the classifier builder never saw. If we go into more detail, we know that it is good methodology in the first phase to split the dataset available into two parts, the training and the testing dataset, or to resort to cross-validation, to make sure that the classifier is reasonably accurate. But in any case, there is a first training phase, clearly separated in time from the prediction phase.

In the online setting, and in particular in streaming, this separation between training, evaluating, and testing is far less clear-cut, and is interleaved. We need to start making predictions before we have all the data, because the data may never end. We need to use the data whose label we predict to keep training the model, if possible. And probably we need to continuously evaluate the model in some way to decide if the model needs more or less aggressive retraining.

Generally speaking, a stream mining classifier is ready to do either one of the following at any moment:

1. Receive an unlabeled example and make a prediction for it on the basis of its current model.

2. Receive the label for an example seen in the past, and use it for adjusting the model, that is, for training.

For example, an online shop may want to predict, for each arriving customer, whether the customer will or will not buy a particular product (prediction). When the customer session ends, say, minutes later, the system gets the "label" indicating whether indeed the customer bought the product or not, and this feedback can be used to tune the predictor. In other cases, the label may never be known; for example, if the task is to determine whether the customer is a robot or a human, the true label may be available for a few customers only. If trying to detect fraudulent transactions in order to block them, transactions predicted to be fraudulent are not executed, so their true labels are never known.

This simple description glosses over a number of important practical issues. First, how many of the unlabeled instances eventually receive their correct label? Clearly, the fewer labels received, the harder the prediction task. How long should we wait for an instance label to arrive, before we drop the instance? Efficiently managing the buffer of instances waiting for their labels is a very delicate implementation problem when dealing with massive, high-speed streams. Finally, should we use all labeled instances for training? If in fact many labels are available, perhaps there is a diminishing return in accuracy for the increased computational cost of training on all instances.

It is difficult to deal with these issues in generic ways, because often the good solution depends too much on the details of a specific practical scenario. For this reason, a large part of the research in stream classification deals with a simplified cycle of training/prediction: we assume that we get the true label of *every* unlabeled instance, and that furthermore we get it *immediately* after making the prediction and before the next instance arrives. In other words, the algorithm executes the following loop:

- Get an unlabeled instance x.
- Make a prediction $\hat{y} = f(x)$ for x's label, where f is the current model.
- Get the true label y for x.
- Use the pair (x, y) to update (train) f, and the pair $(\hat{y}, y)$ to update statistics about classifier performance.
- Proceed to the next instance.

This model is rightly criticized by practitioners as too simple, because it ignores the very real problem of *delayed* and *missing* label feedback. It is however quite useful for comparing learning algorithms in a clean way, provided we have access to, or can simulate, a stream for which we have all labels.

Two variations of these cycles are worth mentioning. In *semi-supervised* learning, we use unlabeled examples for training as well, because at least they provide information on the distribution of the examples. Unfortunately, there is little work on semi-supervised stream learning, even though the abundance of data in high-speed streams makes it promising and a good approach to the delayed/missing label feedback problem. In *active learning*, the algorithm does not expect the labels of all instances but selectively chooses which ones to request. This is a good approach when every label is theoretically available but obtaining it has a cost. In this book we cover active learning in streams but not semi-supervised learning.

2.2.1   Classifier Evaluation in Data Streams

Given this cycle, it is reasonable to ask: How do we evaluate the performance of a classification algorithm? In traditional batch learning, evaluation is typically performed by randomly splitting the data into training and testing sets (holdout); if data is limited, cross-validation (creating several models and averaging results across several random partitions in training and test data) is preferred.

In the stream setting, (effectively) unlimited data tends to make cross-validation too expensive computationally, and less necessary anyway. But it poses new challenges. The main one is to build an accurate picture of accuracy over time. One solution involves taking snapshots at different times during the induction of a model to see how the model accuracy varies. Two main approaches arise:

- **Holdout:** This is measuring performance on a single holdout partition. It is most useful when the division between train and test sets has been predefined, so that results from different studies can be directly compared. However, holdout only gives an accurate estimation of the current accuracy of a classifier if the holdout set is similar to the current data, which may be hard to guarantee in practice.

- **Interleaved test-then-train or prequential:** Each individual example is used to test the model before it is used for training, and from this the accuracy can be incrementally updated. When the evaluation is intentionally performed in this order, the model is always being tested on instances it has not seen. This scheme has the advantage that no holdout set is needed for testing, making maximum use of the available data. It also ensures a smooth plot of accuracy over time, as each individual example will become less and less significant to the overall average. In test-then-train evaluation, all examples seen so far are taken into account to compute accuracy, while in prequential, only those in a sliding window of the most recent ones are.

As data stream classification is a relatively new field, such evaluation practices are not nearly as well researched and established as they are in the traditional batch setting.

Next we name and describe a few of the best-known stream classifiers. The first two are so simple that they are usually only considered baselines for the evaluation of other classifiers.

2.2.2 Majority Class Classifier

The majority class classifier is one of the simplest classifiers. It stores a count for each of the class labels, and predicts as the class of a new instance the most frequent class label.

2.2.3 No-Change Classifier

The no-change classifier is another one of the simplest: predict the last class in the data stream. It exploits autocorrelation in the label assignments, which is very common.

2.2.4 Lazy Classifier

The lazy classifier is based on a very simple idea: the classifier consists of keeping some of the instances seen, and predicting using the class label of the closest instances to the instance whose class label we want to predict. In particular, the k-nearest neighbor or k-NN method outputs the majority class label of the k instances closest to the one to predict.

For this classifier, a predefined notion of closeness or distance is required, and the performance depends on the meaningfulness of this distance with respect to labels.

Example 2.1 Consider the following dataset of tweets, on which we want to build a model to predict the sentiment ($+$ or $-$) of new incoming tweets.

ID	Text	Sentiment
T1	glad happy glad	$+$
T2	glad glad joyful	$+$
T3	glad pleasant	$+$
T4	miserable sad glad	$-$

Assume we want to classify the following new instance:

ID	Text	Sentiment
T5	glad sad miserable pleasant glad	?

The simple classifiers will perform the following predictions:

- *Majority classifier:* The majority class label is $+$, so the prediction is $+$.

- *No-change classifier:* The class label of the last instance (T4) is −, so the prediction is −.
- *Lazy classifier:* If we measure similarity by the number of common words, the tweet closest to T5 is T4, with label −. Therefore, the 1-NN classifier predicts − for T5.

2.2.5 Naive Bayes

The Naive Bayes classifier is a simple classifier based on the use of the Bayes' theorem. The basic idea is to compute a probability for each one of the classes based on the attribute values, and select the class with the highest probability. Under the naive assumption that the attributes are all independent, the class probabilities can be computed by multiplying over all attributes the probability of having that particular class label conditioned on the attribute having a particular value. The independence assumption is almost always false, but it can be shown that weaker assumptions suffice, and Naive Bayes does surprisingly well for its simplicity on a variety of tasks.

2.2.6 Decision Trees

Decision tree learners build a tree structure from training examples to predict class labels of unseen examples. The main advantage of decision trees is that it is easy to understand their predictions. That is why they are among the most used classifiers in settings where black-box classifiers are not desirable, for example, in health-related applications.

In stream mining, the state-of-the art decision tree classifier is the *Hoeffding tree*, due to Domingos and Hulten [88], and its variations. Traditional decision trees scan the entire dataset to discover the best attribute to form the initial split of the data. Once this is found, the data is split by the value of the chosen attribute, and the algorithm is applied recursively to the resulting datasets, to build subtrees. Recursion is applied until some stopping criterion is met. This approach cannot be adopted directly in the stream setting, as we cannot afford the resource cost (time and memory) of storing instances and repeatedly scanning them.

The Hoeffding tree is based on the idea that, instead of looking at previous (stored) instances to decide what splits to do in the trees, we can wait to receive enough instances and make split decisions when they can be made confidently. The main advantage of this approach is that it is not necessary to store

instances. Instead, sufficient statistics are kept in order to make splitting decisions. The sufficient statistics make it easy to incorporate Naive Bayes models
into the leaves of the tree.

The *Hoeffding adaptive tree* [33] is an extension of the Hoeffding tree that
is able to create and replace new branches when the data stream is evolving
and the class label distribution or instance distribution is changing.

2.2.7   Ensembles

Ensembles are sets of classifiers that, when combined, can predict better than
any of them individually. If we use the same algorithm to build all the classifiers in the ensemble, we will need to feed the algorithm with different subsets
of the data to make them different. *Bagging* is an ensemble method that (1)
uses as input for each run of the classifier builder a subset obtained by sampling with repetition of the original input data stream, and (2) uses majority
voting of the classifiers as a prediction strategy.

The *ADWIN bagging* method [38], implemented as OZABAGADWIN in
MOA, is an extension of bagging that it is able to create and replace new
classifiers when the data stream is evolving and the class label distribution
is changing.

2.3   Regression

As in classification, the goal in a regression task is to learn a model that predicts
the value of a label attribute for instances where the label is not (yet) known.
However, here the label is a real value, and not one of a discrete set of values.
Predicting the label exactly is irrealistic, so the goal is to be close to the correct
values under some measure, such as average squared distance.

Several classification algorithms have natural counterparts for regression,
including lazy learning and decision trees.

2.4   Clustering

Clustering is useful when we have unlabeled instances and we want to
find homogeneous groups or clusters in them, according to their similarities
or affinities. The main difference from classification is that the groups are
unknown before the learning process, and we do not know whether they are

the "correct" ones after it. This is why it is a case of so-called *unsupervised* learning. Uses of clustering include segmentation of customers in marketing and finding communities in social networks.

We can see clustering as an optimization problem where we want to minimize a cost function that evaluates the "badness" of a partition of examples into clusters. Some clustering methods need to be told the desired number of clusters to find in the data, and others will find some number of clusters by themselves.

The k-means clustering method is one of the most used methods in clustering, due to its simplicity. It starts by selecting k centroids in a random way. After that, two steps are repeated: first, assign each instance to the nearest centroid, and second, recompute the cluster centroids by taking the center of mass of the instances assigned to it. This is repeated until some stopping criterion is met, such as no changes in the assignments. It is not a streaming method, as it requires several passes over the same data.

Streaming methods for clustering typically have two levels, an online one and an offline one. At the online level, a set of microclusters is computed and updated from the stream efficiently; in the offline phase, a classical batch clustering method such as k-means is performed on the microclusters. The online level only performs one pass over the data; the offline phase performs several passes, but not over all the data, only over the set of microclusters, which is usually a pretty small set of controllable size. The offline level can be invoked once, when (if) the stream ends, or periodically as the stream flows to update the set of clusters.

2.5   Frequent Pattern Mining

Frequent pattern mining is an important task in unsupervised learning. It can be used to simply describe the structure of the data, to find association rules, or to find discriminative features that can be used for classification or clustering tasks. Examples of pattern classes are itemsets, sequences, trees, and graphs [255].

The problem is as follows: given a source of data (a batch dataset or a stream) that contains patterns, and a threshold σ, find all the patterns that appear as a subpattern in a fraction σ of the patterns in the dataset. For example, if our source of data is a stream of supermarket purchases, and $\sigma = 10\%$, we would call $\{cheese, wine\}$ frequent if at least 10% of the purchases contain at least cheese *and* wine, and perhaps other products. For graphs, a triangle could be a graph pattern, and if we have a database of graphs, this pattern would be frequent if at least a fraction σ of the graphs contain at least one triangle.

In the batch setting, Apriori, Eclat, and FP-growth are three of the best-known algorithms for finding frequent itemsets in databases, where each item is a set. Similar algorithms exist for data structures such as sequences and graphs. However, it is difficult to translate them directly to the stream setting, either because they perform several passes over the data or because they store too much information.

Algorithms for frequent pattern mining on streams typically use a batch miner as a base, but need to implement other ideas; furthermore, they are often approximate rather than exact. Moment and IncMine are algorithms for frequent itemset mining in data streams.

3 Hands-on Introduction to MOA

In this chapter, we are going to start using MOA, learn its basics, and run a simple example comparing two classifiers. If you have some background in data mining for the nonstreaming setting, this quick start should let you explore other options, such as clustering and frequent pattern mining. Otherwise, it is probably best to continue with part II which covers these techniques.

Figure 3.1
MOA graphical user interface.

3.1 Getting Started

First, we need to download the lastest release of MOA from `https://moa.cms.waikato.ac.nz`. It is a compressed zip file that contains the `moa.jar` file, an executable Java jar file that can be used either as a Java application or from the command line. The release also contains the jar file `sizeofag.jar`, which is used to measure the memory used running the experiments. The scripts `bin\moa.bat` in Windows and `bin/moa.sh` in Linux and Mac are the easy way to start the graphical user interface of MOA (figure 3.1).

Click *Configure* to set up a task; when ready to launch a task, click *Run*. Several tasks can be run concurrently. Click on different tasks in the list and control them using the buttons underneath. If textual output from a task is available, it will be displayed in the center of the GUI, and can be saved to disk.

Note that the command line text box displayed at the top of the window represents textual commands that can be used to run tasks on the command line. The text can be selected, then copied onto the clipboard. At the bottom of the GUI there is a graphical display of the results. It is possible to compare the results of two different tasks: the current task is displayed in red, and the previously selected task is in blue.

As an example, let us compare two different classifiers, a Naive Bayes and a decision tree, using prequential evaluation on $1,000,000$ instances generated by the default `RandomTreeGenerator` stream generator (figure 3.2):

```
EvaluatePrequential -i 1000000 -f 10000 -l bayes.NaiveBayes

EvaluatePrequential -i 1000000 -f 10000 -l trees.HoeffdingTree
```

Remember that the prequential evaluation is an online evaluation technique distinct from the standard cross-validation used in the batch setting. Each time a new instance arrives, it is first used to test, then to train.

You can use streams from ARFF files, a convenient data format defined by the WEKA project. Sample ARFF datasets are available from `https://moa.cms.waikato.ac.nz`.

```
EvaluatePrequential -s (ArffFileStream -f elec.arff)
```

Also, you can generate streams with concept drift, joining several different streams. For example, the SEA concepts dataset is generated joining four different streams with a different SEA concept in each one:

```
EvaluatePrequential
  -s (ConceptDriftStream
      -s (generators.SEAGenerator -f 1) -d (ConceptDriftStream
          -s (generators.SEAGenerator -f 2) -d (ConceptDriftStream
              -s generators.SEAGenerator
```

Figure 3.2
MOA GUI running two different tasks.

```
        -d (generators.SEAGenerator -f 4)
         -w 50 -p 250000 )
    -w 50 -p 250000)
-w 50 -p 250000)
```

3.2   The Graphical User Interface for Classification

We start by comparing the accuracy of two classifiers.

Exercise 3.1 Compare the accuracies of the Hoeffding tree and the Naive Bayes classifiers, for a `RandomTreeGenerator` stream of $1,000,000$ instances, using interleaved test-then-train evaluation. Use a sample frequency of $10,000$ instances to output the evaluation results every $10,000$ instances.

We configure and run the following tasks:

```
EvaluateInterleavedTestThenTrain -l bayes.NaiveBayes
    -i 1000000 -f 10000

EvaluateInterleavedTestThenTrain -l trees.HoeffdingTree
    -i 1000000 -f 10000
```

The results are shown in figure 3.3.

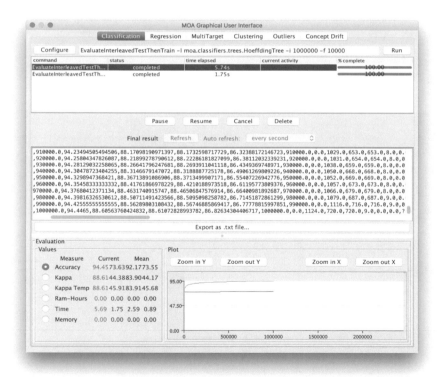

Figure 3.3
Exercise 3.1, comparing the Naive Bayes Classifier and the Hoeffding tree.

Exercise 3.2 Compare and discuss the accuracy for the stream in the previous example using three different evaluations with a Hoeffding tree:

- Periodic holdout with 1,000 instances for testing
- Interleaved test-then-train
- Prequential with a sliding window of 1,000 instances

The tasks needed for this example are the following:

- Periodic holdout with 1,000 instances for testing:

```
EvaluatePeriodicHeldOutTest -n 1000 -i 1000000 -f 10000
```

- Interleaved test-then-train:

```
EvaluateInterleavedTestThenTrain -l trees.HoeffdingTree
    -i 1000000 -f 10000
```

- Prequential with a sliding window of 1,000 instances:

```
EvaluatePrequential -l trees.HoeffdingTree -i 1000000 -f 10000
```

The comparison between the first two is shown in figure 3.4.

3.2.1   Drift Stream Generators

MOA streams are built using generators, reading ARFF files, joining several streams, or filtering streams. MOA stream generators allow us to simulate potentially infinite sequences of data.

It is possible to build streams that exhibit concept drift, or concept change over time. Two examples are the rotating hyperplane and the random RBF generator. The rate of change in these streams is determined by a parameter, and their operation will be explained in chapter 12.

We can also introduce concept drift or change by joining several streams. In MOA this is done by building a weighted combination of two pure distributions that characterizes the target concepts before and after the change. MOA uses the sigmoid function as an elegant and practical solution to define the probability that each new instance of the stream belongs to the new concept after the drift. The sigmoid function introduces a gradual, smooth transition whose duration is controlled with two parameters: p, the position where the change occurs, and the length w of the transition, as can be seen in figure 3.5.

An example is:

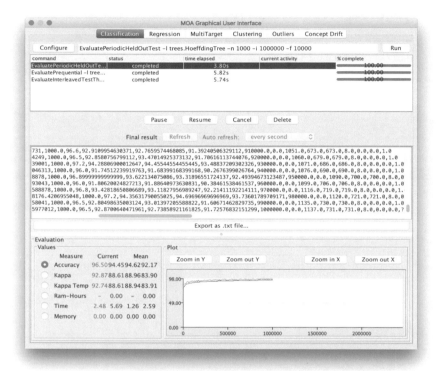

Figure 3.4
Exercise 3.2, comparing three different evaluation methods on the same classifier.

```
ConceptDriftStream -s (generators.AgrawalGenerator -f 7)
    -d (generators.AgrawalGenerator -f 2) -w 1000000 -p 900000
```

where the parameters of `ConceptDriftStream` are:

- `-s` : Initial stream generator
- `-d` : Generator of the stream after drift or change
- `-p` : Central position of the change
- `-w` : Width of the change period

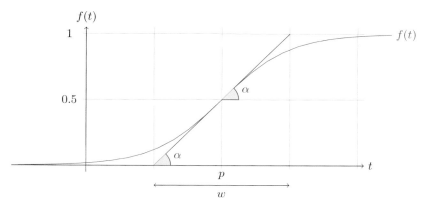

Figure 3.5
A sigmoid function $f(t) = 1/(1 + e^{-4(t-p)/w})$.

Exercise 3.3 Compare the accuracy of the Hoeffding tree with the Naive Bayes classifier, for a `RandomRBFGenerator` stream of 1,000,000 instances with speed change of 0.001 using interleaved test-then-train evaluation.
The tasks needed for this example are:

```
EvaluateInterleavedTestThenTrain -l bayes.NaiveBayes
  -s (generators.RandomRBFGeneratorDrift -s 0.001)
  -i 1000000 -f 10000

EvaluateInterleavedTestThenTrain -l trees.HoeffdingTree
  -s (generators.RandomRBFGeneratorDrift -s 0.001)
  -i 1000000 -f 10000
```

The comparison between the two classifiers is shown in figure 3.6.

Exercise 3.4 Compare the accuracy for the stream of the previous exercise using three different classifiers:

- Hoeffding tree with majority class at the leaves
- Hoeffding adaptive tree
- ADWIN bagging (`OzaBagAdwin`) on ten Hoeffding trees

The tasks needed for this example are:

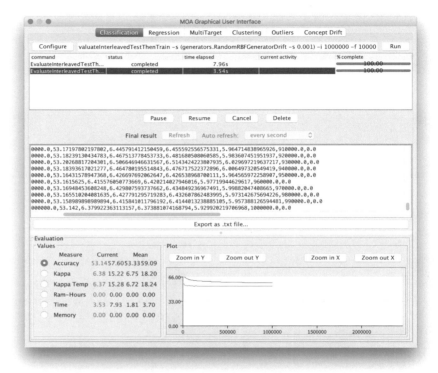

Figure 3.6

Exercise 3.3, comparing the Hoeffding tree and Naive Bayes classifiers on a nonstationary stream.

```
EvaluateInterleavedTestThenTrain -l (trees.HoeffdingTree -l MC)
  -s (generators.RandomRBFGeneratorDrift -s 0.001)
  -i 1000000 -f 10000

EvaluateInterleavedTestThenTrain -l trees.HoeffdingAdaptiveTree
  -s (generators.RandomRBFGeneratorDrift -s 0.001)
  -i 1000000 -f 10000

EvaluateInterleavedTestThenTrain -l meta.OzaBagAdwin
  -s (generators.RandomRBFGeneratorDrift -s 0.001)
  -i 1000000 -f 10000
```

The comparison of these three classifiers is shown in figure 3.7. We observe that the two adaptive classifiers perform much better than the standard Hoeffding tree, since the data stream is evolving and changing.

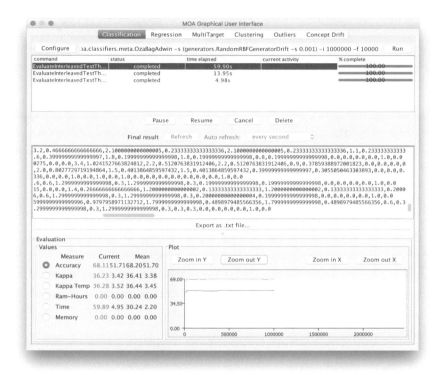

Figure 3.7
Exercise 3.4, comparing three different classifiers.

3.3   Using the Command Line

An easy way to use the command line is to copy and paste the text in the *Configure* line of the GUI. For example, suppose we want to execute the task

```
EvaluatePrequential -l trees.HoeffdingTree -i 1000000 -w 10000
```

from the command line. We can simply write

```
java -cp moa.jar -javaagent:sizeofag.jar moa.DoTask
"EvaluatePrequential -l trees.HoeffdingTree -i 1000000 -w 10000"
```

Note that some parameters are missing, so default values will be used. We explain this line in the following paragraphs.

The class moa.DoTask is the main one for running tasks on the command line. It will accept the name of a task followed by any appropriate parameters. The first task used is the LearnModel task. The -l parameter specifies the learner, in this case the HoeffdingTree class. The -s parameter specifies the stream to learn from, in this case generators.WaveformGenerator, which is a data stream generator that produces a three-class learning problem of identifying three types of waveform. The -m option specifies the maximum number of examples to train the learner with, in this case $1,000,000$ examples. The -O option specifies a file to output the resulting model to:

```
java -cp moa.jar -javaagent:sizeofag.jar moa.DoTask
  LearnModel -l trees.HoeffdingTree
  -s generators.WaveformGenerator -m 1000000 -O model1.moa
```

This will create a file named model1.moa that contains a decision tree model that was induced during training.

The next example will evaluate the model to see how accurate it is on a set of examples that are generated using a different random seed. The EvaluateModel task is given the parameters needed to load the model produced in the previous step, generate a new waveform stream with random seed 2, and test on $1,000,000$ examples:

```
java -cp moa.jar -javaagent:sizeofag.jar moa.DoTask
  "EvaluateModel -m file:model1.moa
  -s (generators.WaveformGenerator -i 2) -i 1000000"
```

Note that we are nesting parameters using brackets. Quotes have been added around the description of the task, otherwise the operating system might be confused about the meaning of the brackets.

After evaluation the following statistics are displayed:

```
classified instances = 1,000,000
classifications correct (percent) = 84.474
Kappa Statistic (percent) = 76.711
```

Note that the two steps above can be rolled into one, avoiding the need to create an external file, as follows:

```
java -cp moa.jar -javaagent:sizeofag.jar moa.DoTask
  "EvaluateModel -m (LearnModel -l trees.HoeffdingTree
  -s generators.WaveformGenerator -m 1000000)
  -s (generators.WaveformGenerator -i 2) -i 1000000"
```

The task `EvaluatePeriodicHeldOutTest` will train a model while taking snapshots of performance using a holdout test set at periodic intervals. The following command creates a *comma-separated value* (CSV) file, training the `HoeffdingTree` classifier on the `WaveformGenerator` data, using the first 100,000 examples for testing, training on a total of $100,000,000$ examples, and testing every $1,000,000$ examples:

```
java -cp moa.jar -javaagent:sizeofag.jar moa.DoTask
  "EvaluatePeriodicHeldOutTest -l trees.HoeffdingTree
  -s generators.WaveformGenerator
  -n 100000 -i 10000000 -f 1000000" > dsresult.csv
```

These are examples of how we can use MOA from the command line. In part II of the book we discuss the classifiers that appear here. In part III we explain the generators used here, and see how to use the MOA API from source code written in Java.

II STREAM MINING

4   **Streams and Sketches**

Streams can be seen as read-once sequences of data. Algorithms on streams must work under what we call the *data stream axioms*, already stated in chapter 2:

1. Only one pass is allowed on the stream; each stream item can be observed only once.
2. The processing time per item must be low.
3. Memory use must be low as well, certainly sublinear in the length of the stream; this implies that only a few stream items can be explicitly stored.
4. The algorithm must be able to provide answers at any time.
5. Streams evolve over time, that is, they are nonstationary data sources.

The concern of this chapter is the design of algorithms that satisfy the first four axioms. We make *no probabilistic assumption* on the stream, on the process that generates the stream items, or on any statistical laws it may obey. Streams are generated *adversarially*, that is, following the patterns that are hardest for the algorithm. Thus, axiom 5 is irrelevant in this chapter. In contrast, in chapter 5 we will define a more benign model of stream generation where items are generated according to some stochastic process, and therefore obey statistical laws. This assumption lets us formalize axiom 5 and is implicit in most available stream ML and data mining algorithms.

Many solutions to streaming problems use the notion of a stream *sketch* or *summary*. A sketch is a data structure plus accompanying algorithms that read a stream and store sufficient information to be able to answer one or more predefined queries about the stream. We will view sketches as building blocks for higher-level learning and mining algorithms on streams. In this light, the requirement to use little memory is particularly pressing, because the mining algorithm will often create not a single sketch, but many, for keeping track of many different statistics on the data simultaneously.

4.1   Setting: Approximation Algorithms

We first fix some notation used throughout the rest of the book. We use $E[X]$ and $Var(X)$ to denote the expected value and the variance, respectively, of random variable X. A $\log$ without a subscript denotes a logarithm in base 2, and $\ln$ denotes a natural logarithm. A function f is $O(g)$ if there is a constant $c > 0$ such that for every x we have $f(x) \leq c \cdot g(x)$. The cardinality of a set A

is denoted $|A|$. In pseudocode, $\leftarrow$ denotes variable assignment, and $\triangleright$ starts a comment line.

In streaming, an *item* is simply an element of a universe of items I without any relevant inner structure. Set I is potentially very large, which means that it is unfeasible to use memory proportional to $|I|$. We will sometimes assume that storing an element of I takes one unit of memory; this is necessary when I is infinite—for instance, the set of real numbers. In other cases we will go into more detail and count the number of bits required to store an item, which is at least $\log |I|$.

We define a *sketching* algorithm by giving three operations: an $Init(\ldots)$ operation that initializes the data structure, possibly with some parameters such as the desired approximation or the amount of memory to be used; an $Update(item)$ operation that will be applied to every item on the stream; and a $Query(\ldots)$ operation that returns the current value of a function of interest on the stream read so far (and may or may not have parameters). In general, a sketch may implement several types of queries.

Many functions that can be computed easily on offline data are impossible to compute *exactly* on streams in sublinear memory. For example, computing the number of distinct items seen requires linear memory in the length of the stream, in the worst case and large enough item universes. On the other hand, for many functions there are algorithms that provide *approximate* solutions and obtain large gains in memory and time with only a small loss in accuracy, which is often acceptable in applications. We next introduce some formalism for discussing approximate computation.

Let f and g be two real-valued functions. We think of g as an approximation of f. For an *accuracy* value ϵ, we say that g is

- an *absolute* or *additive* ϵ-approximation of f if $|f(x) - g(x)| \leq \epsilon$ for every input x;
- a *relative* or *multiplicative* ϵ-approximation of f if $|f(x) - g(x)| \leq \epsilon|f(x)|$ for every input x.

Many approximate algorithms on streams are also *randomized*, meaning that they have access to a source of random bits or numbers to make their choices. Their output on a fixed input is not uniquely defined, as it may be different on different runs. It should therefore be treated as a *random variable g* that hopefully is close to the desired f in most places. The definition of (absolute or relative) (ϵ, δ)-approximation is like that of ϵ-approximation as above, but requiring only that the approximation above holds with probability at least $1 - \delta$ over the runs of the algorithm, rather than in every single run. For example, to say that the output g of an algorithm is an absolute $(0.1, 0.01)$-approximation of a desired function f, we require that, for every x, $g(x)$ is within ± 0.1 of $f(x)$ at least 99% of the times we run the algorithm. The value $1 - \delta$ is usually called *confidence*.

This framework is similar to the PAC learning model [146] used to formalize prediction learning problems, where PAC stands for "probably approximately correct." It should be noted that, usually, the approximation guarantees only hold when the updates and queries made do not depend on the answers returned by previous queries. That is, we cannot apply these guarantees for *adaptive queries*, which are common in exploratory data analysis.

In statistics, the traditional way of approximately describing a random variable X is by giving its expected value $\mathrm{E}[X]$ and its variance $\mathrm{Var}(X)$. Suppose we have a randomized algorithm g that approximates a desired function f, in the sense that $\mathrm{E}[g(x)] = f(x)$ with some variance $\mathrm{Var}(g) = \sigma^2$. In that case, we can design, on the basis of g, another algorithm h that approximates f in the seemingly stricter sense of (ϵ, δ)-approximation. The new algorithm h takes any ϵ and δ as parameters, in addition to x, and uses $O((\sigma^2/\epsilon^2)\ln(1/\delta))$ times the memory and running time of f. As we might expect, it uses more resources as more accuracy and more confidence are required. The details of the conversion are given in section 4.9.2, but we describe next the main ingredient, as it is ubiquitous in stream algorithmics and stream mining.

4.2   Concentration Inequalities

While processing a stream, algorithms often need to make decisions based on the information they have seen, such as deciding the value to output or choosing among some finite number of options. If a decision has to be made around accumulated statistics, then a useful tool would be a method to establish the likelihood of an undesired event occurring. In other words, one could ask the question: If I make a decision at this point in time about the model I am constructing, what is the chance that I will be wrong in the long run? Such decision-making leans heavily on concentration inequalities.

Inequalities stating that random variables are concentrated around the mean with high probability are known as *concentration inequalities* or *large-deviation bounds*. They can also be regarded as providing *confidence bounds* for the variables. An example is the law of large numbers of classical probability theory, or the three-sigma rule, which states that for a normal distribution nearly all (99.73%) of the probability mass lies within three standard deviations of the mean.

The most basic concentration inequality is *Markov's inequality*, which states that for any nonnegative random variable X, and $t > 0$,

$$\Pr[X \geq t] \leq \mathrm{E}[x]/t.$$

Chebyshev's inequality is an application of Markov's inequality and states that for any nonnegative random variable X, and $t > 0$,

$$\Pr[X - \mathrm{E}[X] \geq t] \leq \mathrm{Var}[X]/t^2.$$

Often, we want to estimate $\mathrm{E}[X]$ by averaging several copies of X. Averages, a special kind of random variable, converge to their expectation much faster than stated by Chebyshev's inequality, as the number of copies grows. For any n, define $X = \left(\sum_{i=1}^{n} X_i\right)/n$ where $X_1, \ldots, X_n$ are independent variables taking values in $[0, 1]$ with $\mathrm{E}[X] = p$. Then:

1. **Chernoff's bound:** For all $\epsilon \in (0, 1)$,

   $$\Pr[|X - p| > \epsilon p] \leq 2\exp\left(-\epsilon^2 pn/3\right).$$

2. **Hoeffding's bound:** For all $\epsilon > 0$,

   $$\Pr[|X - p| > \epsilon] \leq 2\exp\left(-2\epsilon^2 n\right).$$

3. **The normal approximation:** If in a draw of $X_1, \ldots, X_n$ we obtain $X = \hat{p}$, then $|p - \hat{p}| > \epsilon$ happens with probability about $2(1 - \Phi(\epsilon\sqrt{n/(\hat{p}(1 - \hat{p}))}\,))$, where $\Phi(z)$ is the probability that a normally distributed variable with average 0 and standard deviation 1 is less than z. The function $\Phi(z)$ equals $\frac{1}{2}(1 + \mathrm{erf}(z/\sqrt{2}))$, where erf is the error function available in most programming languages.

We can apply the bounds in the reverse direction and derive a formula relating the deviation from the mean and its probability. For example, if $\epsilon = \sqrt{\log(2/\delta)/2n}$, Hoeffding's bound gives $\Pr[|X - p| > \epsilon] \leq \delta$. This is useful for obtaining additive (ϵ, δ)-approximations. Chernoff's bound gives multiplicative approximations instead, but has the disadvantage that the bound mentions $p = \mathrm{E}[X]$, the unknown value that we want to estimate; also, it applies only to $\epsilon < 1$.

The normal approximation is based on the fact that, as n tends to infinity, the variable nX tends to a normal with mean pn and standard deviation at most $\sqrt{p(1-p)n}$; notice that 0/1-valued or Bernoulli variables are the worst case and lead to this variance exactly. It is not completely rigorous, both because n is finite and because it permutes the roles of p and $\hat{p}$. However, folklore says that the approximation is correct enough for all practical purposes when $\hat{p}n$ and $(1-\hat{p})n$ are larger than about 30, and tighter than Hoeffding's and Chernoff's bounds, which require larger n to reach the same uncertainty ϵ. It is thus preferable in most practical settings, except when we are interested in proving rigorous theorems about the performance of algorithms.

Many more inequalities are known. For example, Bernstein's inequality generalizes both Chernoff's and Hoeffding's (up to constant factors) using the variance of the variables X_i. McDiarmid's inequality applies to functions of the X_is other than the sum, as long as no single X_i determines the function too much. Other inequalities relax the condition that the X_is are fully independent. There are also approximate bounds other than the normal one, such as the Agresti-Coull bound, which is better for values of p close to 0 or to 1 and small n.

In the following sections, we will consider these problems in detail:

- Sampling

- Counting items and distinct items

- Frequency problems

- Counting within a sliding window

- Merging sketches computed distributedly

For readability, some technical details and references are deferred to section 4.9.

4.3   Sampling

Sampling is an obvious approach to dealing with streams: for each item in the stream, process it with probability α, and ignore it with probability $1 - \alpha$.

For many tasks, including many in learning and data mining contexts, we can obtain quite good approximations while reducing computational cost by computing the function on the fraction α of sampled elements. But be warned that sampling is not a universal solution, as it does perform poorly in some

tasks. For example, for the problem of estimating the number of distinct elements, rare elements may be missed entirely and their numbers are typically
underestimated.

Often, we want to reduce the number of items to be processed, yet maintain
a representative sample of the stream of a given size k. *Reservoir sampling*,
due to Vitter [240], is a simple and efficient technique for achieving this. It is
presented in figure 4.1.

RESERVOIR SAMPLING

```
1   Init(k):
2        create a reservoir (array[0...k − 1]) of up to k items
3        fill the reservoir with the first k items in the stream
4        t ← k        ▷ t counts the number of items seen so far
5   Update(x):
6        select a random number r between 0 and t − 1
7        if r < k
8             replace the rth item in the reservoir with item x
9        t ← t + 1
10  Query():
11       return the current reservoir
```

Figure 4.1
The RESERVOIR SAMPLING sketch.

Reservoir sampling has the property that no matter how many stream elements t have been read so far, each of them is currently in the reservoir with
the same probability, k/t. That is, it is equally biased toward early elements
and late elements. To see that this is true, use induction on t. It is clearly true
after the first t steps, for $t \leq k$. At a later time $t > k$, the probability that the tth
item in the stream is in the reservoir is k/t because it is added with that probability. For item number i (with $i < t$) to be in the reservoir, (1) it must happen that it was in the reservoir at time $t − 1$, which inductively happens with
probability $k/(t − 1)$, and (2) it must *not* happen that the tth item is selected
(probability k/t) *and* that it is placed in the position of the reservoir where the
ith item is (probability $1/k$). All this occurs, as desired, with probability

$$\frac{k}{t-1} \cdot \left(1 - \frac{k}{t} \cdot \frac{1}{k}\right) = \frac{k}{t-1} \cdot \frac{t-1}{t} = \frac{k}{t} \ .$$

A variant called *skip counting* is better when the time for processing one item exceeds the arrival time between items. The idea is to randomly choose at time t the index $t' > t$ of the next item that will be included in the sample, and skip all records before it with no computation—in particular, without the relatively costly random number generation. Rules for randomly choosing t' given t and k can be derived so that the output of this method is probabilistically identical to that of reservoir sampling [240].

4.4   Counting Total Items

Counting the total number of items seen so far is perhaps the most basic question one can imagine on a stream. The trivial solution keeps a standard integer counter, and has the update operation just increment the counter. Typical programming languages implement integers with a fixed number of bits, such as 16, 32, or 64, which is supposed to be at least $\log t$ to count up to t.

A more economical solution is *Morris's approximate counter* [183]. It is a randomized, approximate counter that counts up to t using $\log \log t$ bits, instead of $\log t$. This means that it can count up to 10^9 with $\log \log 10^9 = 5$ bits, and to any practical number of items in 6 bits. The tradeoff is, of course, that the counting is only approximate.

The initial idea is to use uniform sampling as we have described it before: fix some probability p that is a power of 2, say 2^{-k}. Use an integer counter c as before, but upon receiving an item, increment the counter with probability p, and do nothing with probability $1 - p$. Now, the expected value of c after t items is pt, so c/p should be a good approximation of t. The sketch uses $\log(pt) = \log t - k$ bits instead of $\log t$ bits; for example, with $p = 1/8$, 3 bits are saved. The returned value will be inaccurate, though, because of the random fluctuations of c around pt.

Morris's simple but clever idea is as follows: instead of fixing k a priori and counting up to 2^k, use c in the place of k. The algorithm is shown in figure 4.2; observe that it does not mention k.

More precisely, it can be shown [103] that after reading t stream elements the expected value of 2^c is $t + 1$ and its variance is $t(t-1)/2$. That is, it returns the right value in expectation, although with a large variance. Only the value of c needs to be stored, which uses $\log c \simeq \log \log t$ bits, with an additional copy of c alive only during the *Update* procedure.

MORRIS'S COUNTER

1 *Init*():
2      $c \leftarrow 0$
3 *Update*(*item*):
4   increment c with probability 2^{-c}
5   ▷ and do nothing with probability $1 - 2^{-c}$
6 *Query*():
7   **return** $2^c - 1$

Figure 4.2
Morris's approximate counting algorithm.

We can reduce the variance by running several copies of the algorithm and taking averages. But in this case, there is an ad-hoc more efficient method. Intuitively, c is incremented about once every time that t doubles—that is why we have $t \simeq 2^c$; the sketch is probabilistically placing t in intervals of the form $(2^c, 2^{c+1})$. If we replace the 2s in the algorithm with a smaller base $b < 2$, intuitively we are increasing the resolution to finer intervals of the form (b^c, b^{c+1}). It can be shown [103] that the expected value of b^c is $(b-1)t+1$ and its variance $(b-1)t(t-1)/2$. The number of bits required is roughly $\log c = \log\log t - \log\log b$. For example, taking $b = 1.08$, we can count up to $t \simeq 10^9$ with 1 byte of memory and standard deviation $0.2t$.

As an example of application, Van Durme and Lall [94] addressed the problem of estimating the frequencies of k-grams in large textual corpora by using a variant of Morris's counter. The number of occurring k-grams may be huge even for moderate values of k and they have to be kept in RAM for speed, so it is important to use as few bits as possible for each counter.

4.5   Counting Distinct Elements

A more challenging problem is counting the number of *distinct* elements observed in the stream so far (also somewhat incorrectly called *unique* elements, perhaps by analogy with the Unix `uniq` command). The difficulty is that an item may appear only once and another item millions of times, but both add the same, 1, to the distinct element count.

As motivation, consider the problem of counting the number of distinct flows (source-destination IP address pairs) seen by an Internet link. The number of potential items is huge: an IPv6 address is 64 bits, so there are $2^{128} \simeq 10^{38}$ potential items, or address pairs. The direct solution is to keep some associative table, such as a hash table, and record the pairs that have actually been seen. This may quickly become too large for busy links. Fortunately, we can often trade off approximation quality for memory usage.

4.5.1   Linear Counting

Several methods for distinct element counting are variations of the classical idea of *Bloom filter*. As an example, we discuss LINEAR COUNTING, due to Whang et al. [246], which is presented in figure 4.3.

LINEAR COUNTING

```
1   Init(D, ρ):
2       ▷ D is an upper bound on the number of distinct elements
3       ▷ ρ > 0 is a load factor
4       s ← D/ρ
5       choose a hash function h from items to {0, . . . , s − 1}
6       build a bit vector B of size s
7   Update(x):
8       B[h(x)] ← 1
9   Query():
10      let w be the fraction of 0s in B
11      return s · ln(1/w)
```

Figure 4.3
The LINEAR COUNTING sketch.

Parameter D in the initialization is an upper bound on the number of distinct elements d in the stream, that is, we assume that $d \leq D$. A *hash function* between two sets, intuitively, maps every element x in the first set to a "random" element in the second set. The technical discussion on what exactly this means, and how to build "good enough" hash functions that can be stored in few bits is left for section 4.9.1. Let us say only that hash functions that are random enough for our purposes and map $\{0, . . . , m − 1\}$ to itself can be obtained from $O(\log m)$ truly random bits, and stored with $O(\log m)$ bits.

Each item present in the stream sets to 1 an entry of table B, the same one regardless of how many times it occurs. Intuitively, a good hash function ensures that the distinct items appearing in the stream are uniformly allocated to the entries of B. Then, the expected value returned by *Query* is the number of distinct values seen in the stream plus a tiny bias term, whose standard deviation is $\sqrt{D\rho(e^\rho - \rho - 1)}$. For a reasonably large number of distinct elements ($d \gg \sqrt{D}$) this is much smaller than d itself, which means that LINEAR COUNTING will be pretty accurate in relative terms.

4.5.2   Cohen's Logarithmic Counter

Cohen's counter [74] builds on this idea but moves to logarithmic space using the following observation. The average gap between two consecutive 1s in B is determined by the number of 1 bits in the stream, and is approximately s/d. This is true in particular for the first gap, or equivalently for the position of the first 1. Conveniently, it only takes $\log s$ bits to store this first position, because it is the minimum of the observed values of the hash function. The sketch is shown in figure 4.4. Cohen's counter only uses $\log D$ bits to store p.

COHEN'S COUNTER

```
1   Init(D):
2       ▷ D is an upper bound on the number of distinct elements
3       p ← D
4       choose a hash function h from items to {0, . . . , D − 1}
5   Update(x):
6       p ← min( p, h(x) )
7   Query():
8       return D/p
```

Figure 4.4
Cohen's counting algorithm.

It can be shown that the expected value of p is D/d and that the *Query* procedure returns d in expectation. Its variance is large, roughly $(D/d)^2$. It can be reduced by running several copies in parallel and averaging, but this requires building several independent and "good" hash functions, which is problematic. An alternative method using a single hash function will be presented as part of the next sketch.

4.5.3 The Flajolet-Martin Counter and HyperLogLog

A series of algorithms starting with the Flajolet-Martin counter [105] and culminating in HyperLogLog [104], achieve relative approximation ϵ with even fewer bits, $O((\log \log D)/\epsilon^2)$, plus whatever is required to store a hash function. The intuition of this method is the following: let D be 2^k. Select without repetition numbers in the range $[0, 2^k - 1]$ uniformly at random; this is what we obtain after applying a good hash function to stream items. All these numbers can be written with k bits in binary; half of these numbers have 0 as the first bit, one-quarter have two leading 0s, one-eighth start with 000, and so on. In general, a leading pattern $0^i 1$ appears with probability $2^{-(i+1)}$, so if $0^i 1$ is the longest such pattern in the hash values drawn so far, then we may expect d to be around 2^{i+1}. Durand and Flajolet [93], in their improvements of Flajolet-Martin, realized that one only needs to remember k, with $\log k = \log \log D$ bits, to keep track of the longest pattern, or largest i. The basic Flajolet-Martin probabilistic counter with this improvement is given in pseudocode in figure 4.5.

PROBABILISTIC COUNTER

```
1   Init(D):
2          ▷ D is an upper bound on the number of distinct elements
3          L ← log D
4          choose a hash function h from items to {0, ..., L − 1}
5          p ← L
6   Update(x):
7          let i be such that h(x) in binary starts with 0^i 1
8          p ← min(p, i)
9   Query():
10         return 2^p/0.77351
```

Figure 4.5
The basic Flajolet-Martin probabilistic counter.

The method needs a hash function h that transforms each item into an integer between 0 and $L - 1$, as randomly as possible. It was shown in [105] that, if d distinct items have been read, the expected value of p is $\log(0.77351\, d)$ and its standard deviation is $1.12127\ldots$ The sketch only requires memory to store p, whose value is at most $L = \log D$, and so requires $\log \log D$ bits.

The main drawback of this method is the relatively large error in the estimation, on the order of d. It can be reduced by averaging several copies, as discussed before. But this has two problems: one, it multiplies the computation time of the update operation accordingly. Two, obtaining several truly independent hash functions is hard.

Flajolet and Martin propose instead the technique they call *stochastic averaging*: Conceptually divide the stream into $m = 2^b$ substreams, each one feeding a different copy of the sketch. For each item x, use the first $b = \log m$ bits of $h(x)$ to decide the stream to which x is assigned, and the other $m - \log m$ of bits of $h(x)$ to feed the corresponding sketch. A single hash function can be used now, because items in different substreams see independent parts of the same function, and update time is essentially the same as for a single sketch. Memory use is still multiplied by m.

Different variants of the algorithm differ in how they combine the results from the m copies into a single estimation.

- LogLog [93] returns the geometric average of their estimations, which is 2 to the arithmetic average of their variables p, times a constant.

- SuperLogLog [93] removes the top 30% of the estimations before doing the above; this reduces the effect of outliers.

- HyperLogLog, by Flajolet et al. [104], returns instead the harmonic average of the m estimations, which also smooths out large outliers.

The variants above achieve standard deviations $1.3d/\sqrt{m}$, $1.05d/\sqrt{m}$, and $1.04d/\sqrt{m}$, respectively, and use memory $O(m \log \log D)$, plus $O(\log D)$ bits to store a hash function that can be shared among all instances of the counter. By using Chebyshev's inequality, we obtain an (ϵ, δ)-approximation provided that $m = O(1/(\delta\epsilon^2))$; note that it is not clear how to apply Hoeffding's bound because the estimation is not an average. Stated differently, taking $\epsilon = O(1/\sqrt{m})$, we achieve relative approximation ϵ for fixed confidence using $O((\log \log D)/\epsilon^2)$ bits of memory.

In more concrete terms, according to [104], HyperLogLog can approximate cardinalities up to 10^9 within, say, 2% using just 1.5 kilobytes of memory. A discussion of practical implementations of HyperLogLog for large applications can be found in [134].

4.5.4   An Application: Computing Distance Functions in Graphs

Let us mention a nonstreaming application of the Flajolet-Martin counter, to illustrate that streaming algorithms can sometimes be used to improve time or memory efficiency in nonstreaming problems.

Boldi et al. [47], improving on [192], proposed the HyperANF counter, which uses HyperLogLog to approximate the *neighborhood function* N of graphs. For a node v and distance d, $N(v, d)$ is defined as the number of nodes reachable from node v by paths of length at most d. The probabilistic counter allows for a memory-efficient, approximate calculation of $N(., d)$ given the values of $N(., d-1)$, and one sequential pass over the edges of the graph in the arbitrary order in which they are stored in disk, that is, with no expensive disk random accesses.

We give the intuition of how to achieve this. The first key observation is that a vertex is reachable from v by a path of length at most d if it is either reachable from v by a path of length at most $d-1$, or reachable by a path of length at most $d-1$ from a vertex u such that (v, u) is an edge. The second key observation is that HyperLogLog counters are mergeable, a concept we will explore in section 4.8. It means that, given two HyperLogLog counters H_A and H_B that result from processing two streams A and B, there is a way to obtain a new HyperLogLog counter $merge(H_A, H_B)$ identical to the one that would be obtained by processing the concatenation of C of A and B. That is, it contains the number of distinct items in C. Then, suppose inductively that we have computed for each vertex v a HyperLogLog counter $H_{d-1}(v)$ that (approximately) counts the number of vertices at distance at most $d-1$ from v, or in other words, approximates $N(v, d-1)$. Then compute $H_d(v)$ as follows:

1. $H_d(v) \leftarrow H_{d-1}(v)$.

2. For each edge (v, u) (in arbitrary order) do

$$H_d(v) \leftarrow merge(H_d(v), H_{d-1}(u)).$$

Using the first key observation above, it is clear that $H_d(v)$ equals $N(v, d)$ if the counts are exact; errors due to approximations might in principle accumulate and amplify as we increase d, but experiments in [47] do not show this effect. We can discard the H_{d-1} counters once the H_d are computed, and reuse the space they used. Thus we can approximate neighborhood functions up to distance d with d sequential scans of the edge database and memory $O(n \log \log n)$.

Using this idea and a good number of clever optimizations, Backstrom et al. [21] were able to address the estimation of distances in the Facebook graph, the graph where nodes are Facebook users and edges their direct friendship relationships. The graph had 721 million users and 69 billion links. Remarkably, their computation of the average distance between users ran in a few hours on a single machine, and resulted in average distance 4.74, corresponding to 3.74 intermediaries or "degrees of separation." Informally, this confirms the celebrated experiment by S. Milgram in the 1960s [177], with physical letters and the postal service, hinting that most people in the world were at the time no more than six degrees of separation apart from each other.

A unified view of sketches for distance-related queries in massive graphs is presented in [75].

4.5.5 Discussion: Log vs. Linear

More details on algorithms for finding distinct elements can be found in [176], which also provides empirical evaluations. It focuses on the question of when it is worth using the relatively sophisticated sublinear sketches rather than simple linear counting. The conclusion is that linear sketches are preferable when extremely high accuracy, say below $\epsilon = 10^{-4}$, is required. Logarithmic sketches typically require $O(1/\epsilon^2)$ space for multiplicative error ϵ, which may indeed be large for high accuracies.

In data mining and ML applications, relatively large approximation errors are often acceptable, say within $\epsilon = 10^{-1}$, because the model mined is the combination of many statistics, none of which is too crucial by itself, and because anyway data is viewed as a random sample of reality. Thus, logarithmic space sketches may be an attractive option.

Also worthy of mention is that [144] gives a more involved, asymptotically optimal algorithm for counting distinct elements, using $O(\epsilon^{-2} + \log d)$ bits, that is, removing the $\log \log d$ factor in HyperLogLog. HyperLogLog still seems to be faster and smaller for practical purposes.

4.6   Frequency Problems

In many cases, we do not simply want to count all items in a stream, but separately count different types of items in the stream. Estimating the frequencies of all items is impossible to do in general in sublinear memory, but often it suffices to have approximate counts for the most frequent items.

For an initial segment of length t of a stream, the *absolute frequency* of an item x is the number of times it has appeared in the segment, and its *relative frequency* is the absolute frequency divided by t. We will mostly consider the following formulation of the problem:

The heavy hitter problem. Given a threshold ϵ and access to a stream, after reading any number of items from the stream, produce the set of *heavy hitters*, all items whose relative frequency exceeds ϵ.

This problem is closely related to that of computing *iceberg queries* [97] in the database area. A basic observation is that there can be at most $1/\epsilon$ items having relative frequency above ϵ; otherwise relative frequencies add to more than 1, which is impossible.

A first approximation to the heavy hitter problem is to use sampling; for example, use reservoir sampling to draw a uniform sample from the stream, and at all times declare that the frequent elements in the sample are the frequent elements in the stream. This is a valid algorithm, but the sample size required to achieve any fixed confidence is proportional to $1/\epsilon^2$. In this section we will present three algorithms for the heavy hitter problem, each with its own strong points. The first is deterministic and based on counters; the other two are based on hashing.

The surveys [80, 164] discuss and evaluate the algorithms we are going to present, and several others.

In this section we measure memory in words, assuming that an item, integer, pointer, and such simple variables fit in one memory word.

4.6.1   The SPACESAVING **Sketch**

Counter-based algorithms are historically evolutions of a method by Boyer and Moore [50] to find a majority element (one with frequency at least 1/2) when it exists. An improvement of this method was independently discovered by Misra and Gries [179], Demaine et al. [86], and Karp et al. [145]. Usually called FREQUENT now, this method finds a list of elements guaranteed to contain all ϵ–heavy hitters with memory $O(1/\epsilon)$ only.

A drawback of FREQUENT is that it provides the heavy hitters but no reliable estimates of their frequencies, which are often important to have. Other counter-based sketches that do provide approximations of the frequencies include Lossy Counting and Sticky Sampling, both due Manku and Motwani [165, 166], and Space Saving, due to Metwally et al. [175]. We describe Space Saving, reported in [80, 161, 164] to have the best performance among several heavy hitter algorithms. Additionally, it is simple and has intuitive rigorous guarantees on the quality of approximation.

Figure 4.6 shows the pseudocode of SPACESAVING. It maintains in memory a set of at most k pairs (item, count), initialized with the first k distinct elements and their counts. When a new stream item arrives, if the item already has an entry in the set, its count is incremented. If not, this item replaces the item with the lowest count, which is then incremented by 1. The nonintuitive part is that this item inherits the counts of the element it evicts, even if this is its first occurrence. However, as the following claims show, the error is never too large, and can neither make a rare element look too frequent nor a true heavy hitter look too infrequent.

SPACESAVING

```
1   Init(k):
2          create an empty set S of pairs (item,count) able to hold up to k pairs
3   Update(x):
4          if item x is in S
5                 increase its count by 1
6          else if S contains less than k entries
7                 add (x, 1) to S
8          else
9                 let (y, count) be an entry in S with lowest count
10                replace the entry (y, count) with (x, count + 1) in S
11  Query():
12         return the list of pairs (x, count(x)) currently in S
```

Figure 4.6
The SPACESAVING sketch.

Let $f_{t,x}$ be the absolute frequency of item x among the first t stream elements, and if x is in the sketch at time t, let $count_t(x)$ be its associated count; we omit the subindex t when it is clear from the context. The following are true for every item x and at all times t:

1. The value of the smallest counter min is at most t/k.
2. If $x \notin S$, then $f_x \leq min$.
3. If $x \in S$, then $f_x \leq count(x) \leq f_x + min$.

(1) and (2) imply that every x with frequency above t/k is in S, that is, the sketch contains all $(1/k)$–heavy hitters. (3) says that the counts for elements in S do not underestimate the true frequencies and do not overestimate them by more than t/k. The value t/k can be seen as the minimum resolution: counts are good approximations only for frequencies substantially larger than t/k, and an item with frequency 1 may have just made it into the sketch and have associated count up to t/k.

The *Stream-Summary* data structure proposed in [175] implements the sketch, ensuring amortized constant time per update. For every count value c present in the sketch, a bucket is created that contains c and a pointer to a doubly linked list of all the items having count c. Buckets are kept in a doubly linked list, sorted by their values c. The nodes in the linked lists of items all contain a pointer to their parent bucket, and there is a hash table that, given an item, provides a pointer to the node that contains it. The details are left as an exercise.

All in all, taking $k = \lceil 1/\epsilon \rceil$, SPACESAVING finds all ϵ–heavy hitters, with an approximation of their frequencies that is correct up to ϵ, using $O(1/\epsilon)$ memory words and constant amortized time.

SPACESAVING, FREQUENT, Lossy Counting, and Sticky Sampling are all deterministic algorithms; they do not use hash functions or randomization, except perhaps inside the hash table used for searching the set. It is easy to adapt SPACESAVING to updates of the form (x, c), where x is an item, c any *positive* weight, and the pair stands for the assignment $f_x \leftarrow f_x + c$, with no significant impact on memory or update time. But it cannot simulate item deletions or, equivalently, updates with *negative* weights.

4.6.2   The CM-Sketch Algorithm

The *Count-Min sketch* or *CM-sketch* is due to Cormode and Muthukrishnan [81] and can be used to solve several problems related to item frequencies, among them the heavy hitter problem. Unlike FREQUENT and SPACE-SAVING, it is probabilistic and uses random hash functions extensively. More importantly for some applications, it can deal with updates having positive and negative weights, in particular, with item additions and subtractions.

We first describe what the sketch achieves, then its implementation. We consider streams with elements of the form (x, c) where x is an item, c any positive or negative weight update to f_x. We use F to denote the total weight $\sum_x f_x$ at a given time.

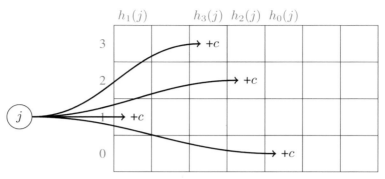

Figure 4.7

Example CM-sketch structure of width 7 and depth 4, corresponding to $\epsilon = 0.4$ and $\delta = 0.02$.

The CM-sketch creation function takes two parameters, the *width* w and the *depth* d. Its update function receives a pair (x, c) as above. Its *Query* function takes as parameter an item x, and returns a value $\hat{f}_x$ that satisfies, with probability $1 - \delta$, that

$$f_x \leq \hat{f}_x \leq f_x + \epsilon F \tag{4.1}$$

provided $w \geq \lceil e/\epsilon \rceil$ and $d \geq \lceil \ln(1/\delta) \rceil$. This holds at any time, no matter how many items have been added and then deleted before.

We assume from now on that $F > 0$ for the inequality above to make sense, that is, the negative weights are smaller than the positive weight. Like in SPACESAVING, this means that $\hat{f}_x$ is a reasonable approximation of f_x for heavy items, that is, items whose weight is a noticeable fraction of F. Additionally, the memory used by the algorithm is approximately wd counters or accumulators. In summary, values f_x are approximated within an additive factor of ϵ with probability $1 - \delta$ using $O(\ln(1/\delta)/\epsilon)$ memory words.

Let us now describe the implementation of the sketch. A CM-sketch with parameters w, d consists of a two-dimensional array of counters with d rows and w columns, together with d independent hash functions $h_0, \ldots, h_{d-1}$ mapping items to the interval $[0 \ldots w - 1]$. Figure 4.7 shows an example of the CM-sketch structure for $d = 4$ and $w = 7$, and figure 4.8 shows the pseudocode of the algorithm.

It can be seen that both *Update* and *Query* operations perform $O(d)$ operations. We do not formally prove the approximation bounds in inequality (4.1), but we provide some intuition of why they hold. Observe first that for a row i and column j, $A[i, j]$ contains the sum of the weights in the stream of all

CM-SKETCH

```
1  Init(w, d):
2        create a d × w array of counters A, all initialized to 0
3        choose d hash functions h_0, ..., h_{d-1} from items to {0, ..., w - 1}
4  Update(x, c):
5        for i ← 0 ... d - 1
6              A[i, h_i(x)] ← A[i, h_i(x)] + c
7  Query(x):
8        return min{A[i, h_i(x)] : i = 0 ... d - 1}
```

Figure 4.8

The CM-SKETCH algorithm.

items x such that $h_i(x) = j$. This alone ensures that $f_x \leq A[i, h_i(x)]$ and therefore that $f_x \leq Query(x)$. But $A[i, h_i(x)]$ may overestimate f_x if there are other items y that happen to be mapped to the same cell of that row, that is $h_i(x) = h_i(y)$. The total weight to be distributed among the w cells in the row is F, so the expected weight falling on any particular cell is F/w. One can show that it is unlikely that any cell receives much more than this expected value. Intuitively, this may happen if a particularly heavy item is mapped in the cell, but the number of heavy items is limited, so this happens rarely; or else if too many light items are mapped to the cell, but this is also unlikely because the hash function places items more or less uniformly among all w cells in the row. Markov's inequality is central in the proof.

Returning to the heavy hitter problem, the CM-sketch provides a reasonable approximation of the frequency of elements that are heavy hitters, but there is no obvious way to locate them from the data structure. A brute-force search that calls $Query(x)$ for all possible x is unfeasible for large item universes. The solution uses an efficient implementation of so-called *Range-Sum queries*, which are of independent interest in many situations.

A Range-Sum query is defined on sets of items that can be identified with integers in $\{1, ..., |I|\}$. The range-sum query with parameters $[x, y]$ returns $f_x + f_{x+1} + \cdots + f_{y-1} + f_y$. As an example, consider a router handling packets destined to IP addresses. A range-sum query for the router could be "How many packets directed to IPv4 addresses in the range 172.16.aaa.bbb have you seen?" We expect to solve this query faster than iterating over the 2^{16} addresses in the range.

Range-sum queries can be implemented using CM-sketches as follows: Let $|I| = 2^n$ be the number of potential items. For every power of two 2^i, $0 \leq i \leq n$, create a CM-sketch C_i that range-sums items in intervals of size 2^i. More precisely, $Query(j)$ to C_i will return the total count of items in the interval $[j2^i \ldots (j+1)2^i - 1]$. Alternatively, we can imagine that at level i each item x belongs to the "superitem" $x \bmod 2^{n-i}$. In particular, C_0 stores individual item counts and C_n the sum of all counts. Then we can answer the range-sum query (x, y) to C_i, for x and y in the same interval of size 2^i, with the following recursion: If x and y fall in the same interval of size 2^{i-1}, we query (x, y) to C_{i-1} and return its answer. If, on the other hand, there is some j such that $x < j2^{i-1} \leq y$ (that is, x and y do not belong to the same interval of size 2^{i-1}), we ask the range-sum queries $(x, j2^{i-1} - 1)$ and $(j2^{i-1}, y)$ to C_{i-1}, and then return the sum of the answers. Sketch C_0 is the base of the recursion.

Now, the heavy hitter problem with parameter k can be solved by exploring the set of intervals $[j2^i, (j+1)2^i - 1]$ by depth. If the weight of the interval is below F/k, no leaf below it can be a heavy hitter, so the empty list is returned. Otherwise, it is divided into two equal-size intervals that are explored separately, and the lists returned are concatenated. When a leaf is reached, it is returned if and only if it is a heavy hitter, that is, its weight is F/k or more. Also, at each level of the tree there can be at most k nodes of weight F/k or more, so at most $k \log |I|$ nodes of the tree are explored. All in all, heavy hitters are found using $O((\log |I|) \ln(1/\delta)/\epsilon)$ memory words.

As already mentioned, the CM-sketch can be used for solving several other problems on streams efficiently [81], including quantile computations, item frequency histograms, correlation, and the inner product of two streams. For the case of quantile computation, however, the specialized sketch FrugalStreaming [163] is considered the state of the art. We will describe another quantile summary in section 6.4.3 when describing the management of numeric attributes in classification problems.

4.6.3   CountSketch

The COUNTSKETCH algorithm was proposed by Charikar et al. [64]. Like CM-SKETCH, it supports updates with both positive and negative weights. It uses memory $O(1/\epsilon^2)$, but it finds the so-called F_2–heavy hitters, which is an interesting superset of the regular heavy hitters, or F_1–heavy hitters.

The F_2 norm of a stream is defined as $\sum_{x \in I} f_x^2$. Item x is an F_2–heavy hitter with threshold ϵ if $f_x \geq \epsilon\sqrt{F_2}$. Some easy algebra shows that every F_1–heavy hitter is also an F_2–heavy hitter.

In its simplest form, COUNTSKETCH can be described as follows. It chooses two hash functions. Function h maps items to a set of w buckets $\{0, \ldots, w - 1\}$. Function σ maps items to $\{-1, +1\}$. Both are assumed to be random enough. In particular, an important property of σ is that for different x and y, $\sigma(x)$ and $\sigma(y)$ are independent, which means that $\Pr[\sigma(x) = \sigma(y)] = 1/2$, which means that $\mathrm{E}[\sigma(x) \cdot \sigma(y)] = 0$.

The algorithm keeps an array A of w accumulators, initialized to 0. For every pair (x, c) in the stream, it adds to $A[h(x)]$ the value $\sigma(x) \cdot c$. Note that updates for a given x are either all added or all subtracted, depending on $\sigma(x)$. When asked to provide an estimation of f_x, the algorithm returns $Query(x) = \sigma(x) \cdot A[h(x)]$. This estimation would be exact if no other item y was mapped to the same cell of A as x, but this is rarely the case. Still, one can prove that the expectation over random choices of the hash functions is the correct one. Indeed:

$$\mathrm{E}[Query(x)] = \mathrm{E}[\sigma(x) \cdot \sum_{y:h(y)=h(x)} \sigma(y)f_y]$$

$$= \mathrm{E}[\sigma(x)^2 f_x] + \sum_{y:h(y)=h(x), y \neq x} \sigma(x)\sigma(y)f_y] = f_x$$

because, as mentioned, $E[\sigma(x)\sigma(y)] = 0$ for $x \neq y$, and $\sigma(x)^2 = 1$. Similar algebra shows that $\mathrm{Var}(Query(x)) \leq F_2/w$.

Now we can use a strategy like the one described in section 4.9.2 to improve first accuracy, then confidence: take the average of $w = 12/(5\epsilon^2)$ independent copies; by Chebyshev's inequality, this estimates each frequency with additive error $\epsilon/2 \cdot \sqrt{F_2}$ and probability $5/6$. Then do this $d = O(\ln(1/\delta))$ times independently and return the median of the results; Hoeffding's inequality shows (see exercise 4.9) that this lifts the confidence to $1 - \delta$. Therefore, the set of x's such that $Query(x) > \epsilon/2 \cdot \sqrt{F_2}$ contains each F_2–heavy hitter with high probability. Note that, unlike in CM-SKETCH and SPACESAVING, there may be false negatives besides false positives, because the median rather than the min is used. Memory use is $O(\ln(1/\delta)/\epsilon^2)$ words.

At this point, we can view the d copies of the basic algorithm as a single algorithm that resembles CM-SKETCH: it chooses hash functions

$h_0, \ldots, h_{d-1}$, $\sigma_0, \ldots, \sigma_{d-1}$, and maintains an array A with d rows and w columns. The pseudocode is shown in figure 4.9. To recover the heavy hitters efficiently, COUNTSKETCH also maintains a heap of the most frequent elements seen so far on the basis of the estimated weights.

COUNTSKETCH

1 *Init*(w, d):
2   create a $d \times w$ array of counters A, all initialized to 0
3   choose d hash functions $h_0, \ldots, h_{d-1}$ from items to $\{0, \ldots, w-1\}$
4   choose d hash functions $\sigma_0, \ldots, \sigma_{d-1}$ from items to $\{-1, +1\}$
5   create an empty heap
6 *Update*(x, c):
7   **for** $i \leftarrow 0 \ldots d - 1$
8          $A[i, h_i(x)] \leftarrow A[i, h_i(x)] + \sigma(i) \cdot c$
9   **if** x is in the heap, increment its count there by c
10   **else if** *Query*$(y) <$ *Query*(x) where y has smallest weight in the heap
11   remove y from the heap and add (x, c) to the heap
12 *Query*(x):
13   **return** median$\{A[i, h_i(x)] : i = 0 \ldots d - 1\}$

Figure 4.9
The COUNTSKETCH algorithm.

Improvements of COUNTSKETCH are presented in [51, 249].

As a brief summary of the heavy hitter methods, and following [164], if an application is strictly limited to discovering frequent items, counter-based techniques such as Lossy Counting or Space Saving are probably preferable in time, memory, and accuracy, and are easier to implement. For example, COUNTSKETCH and CM-SKETCH were found to be less stable and perform worse for some parameter ranges. On the other hand, hash-based methods are the only alternative to support negative item weights, and provide useful information besides simply the heavy hitters.

4.6.4 Moment Computation

Frequency moments are a generalization of item frequency that give different information on the distribution of items in the stream. The pth moment of a stream where each item x has absolute frequency f_x is defined as

$$F_p = \sum_x f_x^p.$$

Observe that F_1 is the length of the stream and that F_0 is the number of distinct items it contains (if we take 0^0 to be 0, and $f^0 = 1$ for any other f). F_2 is of particular interest, as it can be used to compute the variance of the items in the stream. The limit case is F_∞, defined as

$$F_\infty = \lim_{p \to \infty} (F_p)^{1/p} = \max_x f_x$$

or, in words, the frequency of the most frequent element.

Alon et al. [14] started the study of streaming algorithms for computing approximations of frequency moments. Their sketch for $p \geq 2$ (known as the Alon-Matias-Szegedy or AMS sketch) uses a technique similar to the one in CM-SKETCH: take hash functions that map each item to $\{-1, +1\}$, use them to build an unbiased estimator of the moment with high variance, then average and take medians of several copies to produce an arbitrarily accurate estimation.

Their work already indicated that there was an abrupt difference in the memory requirements for computing F_p for $p \leq 2$ and for $p > 2$. After a long series of papers it was shown in [141] that, considering relative approximations,

- for $p \leq 2$, F_p can be approximated in a data stream using $O(\epsilon^{-2}(\log t + \log m) \ln(1/\delta))$ bits of memory, and

- for $p > 2$, F_p can be approximated in a data stream using $O(\epsilon^{-2} t^{1-2/p} \ln(1/\delta))$ bits,

up to logarithmic factors, where t is the length of the stream and $m = |I|$ is the size of the set of items. Furthermore, memory of that order is in fact *necessary* for every p other than 0 and 1. Later work has essentially removed the logarithmic gaps as well. In particular, for F_∞ or the maximum frequency, linear memory in the length of the stream is required. Observe that for the special cases $p = 0$ and $p = 1$ we have given algorithms using memory $O(\log \log t)$ rather than $O(\log t)$ in previous sections.

4.7 Exponential Histograms for Sliding Windows

Often, more recent items in the stream should be considered more important for analysis. We will model this idea in several ways in chapter 5, but here we consider the simplest model, the *sliding window*: At all times, we only consider relevant the last W items received, where W is the window size; all previous items are irrelevant. Alternatively, we fix a time duration T (such as one week, one hour, or one minute) and consider only the items that have arrived within time T from now. We will consider mostly the first model, but adaptation to the second is easy.

Consider the problem of maintaining the sum of the last W values in a stream of real numbers. The natural solution is to use a circular buffer of size W; every arriving element is added to the sum; it evicts the oldest element from the buffer, which is subtracted from the sum. The scheme has constant update time, but uses memory W. In fact, one can show that any streaming algorithm that *exactly* solves this problem must use memory at least W.

We will see next a method for maintaining an *approximate* value of the sum storing only $O(\log W)$ values. The *Exponential Histogram* sketch by Datar et al. [83] maintains approximations of aggregate functions on sliding windows of real numbers. We describe in detail only the case in which the aggregate function is the sum and the items are bits.

The sketch partitions the length-W window into a sequence of subwindows, and represents each subwindow by a *bucket*. Intuitively, buckets encode the desired window of size W where older 1s are represented with less and less resolution. Each bucket has a *capacity*, which is a power of 2, and represents a subwindow containing as many 1s as its capacity. It contains an integer value, the *timestamp*, which is the timestamp of the most recent 1 in the subwindow it represents. For a parameter $k > 1$, there are k buckets of capacity 1, delimited by the most recent k 1s, k buckets of capacity 2, k buckets of capacity 4, and so on, up to k buckets of capacity 2^m, where m is the smallest value ensuring that there are enough buckets to hold W items, that is,

$$k \sum_{i=0}^{m-1} 2^i < W \leq k \sum_{i=0}^{m} 2^i.$$

Observe that $m \simeq \log(W/k)$, and so there are $km \simeq k \log(W/k)$ buckets.

The pseudocode of the method is given in figure 4.11 and an example of a sliding window split into buckets is given in figure 4.10. The example shows the partition of the last 29 bits of a stream into 6 buckets at some time t, with $k = 2$. Each bucket contains as many 1s as its capacity. The most recent bit is on the right, with timestamp t. The least recent bit is on the left, with timestamp $t - 28$. The timestamp of each bucket is the timestamp of its most recent 1. If the desired sliding window size W is 25, the true count of 1s within the most recent W bits is 11, as there are 11 1s with timestamps between $t - 24$ and t. The sketch will report the sum of the window to be 12: the total number of 1s in the buckets (14), minus half the capacity of the oldest bucket (2). Therefore the relative error is $(12 - 11)/11 \simeq 9\%$.

Bucket:	1011100	10100101	100010	11	10	1000
Capacity:	4	4	2	2	1	1
Timestamp:	$t - 24$	$t - 14$	$t - 9$	$t - 6$	$t - 5$	$t - 3$

Figure 4.10

Partitioning a stream of 29 bits into buckets, with $k = 2$. Most recent bits are to the right.

EXPONENTIAL HISTOGRAMS

1   *Init*(k, W):
2       $t \leftarrow 0$
3   create a list of empty buckets
4   *Update*(b):
5       $t \leftarrow t + 1$
6   **if** $b = 1$ ▷ do nothing with 0s
7   let t be the current time
8   create a bucket of capacity 1 and timestamp t
9           $i \leftarrow 0$
10   **while** there are more than k buckets of capacity 2^i
11   merge the two oldest buckets of capacity 2^i into a
12   bucket of capacity 2^{i+1}: the timestamp of the new bucket
13   is the largest (most recent) of their two timestamps
14              $i \leftarrow i + 1$
15   remove all buckets whose timestamp is $\leq t - W$
16 *Query*():
17   **return** the sum of the capacities of all existing buckets
18   minus half the capacity of the oldest bucket

Figure 4.11

The EXPONENTIAL HISTOGRAMS sketch.

The error in the approximation is introduced only by the oldest bucket. It must contain at least one 1 with timestamp greater than $t - W$, otherwise it would have been dropped, but possibly also up to $2^m - 1$ 1s whose timestamp is at most $t - W$ and that should not be counted by an exact method. The relative error is therefore at most half the capacity of the oldest bucket over the capacity of all buckets. Since, after some transient, there are either $k - 1$ or k buckets of each size except the largest one, the relative error is at most $(2^m/2)/(2^m + (k-1)(2^{m-1} + \cdots + 1)) \simeq 1/2k$.

If the desired approximation rate is ϵ, it suffices to set $k = 1/2\epsilon$. The number of buckets is then $(\log W)/2\epsilon$. Each bucket contains a timestamp, which is in principle an unbounded number. However, we can reduce the timestamps to the interval $0 \ldots W - 1$ by counting mod W, so a timestamp has $\log W$ bits, giving a total of $O((\log W)^2/\epsilon)$ bits of memory. Update time is $O(\log W)$ in the worst case if the cascade of bucket updates affects all buckets, but this happens rarely; amortized time is $O(1)$. A variant of exponential histograms called *deterministic waves* achieves worst-case $O(1)$ time [122].

The sketch can be adapted to work for nonnegative numbers in a range $[0, B]$ multiplying memory by $\log B$, and also to maintain approximations of other aggregates such as variance, maximum, minimum, number of distinct elements, and histograms [83].

4.8   Distributed Sketching: Mergeability

Most of the sketches discussed so far have the property called *mergeability*, which makes them appropriate for distributed computation. We say that a sketch type is *mergeable* if two sketches built from data streams D_1 and D_2 can be combined efficiently into another sketch of the same type that can correctly answer queries about interleavings of D_1 and D_2. Note that in problems that only depend on item frequencies, the answer is the same for all interleavings of the streams. For other problems, the definition of mergeability can be more complex.

As a simple example, consider a "sketch" consisting of an integer that counts the number of items in the stream. Now we build two such sketches from two streams. If we add their values, the result is—correctly—the number of items in any stream obtained by merging the original two.

Less trivially, taking the OR is a correct merging operation for Linear Counters. For Cohen's and Flajolet-Martin counters and variants, take the minimum of their stored values, componentwise if we use several copies to reduce the variance. For the CM-sketch, add the two arrays of counters component-wise. In these cases, the two sketches to be merged must use the same hash functions. The cases of SPACESAVING and EXPONENTIAL HISTOGRAMS are left for the exercises.

Mergeability allows for distributed processing as follows: suppose we have k different computing nodes, each receiving a different stream—or equivalently some fraction of a large, distributed stream. A central node that wants to build a sketch for this large implicit stream can periodically request the k nodes to send their sketches, and merge them into its own global sketch.

For Morris's counter, Cohen (section 7 of [75]) presents a merging method; it is not as trivial as the ones above, particularly the correctness analysis.

4.9   Some Technical Discussions and Additional Material

4.9.1   Hash Functions

For several sketches we have assumed the existence of hash functions that randomly map a set of items I to a set B. Strictly speaking, a *fully independent* hash function h should be such that the value of h on some value x cannot be guessed with any advantage given the values of h on the rest of the elements of I; formally, for every i,

$$\Pr[h(x_i)|h(x_1), \ldots, h(x_{i-1}), h(x_{i+1}), \ldots, h(x_{|I|})] = \Pr[h(x_i)] = 1/|I|.$$

But it is incorrect to think of $h(x_i)$ as generating a new random value each time it is called—it must always return the same value on the same input. It is thus random, but reproducibly random. To create such an h we can randomly guess and store the value of $h(x_i)$ for each $x_i \in I$, but storing h will use memory proportional to $|I| \log |B|$, defeating the goal of using memory far below $|I|$.

Fortunately, in some cases we can show that weaker notions of "random hash function" suffice. Rather than using a fixed hash function, whenever the algorithm needs to use a new hash function, it will use a few random bits to choose one at random from a *family* of hash functions H. We say that family H is *pairwise independent* if for any two distinct values x and y in I and α, β in B we have

$$\Pr[h(x) = \alpha|h(y) = \beta] = \Pr[h(x) = \alpha] = 1/|I|,$$

where the probability is taken over a random choice of $h \in H$. This means that if we do not know the h chosen within H, and know only one value of h, we cannot guess any other value of h.

Here is a simple construction of a family of pairwise independent hash functions when $|I|$ is some prime p. View I as the interval $[0 \ldots p-1]$. A function h in the family is defined by two values a and b in $[0 \ldots p-1]$ and computes $h(x) = (ax + b) \bmod p$. Note that one such function is described by a and b, so with $2 \log p$ bits. This family is pairwise independent because given x, y and the value $h(y)$, for each possible value $h(x)$ there is a unique solution (a, b) to the system of equations $\{h(x) = ax + b, h(y) = ay + b\}$, so all values of $h(x)$ are equally likely. Note however that if we know x, y, $h(x)$, and $h(y)$, we can solve uniquely for a, b so we know the value $h(z)$ for every other input z. If $|I|$ is a prime power p^b, we can generalize this construction by operating in the finite field of size p^b; be warned that this is *not* the same as doing arithmetic modulo p^b. We can also choose a prime slightly larger than $|I|$ and get functions that deviate only marginally from pairwise independence.

Pairwise independent functions suffice for the CM-sketch. Algorithms for moments require a generalization called 4-wise independence. For other algorithms, such as HyperLogLog, k-wise independence cannot be formally shown to suffice, to the best of our knowledge. However, although no formal guarantee exists, well-known hash functions such as MD5, SHA1, SHA256, and Murmur3 seem to pose no problem in practice [104, 134]. Theoretical arguments have been proposed in [71] for why simple hash functions may do well on data structure problems such as sketching.

4.9.2   Creating (ϵ, δ)-Approximation Algorithms

Let f be a function to be approximated, and g a randomized algorithm such that $\mathrm{E}[g(x)] = f(x)$ for all x, and $\mathrm{Var}(g(x)) = \sigma^2$. Run k independent copies of g, say $g_1, \ldots, g_k$, and combine their outputs by averaging them, and let h denote the result. We have $\mathrm{E}[h(x)] = f(x)$ and, by simple properties of the variance, $\mathrm{Var}(|f(x) - h(x)|) \leq \mathrm{Var}(f(x) - h(x)) = \mathrm{Var}(h(x)) = \sigma^2/k$. Then by Chebyshev's inequality we have $|f(x) - h(x)| > \epsilon$ with probability at most $\sigma^2/(k\epsilon^2)$, for every ϵ. This means that h is an (ϵ, δ)-approximation of f if we choose $k = \sigma^2/(\epsilon^2\delta)$. The memory and update time of h are k times those of g.

A dependence of the form σ^2/ϵ^2 to achieve accuracy ϵ is necessary in general, but the dependence of the form $1/\delta$ can be improved as follows: use the method above to achieve a fixed confidence, say, $(\epsilon, 1/6)$-approximation. Then run ℓ copies of this fixed confidence algorithm and take the *median* of the results. Using Hoeffding's inequality we can show that this new algorithm is an (ϵ, δ)-approximation if we take $\ell = O(\ln(1/\delta))$; see exercise 4.9. The final algorithm therefore uses $k \cdot \ell = O((\sigma^2/\epsilon^2) \ln(1/\delta))$ times the memory and running time of the original algorithm g.

This transformation is already present in the pioneer paper on moment estimation in streams by Alon et al. [14].

4.9.3 Other Sketching Techniques

The sketches presented in this chapter were chosen for their potential use in stream mining and learning on data streams. Many other algorithmic problems on data streams have been proposed, for example solving combinatorial problems, geometric problems, and graph problems. Also, streaming variants of deep algorithmic techniques such as wavelets, low-dimensionality embeddings, and compressed sensing have been omitted in our presentation. Recent comprehensive references include [79, 172].

Algorithms for linear-algebraic problems deserve special mention, given how prominent they are becoming in ML. Advances in online Singular Value Decomposition ([221] and the more recent [159]) and Principal Component Analysis [49] are likely to become highly influential in streaming. The book [248] is an in-depth presentation of sketches for linear algebra; their practical use in stream mining and learning tasks is a very promising, but largely unexplored, direction.

4.10 Exercises

Exercise 4.1 We want to estimate the fraction f of items in a stream that satisfy some boolean property P. We do not have access to the stream itself, but only to a reservoir sampling of it, of capacity k. Let g be the fraction of items in the reservoir that satisfy P. Give the accuracy ϵ of the approximation g to f as a function of k if the desired confidence is 95%. (*Hint*: use Hoeffding's bound.)

Exercise 4.2 Suppose that in Morris's counter we change the threshold 2^{-c} to the exponentially smaller threshold 2^{-2^c}. (1) Argue informally that we obtain an algorithm that can count up to t using memory $O(\log \log \log t)$. (2) Explain why this algorithm is not interesting in practice.

Exercise 4.3 Give pseudocode for (or better, implement) the SPACESAVING algorithm using the Stream Summary data structure outlined in the text.

Exercise 4.4 Complete the proof by induction of the approximation guarantees (1)–(3) given for SPACESAVING.

Exercise 4.5 Give an algorithm for merging two SPACESAVING sketches of the same size k into a sketch of size k', where $k \le k' \le 2k$. Its runtime should be proportional to k, not to the sum of the counts contained in either of the sketches.

Exercise 4.6 Give pseudocode for (or better, implement) the range-sum query algorithm and the heavy hitter algorithm based on CM-SKETCH.

Exercise 4.7 Suppose that we change the Exponential Histograms (for the worse) as follows: 0 bits are now not ignored, but added to the bucket. A bucket, besides a timestamp, has a counter m of the 1s it contains (the number of 0s being its capacity minus m). Explain how buckets should be merged, and argue that querying the sketch returns an *additive* ϵ-approximation of the fraction of 1s in the sliding window of size W, instead of a multiplicative one.

Exercise 4.8 Give a procedure to merge two Exponential Histograms for the sum of two bit streams. The two input sketches and the output sketch must all have the same window length W and the same parameter k. You can start by assuming that the sketches are synchronized, that is, they represent windows with the same set of timestamps. An extension is to do without this assumption.

Exercise 4.9 Complete the proof that the construction of an (ϵ, δ)-approximation algorithm from any approximation algorithm is correct.

First show the following: suppose that a real-valued random variable X satisfies

$$\Pr[a \le X \le b] \ge 5/6.$$

Then the median Z of ℓ independent copies of X, say $X_1, \ldots, X_\ell$, satisfies

$$\Pr[a \leq Z \leq b] \geq 1 - 2\exp(-2\ell/9).$$

To show this, follow these steps:

- For each $i \leq \ell$, define an indicator variable Z_i as 1 if the event "$a \leq X_i$" occurs, and 0 otherwise.
- State the relation between $\sum_{i=1}^{\ell} Z_i$ and the event "$Z < a$."
- Use Hoeffding's inequality to bound the probability that $Z < a$.
- Proceed similarly to bound the probability that $Z > b$, and conclude the proof.

Now take $k = 6\sigma^2/\epsilon^2$ and create an algorithm h that averages k copies of the given approximation algorithm g for f. As shown in the text, h is an $(\epsilon, 1/6)$-approximation algorithm for f. Show that the algorithm that returns the median of ℓ independent copies of h is an (ϵ, δ)-approximation algorithm of f for $\ell = 9/2 \cdot \ln(2/\delta)$. This gives $k\ell = 27\sigma^2/\epsilon^2 \cdot \ln(2/\delta)$.

5 Dealing with Change

A central feature of the data stream model is that streams evolve over time, and algorithms must react to the change. For example, let us consider email spam classifiers, which decide whether new incoming emails are or are not spam. As classifiers learn to improve their accuracy, spammers are going to modify their strategies to build spam messages, trying to fool the classifiers into believing they are not spam. Customer behavior prediction is another example: customers, actual or potential, change their preferences as prices rise or fall, as new products appear and others fall out of fashion, or simply as the time of the year changes. The predictors in these and other situations need to be adapted, revised, or replaced as time passes if they are to maintain reasonable accuracy.

In this chapter we will first discuss the notion of change as usually understood in data streaming research, remarking on the differences with other areas that also consider changing data, then discuss possible types of change, some measures of performance used in the presence of change, and the general strategies for designing change-aware algorithms on streams (section 5.1). We will then consider methods for accurately estimating statistics of evolving data streams (section 5.2), and methods for detecting and quantifying change (section 5.3). We will conclude with some references on time-aware sketches and change detection in multidimensional streams (section 5.4).

There is a vast literature on change detection in data, and we have prioritized methods that are most applicable to data streams, easy to implement, and computationally light, and in particular those that are available in MOA. A comprehensive discussion for all types of data is [27], and an up-to-date discussion for streams is [116]. A framework for experimenting with change detection and management in MOA is presented in [41].

5.1 Notion of Change in Streams

Let us first discuss the notion of change in streams with respect to notions in other paradigms, as well as some nuances that appear when carefully defining change over time.

First, nonstationary distributions of data may also appear in batch data analysis. Data in batch datasets may also be timestamped and vary statistically over time. Algorithms may take this possibility into account when drawing conclusions from the data, but otherwise can perform several passes and examine data from before and after any given recorded time. In streaming, we cannot explicitly store all past data to detect or quantify change, and certainly we cannot use data from the future to make decisions in the present.

Second, there is some similarity to the vast field of time series analysis, where data also consists of a sequence (or a set of sequences) of timestamped items. In time series analysis, however, the analysis process is often assumed to be offline, with batch data, and without the requirements for low memory and low processing time per item inherent to streams. (Of course, we can also consider streaming, real-time time series analysis.) More importantly, in time series analysis the emphasis is often on forecasting the future evolution of the data. For example, if the average increase in sales has been 1% per month in the last six months, it is reasonable to predict that sales next month are going to be 1% higher than this month. In contrast, most of the work in streaming does not necessarily assume that change occurs in predictable ways, or has trends. Change may be arbitrary. The task is to build models describing how the world behaves right now, given what we are observing right now.

Third, the notion of change used in data streaming is different from (or a particular case of) the more general notion of "dataset shift" described in [182]. Dataset shift occurs whenever training and testing datasets come from different distributions. Streaming is one instance of this setting; for example, the predictive model we have built so far is going to be used to predict data that will arrive later, which may follow a different distribution. But it also applies to other situations, for instance where a classifier trained with batch data from a geographical region is applied to predict data coming from another region.

What do we mean exactly when we say that a data stream changes or evolves? It cannot mean that the items we observe today are not exactly the same as those that we observed yesterday. A more reasonable notion is that statistical properties of the data change more than what can be attributed to chance fluctuations. To make this idea precise, it helps to assume that the data is in fact the result of a random process that at each time generates an item according to a probability distribution that is used at that exact time, and that may or may not be the same that is used at any other given time. There is no change when this underlying generating distribution remains stationary. Change occurs whenever it varies from one time step to the next.

Recall that in the previous chapter we assumed an adversarial model, in which no randomness was assumed in the stream—only perhaps in the algorithm if it used random bits and numbers. The algorithm had to perform well even in an adversarially chosen, worst-case input. In contrast, in the randomly generated stream model, it makes sense to consider the "average case" performance of an algorithm by averaging over all possible streams according to their probability under the generating distribution. This notion of a *stochastic data stream* is used almost everywhere in the following chapters. For example, if the stream consists of independently generated bits with 1 having probability $1/2$, then we expect to have 0s and 1s interleaved at random. The unique n-bit sequence containing $n/2$ 1s first and then $n/2$ 0s has negligible probability, but could determine the performance of an algorithm in the adversarial model if it turns out to be its hardest case.

Often, an additional *independence* assumption is implicitly or explicitly used: that the item generated at time t is independent of those generated at previous time steps. In other words, it is common to assume that the process is Markovian. This is admittedly dubious, or patently false: in many situations the stream has memory, and experiences bursts of highly correlated events. For example, a fault in a component of a system is likely to generate a burst of faults in related components. A more relaxed version of the hypothesis is that correlations are somehow short-term and that over long enough substreams the statistics are those of a Markovian process. Designing algorithms that take such autocorrelations into account is an active area of research.

Although changes in the item distribution may be arbitrary, it helps to name a few generic types, which are not exclusive within a stream. The naming is unfortunately not consistent throughout the literature. In fact, change in general is often called *concept drift* in the literature; we try to be more precise in the following.

- *Sudden* change occurs when the distribution has remained unchanged for a long time, then changes in a few steps to a significantly different one. It is often called *shift*.

- *Gradual* or *incremental* change occurs when, for a long time, the distribution experiences at each time step a tiny, barely noticeable change, but these accumulated changes become significant over time.

- Change may be *global* or *partial* depending on whether it affects all of the item space or just a part of it. In ML terminology, partial change might affect only instances of certain forms, or only some of the instance attributes.

- *Recurrent concepts* occur when distributions that have appeared in the past tend to reappear later. An example is seasonality, where summer distributions are similar among themselves and different from winter distributions. A different example is the distortions in city traffic and public transportation due to mass events or accidents, which happen at irregular, unpredictable times.

• In prediction scenarios, we are expected to predict some outcome feature Y of an item given the values of input features X observed in the item. *Real change* occurs when $\Pr[Y|X]$ changes, with or without changes in $\Pr[X]$. *Virtual change* occurs when $\Pr[X]$ changes but $\Pr[Y|X]$ remains unchanged. In other words, in real change the rule used to label instances changes, while in virtual change the input distribution changes.

We should also distinguish the notions of *outliers* and *noise* from that of distribution change. Distinguishing true change from transient outliers and from persistent noise is one of the challenges in data stream mining and learning.

All in all, we need to consider the following requirements on data stream algorithms that build models (e.g., predictors, clusterers, or pattern miners) [116]:

1. Detect change in the stream (and adapt the models, if needed) as soon as possible.

2. At the same time, be robust to noise and outliers.

3. Operate in less than instance arrival time and sublinear memory (ideally, some fixed, preset amount of memory).

Change management strategies can be roughly grouped into three families, or a combination thereof. They can use adaptive estimators for relevant statistics, and then an algorithm that maintains a model in synchrony with these statistics. Or they can create models that are adapted or rebuilt when a change detector indicates that change has occurred. Or they can be ensemble methods, which keep dynamic populations of models. We describe all three approaches in detail next.

The first strategy relies on the fact that many model builders work by monitoring a set of statistics from the stream and then combining them into a model. These statistics may be counts, absolute or conditional probabilities, correlations between attributes, or frequencies of certain patterns, among others. Examples of such algorithms are Naive Bayes, which keeps counts of co-occurrences of attribute values and class values, and the perceptron algorithm, which updates weights taking into account agreement between attributes and the outcome to be predicted. This strategy works by having a dynamic estimator for each relevant statistic in a way that reflects its current value, and letting

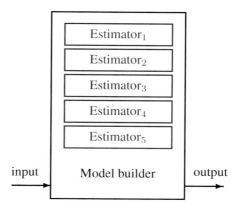

Figure 5.1
Managing change with adaptive estimators. Figure based on [30].

the model builder feed on those estimators. The architecture is presented in Figure 5.1.

In the second strategy, one or more change detection algorithms run in parallel with the main model-building algorithm. When significant change in the stream is detected, they activate a revision algorithm, which may be different if the change is abrupt (where a new model may be built from scratch on new data) or gradual (where recalibration of the current model may be more convenient), local (affecting only parts of the model) or global (affecting all of it). A particular case is when the change is detected by observing the performance of the model—such as decreasing accuracy of a predictor. The architecture of this approach is presented in figure 5.2.

The third strategy is based on the idea of an *ensemble*, used to build complex classifiers out of simpler ones, covered in chapter 7. A single or several model-building algorithms are called at different times, perhaps on different subsets of the data stream. An ensemble manager algorithm contains rules for creating, erasing, and revising the models in its ensemble, as well as for combining the predictions of the models into a single prediction. Here, it is mainly the responsibility of the ensemble manager to detect and react to change, although the individual models may have this capability as well. The architecture of this approach is presented in figure 5.3.

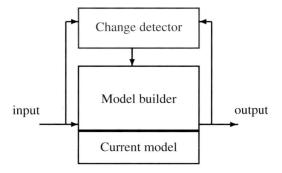

Figure 5.2
Managing change with explicit change detectors for model revision. Figure based on [30]

The next two sections describe some of the methods required to implement the strategies above: estimating statistics on varying streams, and detecting changes.

5.2   Estimators

An *estimator algorithm* estimates one or several statistics on the input data, which may change over time. We concentrate on the case in which such a statistic is (or may be rewritten as) an expected value of the current distribution of the data, which therefore could be approximated by the average of a sample of such a distribution. Part of the problem is that, with the possibility of drift, it is difficult to be sure which past elements of the stream are still reliable as samples of the current distribution, and which are outdated.

There are two kinds of estimators: those that explicitly store a sample of the data stream (we will call this store "the Memory") and memoryless estimators. Among the former we explain the linear estimator over sliding windows. Among the latter, we explain the EWMA and the Kalman filter; other run-time efficient estimators are the autoregressive model and the autoregressive-moving-average estimator.

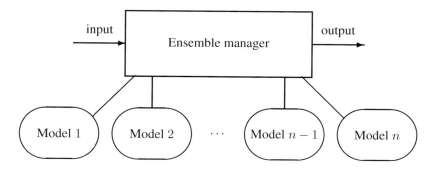

Figure 5.3
Managing change with model ensembles.

5.2.1 Sliding Windows and Linear Estimators

The simplest estimator algorithm for the expected value is the *linear estimator*, which simply returns the average of the data items contained in the Memory. An easy implementation of the Memory is a sliding window that stores the most recent W items received. Most of the time, W is a fixed parameter of the estimator; more sophisticated approaches may change W over time, perhaps in reaction to the nature of the data itself.

The memory used by estimators that use sliding windows can be reduced, for example, by using the Exponential Histogram sketch discussed in section 4.7, at the cost of some approximation error in the estimation.

5.2.2 Exponentially Weighted Moving Average

The exponentially weighted moving average (EWMA) estimator updates the estimation of a variable by combining the most recent measurement of a variable with the EWMA of all previous measurements:

$$A_t = \alpha\, x_t + (1 - \alpha)\, A_{t-1}, \quad A_1 = x_1,$$

where A_t is the moving average at time t, x_t is the latest measurement, and $\alpha \in (0, 1)$ is a parameter that reflects the weight given to the latest measurement. It is often called a *decay* or *fading* factor. Indeed, by expanding the recurrence above, we can see that the estimation at time t is

$$A_t = \sum_{i=2}^{t} \alpha \left(1 - \alpha\right)^{t-i} x_i + \left(1 - \alpha\right)^{t-1} x_1,$$

so the weight of each measurement decays exponentially fast with basis $1 - \alpha$. Larger values of α imply faster forgetting of old measurements, and smaller ones give higher importance to history.

5.2.3   Unidimensional Kalman Filter

The unidimensional Kalman filter addresses the problem of estimating the hidden state $x \in \Re$ of a discrete-time controlled process that is governed by the linear stochastic difference equation

$$x_t = x_{t-1} + w_{t-1}$$

where x is observed indirectly via a measurement $z \in \Re$ that is

$$z_t = x_t + v_t.$$

Here w_t and v_t are random variables representing the process and measurement noise, respectively. They are assumed to be independent of each other and with normal probability distributions

$$w \sim N(0, Q), \quad v \sim N(0, R).$$

In our setting, x_t is the expected value at time t of some property of the stream items, z_t is the value of the property on the item actually observed at time t, and w_t, v_t are the random change in x_t and the observation noise in z_t. The estimation y_t of the state at time t is updated in the Kalman filter as follows, where P and K are auxiliary quantities:

$$K_t \leftarrow P_{t-1} / (P_{t-1} + R),$$
$$y_t \leftarrow y_{t-1} + K_t (z_t - y_{t-1}),$$
$$P_t \leftarrow (1 - K_t) P_{t-1} + Q.$$

The effectiveness of the Kalman filter in any particular application depends on the validity of the stochastic equations, of the Gaussian assumptions on the noise, and on the accuracy of the estimate of the variances Q and R.

This is a very simple version of the Kalman filter. More generally, it can be multidimensional, where x is a vector and each component of x is a linear combination of all its components at the previous time, plus noise. It also allows for control variables that we can change to influence the state and therefore create feedback loops; this is in fact the original and main purpose of the Kalman filter. And it can be extended to nonlinear measurement-to-process relations. A full exposition of the Kalman filter is [245].

5.3   Change Detection

Change detection in data is a vast subject with a long tradition in statistics; see [27]. Not all methods are apt for streaming, typically because they require several passes over the data. We cover only a few streaming-friendly ones.

5.3.1   Evaluating Change Detection

The following criteria are relevant for evaluating change detection methods. They address the fundamental trade-off that such algorithms must face [130], that between detecting true changes and avoiding false alarms. Many depend on the minimum magnitude θ of the changes we want to detect.

- *Mean time between false alarms, MTFA:* Measures how often we get false alarms when there is no change. The false alarm rate (FAR) is defined as 1/MTFA.

- *Mean time to detection, MTD(θ):* Measures the capacity of the learning system to detect and react to change when it occurs.

- *Missed detection rate, MDR(θ):* Measures the probability of not generating an alarm when there has been change.

- *Average run length, ARL(θ):* This measure, which generalizes MTFA and MTD, indicates how long we have to wait before detecting a change after it occurs. We have MTFA = ARL(0) and, for $\theta > 0$, MTD(θ) = ARL(θ).

5.3.2   The CUSUM and Page-Hinkley Tests

The cumulative sum (CUSUM) test [191] is designed to give an alarm when the mean of the input data significantly deviates from its previous value.

In its simplest form, the CUSUM test is as follows: given a sequence of observations $\{x_t\}_t$, define $z_t = (x_t - \mu)/\sigma$, where μ is the expected value of the x_t and σ is their standard deviation in "normal" conditions; if μ and σ are not known a priori, they are estimated from the sequence itself. Then CUSUM computes the indices and alarm:

$$g_0 = 0,$$
$$g_t = \max\ (0, g_{t-1} + z_t - k),$$

if $g_t > h$, declare change and reset $g_t = 0$, and μ and σ.

CUSUM is memoryless and uses constant processing time per item. How its behavior depends on the parameters k and h is difficult to analyze exactly [27]. A guideline is to set k to half the value of the changes to be detected (measured in standard deviations) and h to $\ln(1/\delta)$ where δ is the acceptable false alarm rate; values in the range 3 to 5 are typical. In general, the input z_t to CUSUM can be any filter residual, for instance, the prediction error of a Kalman filter.

A variant of the CUSUM test is the Page-Hinkley test:

$$g_0 = 0,$$
$$g_t = g_{t-1} + z_t - k,$$
$$G_t = \min\{g_t, G_{t-1}\},$$

if $g_t - G_t > h$, declare change and reset $g_t = 0$, G_t, and μ and σ.

These formulations are one-sided in the sense that they only raise alarms when the mean increases. Two-sided versions can be easily derived by symmetry, see exercise 5.3.

5.3.3   Statistical Tests

A statistical test is a procedure for deciding whether a hypothesis about a quantitative feature of a population is true or false. We test a hypothesis of this sort by drawing a random sample from the population in question and calculating an appropriate statistic on its items. If, in doing so, we obtain a value of the statistic that would occur rarely when the hypothesis is true, we would have reason to reject the hypothesis.

To detect change, we need to compare two sources of data and decide whether the hypothesis H_0, that they come from the same distribution, is true. Let us suppose we have estimates $\hat{\mu}_0$, $\hat{\mu}_1$, σ_0^2, and σ_1^2 of the averages and standard deviations of two populations, drawn from equal-sized samples. If the distribution is the same in the two populations, these estimates should be consistent. Otherwise, a hypothesis test should reject H_0. There are several ways to construct such a hypothesis test. The simplest one is to study the difference $\hat{\mu}_0 - \hat{\mu}_1$, which for large samples satisfies

$$\hat{\mu}_0 - \hat{\mu}_1 \in N(0, \sigma_0^2 + \sigma_1^2), \text{ under } H_0.$$

For example, suppose we want to design a change detector using a statistical test with a probability of false alarm of 5%, that is,

$$\Pr\left(\frac{|\hat{\mu}_0 - \hat{\mu}_1|}{\sqrt{\sigma_0^2 + \sigma_1^2}} > h\right) = 0.05.$$

A table of the Gaussian distribution shows that $P(X < 1.96) = 0.975$, so the test becomes

$$\frac{(\hat{\mu}_0 - \hat{\mu}_1)^2}{\sigma_0^2 + \sigma_1^2} > 1.96.$$

In the case of stream mining, the two populations are two different parts of a stream and H_0 is the hypothesis that the two parts have the same distribution. Different implementations may differ on how they choose the parts of the stream to compare. For example, we may fix a reference window, which does not slide, and a sliding window, which slides by 1 unit at every time step. The reference window has average $\hat{\mu}_0$ and the sliding window has average $\hat{\mu}_1$. When change is detected based on the two estimates, the current sliding window becomes the reference window and a new sliding window is created using the following elements. The performance of this method depends, among other parameters, on the sizes of the two windows chosen.

Instead of the normal-based test, we can perform a χ^2-test on the variance, because

$$\frac{(\hat{\mu}_0 - \hat{\mu}_1)^2}{\sigma_0^2 + \sigma_1^2} \in \chi^2(1), \text{ under } H_0$$

from which a standard hypothesis test can be formulated.

Still another test can be derived from Hoeffding's bound, provided that the values of the distribution are in, say, the range $[0, 1]$. Suppose that we have two populations (such as windows) of sizes n_0 and n_1. Define their harmonic mean $n = 1/(1/n_0 + 1/n_1)$ and

$$\epsilon = \sqrt{\frac{1}{2n} \ln \frac{4(n_0 + n_1)}{\delta}}.$$

We have:

- If H_0 is true and $\mu_0 = \mu_1$, then

$$\Pr[|\hat{\mu}_0 - \hat{\mu}_1| > \epsilon/2] < \delta.$$

- Conversely, if H_0 is false and $|\mu_0 - \mu_1| > \epsilon$, then

$$\Pr[\,|\hat{\mu}_0 - \hat{\mu}_1| > \epsilon/2\,] > 1 - \delta.$$

So the test "Is $|\hat{\mu}_0 - \hat{\mu}_1| > \epsilon/2$?" correctly distinguishes between identical means and means differing by at least ϵ with high probability. This test has the property that the guarantee is rigorously true for finite (not asymptotic) n_0 and n_1; on the other hand, because Hoeffding's bound is loose, it has small false alarm rate but large mean time to detection compared to other tests.

5.3.4   Drift Detection Method

The drift detection method (DDM) proposed by Gama et al. [114] is applicable in the context of predictive models. The method monitors the number of errors produced by a model learned on the previous stream items. Generally, the error of the model should decrease or remain stable as more data is used, assuming that the learning method controls overfitting and that the data and label distribution is stationary. When, instead, DDM observes that the prediction error increases, it takes this as evidence that change has occurred.

More precisely, let p_t denote the error rate of the predictor at time t. Since the number of errors in a sample of t examples is modeled by a binomial distribution, its standard deviation at time t is given by $s_t = \sqrt{p_t(1 - p_t)/t}$. DDM stores the smallest value p_{min} of the error rates observed up to time t, and the standard deviation s_{min} at that point. It then performs the following checks:

- If $p_t + s_t \geq p_{min} + 2 \cdot s_{min}$, a warning is declared. From this point on, new examples are stored in anticipation of a possible declaration of change.
- If $p_t + s_t \geq p_{min} + 3 \cdot s_{min}$, change is declared. The model induced by the learning method is discarded and a new model is built using the examples stored since the warning occurred. The values for p_{min} and s_{min} are reset as well.

This approach is generic and simple to use, but it has the drawback that it may be too slow in responding to changes. Indeed, since p_t is computed on the basis of all examples since the last change, it may take many observations after the change to make p_t significantly larger than p_{min}. Also, for slow change, the number of examples retained in memory after a warning may become large.

An evolution of this method that uses EWMA to estimate the errors is presented and thoroughly analyzed in [216].

5.3.5   ADWIN

The ADWIN algorithm (for ADaptive sliding WINdow) [30, 32] is a change detector and estimation algorithm based on the exponential histograms described in section 4.7. It aims at solving some of the problems in the change estimation and detection methods described before. All the problems can be attributed to the trade-off between reacting quickly to changes and having few false alarms.

Often, this trade-off is resolved by requiring the user to enter (or guess) a cutoff parameter. For example, the parameter α in EWMA indicates how to weight recent examples versus older ones; the larger the α, the more quickly the method will react to a change, but the higher the false alarm rate will be due to statistical fluctuations. Similar roles are played by the parameters in the Kalman filters and CUSUM or Page-Hinkley tests. For statistical tests based on windows, we would like to have on the one hand long windows so that the estimates on each window are more robust, but, on the other hand, short windows to detect a change as soon as it happens. The DDM method has no such parameter, but its mean time to detection depends not only on the magnitude of the change, but also on the length of the previous run without change.

Intuitively, the ADWIN algorithm resolves this trade-off by checking change at many scales simultaneously, as if for many values of α in EWMA or for many window lengths in window-based algorithms. The user does not have to guess how often change will occur or how large a deviation should trigger an alarm. The use of exponential histograms allows us to do this more efficiently in time and memory than by brute force. On the negative side, it is computationally more costly (in time and memory) than simple methods such as EWMA or CUSUM: time-per-item and memory are not constant, but logarithmic in the length of the largest window that is being monitored. So it should be used when the scale of change is unknown and this fact might be problematic.

ADWIN solves, in a well-specified way, the problem of tracking the average of a stream of bits or real-valued numbers. It keeps a variable-length window of recently seen items, with the property that the window has the maximal length statistically consistent with the hypothesis "There has been no change in the average value inside the window." More precisely, an old fragment of the window is dropped if and only if there is enough evidence that its average value differs from that of the rest of the window. This has two consequences: one, change is reliably detected whenever the window shrinks; and two, at any time the average over the current window can be used as a reliable estimate of the current average in the stream (barring a very small or recent change that is not yet clearly visible). We now describe the algorithm in more detail.

The inputs to ADWIN are a confidence value $\delta \in (0, 1)$ and a (possibly infinite) sequence of real values $x_1, x_2, x_3, \ldots, x_t, \ldots$ The value of x_t is available only at time t.

The algorithm is parameterized by a test $T(W_0, W_1, \delta)$ that compares the averages of two windows W_0 and W_1 and decides whether they are likely to come from the same distribution. A good test should satisfy the following criteria:

- If W_0 and W_1 were generated from the same distribution (no change), then with probability at least $1 - \delta$ the test says "no change."

- If W_0 and W_1 were generated from two different distributions whose average differs by more than some quantity $\epsilon(W_0, W_1, \delta)$, then with probability at least $1 - \delta$ the test says "change."

ADWIN feeds the stream of items x_t to an exponential histogram. For each stream item, if there are currently b buckets in the histogram, it runs test T up to $b - 1$ times, as follows: For i in $1 \ldots b - 1$, let W_0 be formed by the i oldest buckets, and W_1 be formed by the $b - i$ most recent buckets, then perform the test $T(W_0, W_1, \delta)$. If some test returns "change," it is assumed that change has occurred somewhere and the oldest bucket is dropped; the window implicitly stored in the exponential histogram has shrunk by the size of the dropped bucket. If no test returns "change," then no bucket is dropped, so the window implicit in the exponential histogram increases by 1.

At any time, we can query the exponential histogram for an estimate of the average of the elements in the window being stored. Unlike conventional exponential histograms, the size W of the sliding window is not fixed and can grow and shrink over time. As stated before, W is in fact the size of the longest window preceding the current item on which T is unable to detect any change. The memory used by ADWIN is $O(\log W)$ and its update time is $O(\log W)$.

A few implementation details should be mentioned. First, it is not strictly necessary to perform the tests after each item; in practice it is all right to test every k items, of course at the risk of delaying the detection of a sudden change by time k. Second, experiments show a slight advantage in false positive rate if at most one bucket is dropped when processing any one item rather than all those before the detected change point; if necessary, more buckets will be dropped when processing further items. Third, we can fix a maximum size for the exponential histogram, so that memory does not grow unboundedly if there is no change in the stream. Finally, we need to fix a test T; in [30, 32] and in the MOA implementation, the Hoeffding-based test given in section 5.3.3 is used in order to have rigorous bounds on the performance of the algorithm. However, in practice, it may be better to use the other statistical tests there, which react to true changes more quickly for the same false alarm rate.

5.4   Combination with Other Sketches and Multidimensional Data

The sketches proposed in chapter 4, with the exception of exponential histograms, take into account the information in the whole data stream since the moment the sketch is initialized. This means they contain no forgetting mechanism and do not consider more recent data to be more important. It is possible and natural to combine those sketches with the estimation and change detection algorithms presented in this chapter.

For example, Papapetrou et al. [193] propose ECM, a variant of the CM-Sketch where integer counts are replaced with sliding window structures similar to Exponential Histograms. Muthukrishnan et al. [184] combine the CM-Sketch with sequential testing techniques in order to detect change in multidimensional data.

Change detection in multidimensional data streams is a challenging problem, particularly if one must scale well with the number of dimensions, and if the solution must be generic and not tailored to a specific setting. A quick solution is to reduce the problem to one dimension by monitoring the change in one or more unidimensional statistics of the data, for instance performing random projections or PCA. This typically will reduce the sensitivity to change, particularly if the change is localized in a small subspace of the data. Generic approaches for dealing with multidimensional change directly can be found in [82, 153, 201, 237].

5.5   Exercises

Exercise 5.1   Discuss the differences between distribution change, outliers, anomalies, and noise.

Exercise 5.2   Propose a few strategies for managing ensembles of classifiers in the presence of distribution change. Your strategies should specify mechanisms for creating new classifiers, discarding classifiers, combining their predictions, and managing ensemble size. Think which of your strategies would be more appropriate for gradual and for sudden change. (Note: Ensemble methods will be discussed in chapter 7. Here we encourage you to give your preliminary ideas.)

Exercise 5.3   The CUSUM and Page-Hinkley tests given in the text are one-sided. Give two-sided versions that detect both increases and decreases in the average.

Exercise 5.4   a. We want to keep an array of k EWMA estimators keeping k different statistics of the stream. We know that every item in the stream contributes a 1 to at most one of the estimators, and 0 to all others. For example, the EWMAs track the frequency of k mutually exclusive types of items. The obvious strategy of updating all k estimators uses $O(k)$ time per item. Describe another strategy that uses constant time per item processed and gives the same answers. Query time can be $O(k)$.

b. Replace every integer entry of a CM-Sketch with an EWMA estimator with parameter α. Use the idea in the exercise above to update these estimators. What can you say about the frequency approximations that you get for every item?

c. Can you do something similar for the SPACESAVING sketch?

Exercise 5.5   DDM has the drawback that it may take a long time to react to changes after a long period without change. Suggest a couple of ways to fix this, possibly at the cost of introducing some parameters.

Exercise 5.6   For the mathematically oriented:

- Derive the test for mean difference based on Hoeffding's bound given in section 5.3.3.
- Consider the implementation of ADWIN with the Hoeffding-based test. Analyze and describe how ADWIN will react to:

- A stream with abrupt change: after a long stream of bits with average μ_0, at some time T the average suddenly changes to $\mu_1 \neq \mu_0$.
- Gradual shift: after a long stream of bits with average μ_0, at time T the average starts increasing linearly so that the average at time $t > T$ is $\mu_{t+1} = \mu_t + \Delta$, with Δ a small value.

Deduce when ADWIN will declare change, and how the window length and estimation of the average will evolve from that point on.

Exercise 5.7   For the programming oriented: program a random bit-stream generator in which the probability of getting a 1 changes abruptly or gradually after a long period with no change. Program the Page-Hinkley test, the DDM test, and the three tests in section 5.3.3 with a reference window and a sliding window. Compare the measures described in section 5.3.1 for these tests, including different window sizes for the last three tests. Do not forget to average each experiment over several random runs to get reliable estimates.

6   Classification

Classification is one of the most widely used data mining techniques. In very general terms, given a list of groups (often called *classes*), classification seeks to predict which group a new instance may belong to. The outcome of classification is typically either to identify a single group or to produce a probability distribution of the likelihood of membership for each group. It is the most important case of *supervised* learning, meaning that the labels available to the learning algorithm can be used to guide it. A spam filter is a good example, where we want to predict whether new emails are considered spam or not. Twitter sentiment analysis is another example, where we want to predict whether the sentiment of a new incoming tweet is positive or negative.

More formally, the classification problem can be formulated as follows: we are given a set of labeled *instances* or *examples* of the form (x, y), where $x = x_1, \ldots, x_k$ is a vector of *feature* or *attribute* values, and y is one of n_C different *classes*, regarded also as the value of a discrete attribute called the *class*. The classifier building algorithm builds a classifier or model f such that $y = f(x)$ is the predicted class value for any unlabeled example x. For example, x could be a tweet and y the polarity of its sentiment; or x could be an email message, and y the decision of whether it is spam or not. Most classic methods for classification load all training data into main memory and then build f via multiple passes over the data. In the stream setting, f is typically constructed incrementally, with inspection of data restricted to a single pass with instances presented one at a time.

We start by reviewing how to evaluate classifiers, the most popular classification methods, and how they can be applied in a data stream setting. The two important characteristics of any classification method in the stream setting are: that limitations exist in terms of memory and time (so that we cannot store all instances in memory), and that classification models must be able to adapt to possible changes in the distribution of the incoming data. These characteristics imply that exact solutions are unlikely, so we should expect approximate solutions and therefore expect the associated error to be bounded. Bounds on error are problematic in the sense that, when they themselves make few assumptions about the distribution generating the error, they tend to be conservative (that is, in practice, results are much better than predicted by the bound). When they do make assumptions, they can be much more consistent with experimental results, but are vulnerable to cases where those assumptions simply do not hold.

A third requirement, not covered in this chapter, is the ability to cope with changes in the feature space. In a sensor network, for example, it is likely that one or more sensors providing values to certain features will go offline now and then due to malfunction or replacement. The replacement sensors could be newer models, so they might make measurements differently from the past. In fact, it makes sense that a sensor could be removed permanently. Almost all stream classification algorithms assume that the feature space is fixed and cannot respond easily to this type of change. Aside from the feature space, the set of class labels could also change over time. Thus algorithms would need to be able to cope with the addition of new class labels and the deletion of existing ones. Both these changes in x and y represent fertile ground for the development of new stream classification algorithms.

6.1   Classifier Evaluation

Evaluation is one of the most fundamental tasks in all data mining processes, since it helps to decide which techniques are more appropriate for a specific problem, and to set parameters. The main challenge is to know when a method is outperforming another method only by chance, and when there is a statistical significance to that claim. Some of the methodologies applied in stream mining are the same as in the case of nonstreaming data, where all data can be stored in memory. However, mining data streams poses new challenges and must use modified evaluation methodologies.

One thing worth noting before we continue is that almost all the discoveries made in data mining, and particularly classification, assume that data is independently and identically distributed (IID). Thus a stationary distribution is randomly producing data in no particular order, and the underlying distribution generating the data is not changing. In a streaming environment no part of the IID assumption remains valid. It is often the case, for example, that for certain time periods the labels or classes of instances are correlated. In intrusion detection, there are long periods where all class labels are no-intrusion, mixed with infrequent, short periods of intrusion. This is another aspect of data stream mining that would benefit from further research.

An evaluation framework should be composed of the following parts:

- error estimation,
- evaluation performance measures,
- statistical significance validation, and
- a cost measure of the process.

For evolving data streams, the main difference from traditional data mining evaluation is how to perform the error estimation. Resources are limited and cross-validation may be too expensive. We start by looking at how to define and estimate accuracy, then we look at which measures are the most convenient to measure the performance of the algorithms. Finally we review some statistical techniques for checking significance and measuring the cost of the overall process.

6.1.1 Error Estimation

The evaluation procedure of a learning algorithm determines which examples are used for training the algorithm and which are used for testing the model output by the algorithm.

In traditional batch learning, a first approach is to split the dataset into disjoint training and test sets. If the data is limited, cross-validation is preferable: we create several models and average the results with different random arrangements of training and test data.

In the stream setting, (effectively) unlimited data poses different challenges. Cross-validation typically is computationally too expensive, and not as necessary. On the other hand, creating a picture of accuracy over time is essential. The following main approaches arise:

- **Holdout:** When data is so abundant that it is possible to have test sets periodically, then we can measure the performance on these holdout sets. There is a training data stream that is used to train the learner continuously, and small test datasets that are used to compute the performance periodically. In MOA, the implementation of this concept requires the user to specify two parameters (say, j and k): j is the size of the first window (set of instances) for testing purposes, and k is the frequency of testing—that is, test after every k instances (using a test set of size j).

- **Interleaved test-then-train:** Each individual example can be used to test the model *before* it is used for training, and from this, the accuracy can be incrementally updated. The model is thus always being tested on examples it has not seen. In MOA, this scheme is implemented using a landmark window model (data in the stream is considered from the beginning to now).

- **Prequential:** Like interleaved test-then-train but—in MOA—implements the idea that more recent examples are more important, using a sliding window or a decaying factor. The sizes of the sliding window and the decaying factor are parameters.

- **Interleaved chunks:** Also like interleaved test-then-train, but with chunks of data in sequence. Chunks of different sizes may need to be considered (this is a parameter in the MOA implementation).

Note that if we set the size of the sliding window to the number of instances in the entire dataset, then the middle two schemes are equivalent.

Holdout evaluation more accurately estimates the accuracy of the classifier on more recent data. However, it requires recent test data that is difficult to obtain for real datasets. There is also the issue of ensuring coverage of important change events: if the holdout is during a less volatile period of change, then it might overestimate classifier performance.

Gama et al. [115] propose a forgetting mechanism for estimating holdout accuracy using prequential accuracy: a sliding window of size w with the most recent observations, or fading factors that weigh observations using a decay factor α. The fading factor α is used as follows:

$$E_i = \frac{S_i}{B_i}$$

with

$$S_i = L_i + \alpha \times S_{i-1}, \qquad B_i = n_i + \alpha \times B_{i-1},$$

where n_i is the number of examples used to compute the loss function L_i. We have $n_i = 1$ since the loss L_i is computed for every single example.

The output of the two mechanisms is very similar, as a window of size w may be approximated by a decay factor $\alpha \sim 1/w$. Figure 6.1 shows a comparison of a holdout evaluation, an interleaved test then train evaluation, and a prequential evaluation using a sliding window of size 1,000. Looking at the plot in figure 6.1 it seems that, at least for this dataset, prequential evaluation using a sliding window is a good approximation of holdout evaluation.

6.1.2   Distributed Evaluation

In a distributed data stream setting, we have classifiers that can be trained at the same time. This provides an opportunity to implement something akin to classic k-fold cross-validation. Several approaches to evaluation in this setting

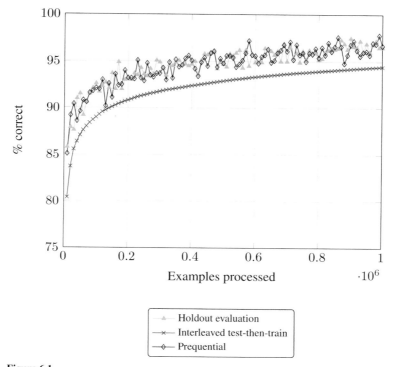

Figure 6.1

Evaluation on a stream of 1,000,000 instances, comparing holdout, interleaved test-then-train, and prequential with sliding window evaluation methods.

have been proposed to cover combinations of data abundance or scarcity, and numbers of classifiers to be compared [40]:

- **k-fold distributed split-validation:** when there is abundance of data and k classifiers. Each time a new instance arrives, it is decided with probability $1/k$ whether it will be used for testing. If it is used for testing, it is used by all the classifiers. If not, then it is used for training and assigned to only one classifier. Thus, each classifier sees different instances, and they are tested using the same data.

- **5x2 distributed cross-validation:** when data is less abundant, and we want to use only, say, ten classifiers. We create five groups of classifier pairs, and for each group, each time a new instance arrives, it is decided with probability $1/2$ which of the two classifiers is used to test; the other classifier of the group is used to train. All instances are used to test or to train, and there is no overlap between test instances and train instances.

- k-**fold distributed cross-validation:** when data is scarce and we have k classifiers. Each time a new instance arrives, it is used for testing in one classifier selected at random, and for training in the others. This evaluation is equivalent to k-fold distributed cross-validation.

6.1.3   Performance Evaluation Measures

In real data streams, the number of instances for each class may be evolving and changing. It may be argued that the prequential accuracy measure is only appropriate when all classes are balanced and have approximately the same number of examples. The Kappa statistic is a more sensitive measure for quantifying the predictive performance of streaming classifiers.

The Kappa statistic κ was introduced by Cohen [76] and defined as follows:

$$\kappa = \frac{p_0 - p_c}{1 - p_c}.$$

The quantity p_0 is the classifier's prequential accuracy, and p_c is the probability that a chance classifier—one that randomly assigns to each class the same number of examples as the classifier under consideration—makes a correct prediction. If the classifier is always correct, then $\kappa = 1$. If its predictions coincide with the correct ones as often as those of a chance classifier, then $\kappa = 0$.

The Kappa M statistic κ_m [40] is a measure that compares against a majority class classifier instead of a chance classifier:

$$\kappa_m = \frac{p_0 - p_m}{1 - p_m}.$$

In cases where the distribution of predicted classes is substantially different from the distribution of the actual classes, a majority class classifier can perform better than a given classifier while the classifier has a positive κ statistic.

An alternative to the Kappa statistic is to compute the area under the receiver operating characteristics curve AUC. Brzezinski and Stefanowski present in [59] an incremental algorithm that uses a sorted tree structure with a sliding window to compute AUC with forgetting. The resulting evaluation measure is called prequential AUC, and is also available in MOA.

Another Kappa measure, the Kappa temporal statistic [42, 262], considers the presence of temporal dependencies in data streams. It is defined as

$$\kappa_{per} = \frac{p_0 - p'_e}{1 - p'_e}$$

where p'_e is the accuracy of the No-change classifier, the classifier that simply echoes the last label received (section 6.2.2), a simple and useful classifier when the same labels appear together in bursts.

Statistic κ_{per} takes values from 0 to 1. The interpretation is similar to that of κ: if the classifier is perfectly correct, then $\kappa_{per} = 1$. If the classifier is achieving the same accuracy as the No-change classifier, then $\kappa_{per} = 0$. Classifiers that outperform the No-change classifier fall between 0 and 1. Sometimes $\kappa_{per} < 0$, which means that the classifier is performing worse than the No-change baseline.

Using κ_{per} instead of κ_m, we can detect misleading classifier performance for data that is not IID. For highly imbalanced but independently distributed data, the majority class classifier may beat the No-change classifier. The κ_{per} and κ_m measures can be seen as orthogonal, since they measure different aspects of the performance.

Other measures that focus on the imbalance among classes are the arithmetic mean and the geometric mean:

$$A = 1/n_c \cdot (A_1 + A_2 + \ldots + A_{n_c}), \qquad G = (A_1 \times A_2 \times \ldots \times A_{n_c})^{1/n_c},$$

where A_i is the testing accuracy on class i and n_c is the number of classes. Note that the geometric accuracy of the majority vote classifier would be 0, as accuracy on the classes other than the majority would be 0. The accuracy of a perfectly correct classifier would be 1. If the accuracies of a classifier are equal for all classes, then both arithmetic and geometric accuracies are equal to the usual accuracy.

Consider the simple confusion matrix shown in table 6.1. From this table, we see that Class+ is predicted correctly 75 times, and Class− is predicted correctly 10 times. So accuracy p_0 is 85%. However, a classifier predicting solely by chance—in the given proportions—will predict Class+ and Class− correctly in 68.06% and 3.06% of cases respectively. Hence, it has accuracy $p_c = 71.12\%$ and $\kappa = 0.48$; the majority class classifier has accuracy $p_m = 75\%$ and $\kappa_m = 0.40$.

Table 6.1

Simple confusion matrix example.

	Predicted Class+	Predicted Class−	Total
Correct Class+	75	8	83
Correct Class−	7	10	17
Total	82	18	100

Table 6.2

Confusion matrix of table 6.1, modified.

	Predicted Class+	Predicted Class−	Total
Correct Class+	75	8	83
Correct Class−	**57**	10	**67**
Total	**132**	18	**150**

The accuracy for Class+ is 90.36% and for Class− is 58.82%. The arithmetic mean A is 74.59%, and the geometric mean G is 72.90%. So we see that $A \geq G$ and that G tends to the lower value.

Imagine that, as shown in table 6.2, the number of misclassified examples of Class− increases to 57. Then, the accuracy for Class− decreases to 14.92%, κ to 0.05, and κ_m to 0.13. The arithmetic mean A changes to 52.64%, and the geometric mean G to 36.72 %.

6.1.4   Statistical Significance

When evaluating classifiers, we should be concerned with the statistical significance of the results. Looking at the performance of only one classifier, it is convenient to give some insights about its statistical significance. We may use *confidence intervals* of parameter estimates to indicate the reliability of our estimate. To do that, we can use Chernoff's or Hoeffding's bounds, which are sharper than Markov's or Chebyshev's inequalities, because the measures we are interested in are averages of evaluations on individual items. For reasonably large numbers of points the approximation by a normal is usually applicable; see section 4.2.

When comparing two classifiers, we need to distinguish between random and nonrandom differences in the experimental accuracies. McNemar's test [173] is the most popular nonparametric test in the stream mining literature to assess the statistical significance of differences in the performance of two classifiers. This test needs to store and update two variables: the number of instances misclassified by the first classifier and not by the second, a, and the number of instances misclassified by the second classifier and not by the first, b. The McNemar statistic is given as $M = |a - b - 1|^2/(a + b)$. The test follows the χ^2 distribution. At 0.99 confidence it rejects the null hypothesis (the performances are equal) if $M > 6.635$.

Although the field of ML is several decades old, there is still much debate around the issue of comparing the performance of classifiers and, consequently, measurements of significant performance difference. The latest contribution is by Berrar [29], who argues that the magnitude of the difference in performance (and reasonable bounds on that difference) should be the focus, not statistical significance. The outcome of this work is a new evaluation tool called confidence curves, curves that show the magnitude difference directly. Issues with null hypothesis significance testing and p-values have also recently led to Bayesian alternatives to the problem being proposed [78]. Thus, it is not possible at this time to give a definitive answer to the question of performance measurement, as further research in classic and streaming ML is still needed. In particular, a measure for estimating the effect size over time for data streams has yet to be proposed.

6.1.5   A Cost Measure for the Mining Process

The issue of measuring three evaluation dimensions simultaneously has led to another important issue in data stream mining, namely, estimating the combined cost of performing the learning and prediction processes in terms of time and memory. As an example, several rental cost options exist:

- Cost per hour of usage: Amazon Elastic Compute Cloud (Amazon EC2) is a web service that provides resizable computing capacity in the cloud. The cost depends on the time and on the size of the machine rented (for example, small instance with 2 GB of RAM, large with 8 GB or extra large with 16 GB).

- Cost per hour and memory used: GoGrid is a web service similar to Amazon EC2, but it charges by RAM-hours. Every GB of RAM deployed for 1 hour equals by definition 1 RAM-hour.

The use of RAM-Hours as defined above was introduced in [37] as an evaluation measure of the resources used by streaming algorithms. Although proposed for learning, it can be applied to the other data mining tasks.

6.2   Baseline Classifiers

Batch learning has led to the development of hundreds of different classifiers that belong to a number of paradigms, such as divide-and-conquer methods, rule learners, lazy learners, kernel methods, graphical models, and so on. If we are to *streamify* methods from these paradigms, we need to consider how to make them both incremental and fast. Some methods are naturally incremental and fast, and we will start with these. Research on the application of batch methods to large datasets tells us to look for methods with good bias management. If a method has high bias, like the ones we will introduce next, then its ability to generalize will be limited. Methods producing more complex models are typically better at generalization but have necessarily higher maintenance costs and should be controlled for overfitting. Producing methods that manage the trade-off well (complexity of model representation versus speed of model update) is the main issue in data stream classification research.

6.2.1   Majority Class

The *Majority Class* algorithm is one of the simplest classifiers: it predicts the class of a new instance to be the most frequent class. It is used mostly as a baseline, but also as a default classifier at the leaves of decision trees. A Majority Class classifier is very easy to compute and maintain, as it only needs to keep an array of counters for each one of the classes.

6.2.2   No-change Classifier

Another simple classifier for data streams is the No-change classifier, which predicts the label for a new instance to be the true label of the previous instance. Like the Majority Class classifier, it does not require the instance features, so it is very easy to implement. In the intrusion detection case where long passages of "no intrusion" are followed with briefer periods of "intrusion," this classifier makes mistakes only on the boundary cases, adjusting quickly to the consistent pattern of labels.

When a temporal dependence among consecutive labels is suspected, it usually pays to add the label(s) of the previous instance(s) as new attributes. This capability, proposed in [42, 262], is available as a generic wrapper TEMPORALLYAUGMENTEDCLASSIFIER in MOA.

6.2.3   Naive Bayes

Naive Bayes is a classification algorithm known for its low computational cost and simplicity. As an incremental algorithm, it is well suited for the data stream setting. However, it assumes independence of the attributes, and that might not be the case in many real data streams.

It is based on Bayes' theorem, which may be stated informally as

$$posterior = \frac{prior \times likelihood}{evidence},$$

that is, it tells how the probability of an event is modified after accounting for evidence. More formally:

$$\Pr(c|d) = \frac{\Pr(c)\Pr(d|c)}{\Pr(d)},$$

where $\Pr(c)$ is the prior, the initial probability of event c, $\Pr(c|d)$ is the posterior, the probability after accounting for d, $\Pr(d|c)$ is the likelihood of event d given that event c occurs, and $\Pr(d)$ is the probability of event d. It is based on the definition of conditional probability, by which $\Pr(c \cap d) = \Pr(c)\Pr(d|c) = \Pr(d)\Pr(c|d)$.

The Naive Bayes model is built as follows: Let $x_1, \ldots, x_k$ be k discrete attributes, and assume that x_i can take n_i different values. Let C be the class attribute, which can take n_C different values. Upon receiving an unlabeled instance $I = (x_1 = v_1, \ldots, x_k = v_k)$, the Naive Bayes classifier computes a "probability" of I being in class c as:

$$\Pr(C = c|I) \cong \Pr(C = c) \cdot \prod_{i=1}^{k} \Pr(x_i = v_i|C = c)$$

$$= \Pr(C = c) \cdot \prod_{i=1}^{k} \frac{\Pr(x_i = v_i \wedge C = c)}{\Pr(C = c)}.$$

The values $\Pr(x_i = v_j \wedge C = c)$ and $\Pr(C = c)$ are estimated from the training data. Thus, the summary of the training data is simply a 3-dimensional table that stores for each triple (x_i, v_j, c) a count $n_{i,j,c}$ of training instances with $x_i = v_j$ and class c, together with a 1-dimensional table for the counts of $C = c$. This algorithm is naturally incremental: upon receiving a new example (or a batch of new examples), simply increment the relevant counts. Predictions can be made at any time from the current counts.

Example 6.1   Suppose we have the following dataset of tweets, and that we want to build a model to predict the polarity of newly arriving tweets.

ID	Text	Sentiment
T1	glad happy glad	$+$
T2	glad glad joyful	$+$
T3	glad pleasant	$+$
T4	miserable sad glad	$-$

First, we transform the text associated with each instance to a vector of attributes.

Id	glad	happy	joyful	pleasant	miserable	sad	Sentiment
T1	1	1	0	0	0	0	$+$
T2	1	0	1	0	0	0	$+$
T3	1	0	0	1	0	0	$+$
T4	1	0	0	0	1	1	$-$

Now, we can build a table with the counts for each class:

Class	Value	glad	happy	joyful	pleasant	miserable	sad
$+$	**1**	3	1	1	1	0	0
$+$	**0**	0	2	2	2	3	3
$-$	**1**	1	0	0	0	1	1
$-$	**0**	0	1	1	1	0	0

Assume we have to classify the following new instance:

ID	Text	Sentiment
T5	glad sad miserable pleasant glad	?

First, we convert it to a vector of attributes.

ID	glad	happy	joyful	pleasant	miserable	sad	Sentiment
T5	1	0	0	1	1	1	?

And now we compute the probabilities as follows:

- $\Pr(+|T5) = \Pr(+) \cdot \Pr(glad = 1|+) \cdot \Pr(happy = 0|+) \cdot \Pr(joyful = 0|+) \cdot \Pr(pleasant = 1|+) \cdot \Pr(miserable = 1|+) \cdot \Pr(sad = 1|+)$, so

$$\Pr(+|T5) = \frac{3}{4} \cdot \frac{3}{3} \cdot \frac{2}{3} \cdot \frac{2}{3} \cdot \frac{1}{3} \cdot \frac{0}{3} \cdot \frac{0}{3} = 0.$$

- $\Pr(-|T5) = Pr(-) \cdot \Pr(glad = 1|-) \cdot \Pr(happy = 0|-) \cdot \Pr(joyful = 0|-) \cdot \Pr(pleasant = 1|-) \cdot \Pr(miserable = 1|-) \cdot \Pr(sad = 1|-)$, so

$$\Pr(-|T5) = \frac{1}{4} \cdot \frac{1}{1} \cdot \frac{1}{1} \cdot \frac{1}{1} \cdot \frac{0}{1} \cdot \frac{1}{1} \cdot \frac{1}{1} = 0.$$

We see that the probabilities are equal to 0 the moment a single term is 0, which is too drastic. A way to avoid this is using the *Laplace correction*, which is adding, for example, 1 to the numerator and the number of classes to the denominator to allow for unseen instances:

$$\Pr(d|c) = \frac{n_{dc} + 1}{n_d + n_c}.$$

In practice, this is done by initializing the counters to 1. In our example, the table of counts for each class becomes:

Class	Value	glad	happy	joyful	pleasant	miserable	sad
+	1	4	2	2	2	1	1
+	0	1	3	3	3	4	4
−	1	2	1	1	1	2	2
−	0	1	2	2	2	1	1

And recomputing the probabilities we get:

- $\Pr(+|T5) = \Pr(+) \cdot \Pr(glad = 1|+) \cdot \Pr(happy = 0|+) \cdot \Pr(joyful = 0|+) \cdot \Pr(pleasant = 1|+) \cdot \Pr(miserable = 1|+) \cdot \Pr(sad = 1|+)$, so

$$\Pr(+|T5) = \frac{3}{4} \cdot \frac{4}{5} \cdot \frac{3}{5} \cdot \frac{3}{5} \cdot \frac{2}{5} \cdot \frac{1}{5} \cdot \frac{1}{5} = 0.0128.$$

- $\Pr(-|T5) = \Pr(-) \cdot \Pr(glad = 1|-) \cdot \Pr(happy = 0|-) \cdot \Pr(joyful = 0|-) \cdot \Pr(pleasant = 1|-) \cdot \Pr(miserable = 1|-) \cdot \Pr(sad = 1|-)$, so

$$\Pr(-|T5) = \frac{1}{4} \cdot \frac{2}{3} \cdot \frac{2}{3} \cdot \frac{2}{3} \cdot \frac{1}{3} \cdot \frac{2}{3} \cdot \frac{2}{3} = 0.0987.$$

We see that $\Pr(-|T5) > \Pr(+|T5)$ and the Naive Bayes classifier predicts that the new tweet has negative polarity.

Observe that the two probabilities do not add up to 1 as they should, because we have ignored the term $\Pr(d)$ in Bayes' theorem. It is normally impossible to assess the probability of a specific data point from a sample. We, can, however normalize by the sum to obtain figures that add up to 1.

6.2.4   Multinomial Naive Bayes

The Multinomial Naive Bayes classifier [171] is an extension of Naive Bayes for document classification that often yields surprisingly good results. Multinomial Naive Bayes considers a document as a bag of words, so it takes into account the frequency of each word in a document and not just its presence or absence. Since word frequency is usually relevant for text classification, this method is preferred over Naive Bayes for text mining.

Let n_{wd} be the number of times word w occurs in document d. Then the probability of class c given a test document is calculated as follows:

$$\Pr(c|d) = \frac{\Pr(c) \prod_{w \in d} \Pr(w|c)^{n_{wd}}}{\Pr(d)},$$

where $\Pr(d)$ can be thought of as a normalization factor.

But a key difference with Naive Bayes is the interpretation of $\Pr(w|c)$: here it is the ratio between the number of occurrences of w in documents of class c over the total number of words in documents of class c. In other words, it is the probability of observing word w at any position of a document belonging to class c. Observe that, again unlike Naive Bayes, the absence of a word in a document does not make any class more likely than any other, as it translates to a 0 exponent.

Conveniently, n_{wd}, $\Pr(w|c)$ and $\Pr(c)$ are trivial to estimate on a data streams by keeping the appropriate counters. Laplace correction can be added by initializing all the counts to 1 instead of 0.

Example 6.2   Suppose we want to build a Multinomial Naive Bayes classifier using the tweets in example 6.1. First we compute the number of occurrences of each word in each document. We use Laplace correction, setting each entry to 1 before starting to count occurrences:

Class	glad	happy	joyful	pleasant	miserable	sad	Total
+	6	2	2	2	1	1	**8+6=14**
−	2	1	1	1	2	2	**3+6=9**

And now the probabilities for each class are:

- $\Pr(+|T5) =$
  $\Pr(+) \cdot \Pr(glad|+) \cdot \Pr(pleasant|+) \cdot \Pr(miserable|+) \cdot \Pr(sad|+),$

$$\Pr(+|T5) = \frac{3}{4} \cdot \left(\frac{6}{14}\right)^2 \cdot \left(\frac{2}{14}\right)^1 \cdot \left(\frac{1}{14}\right)^1 \cdot \left(\frac{1}{14}\right)^1 = 10.04 \cdot 10^{-5}.$$

- $\Pr(-|T5) =$
  $\Pr(-) \cdot \Pr(glad|-) \cdot \Pr(pleasant|-) \cdot \Pr(miserable|-) \cdot \Pr(sad|-),$

$$\Pr(-|T5) = \frac{1}{4} \cdot \left(\frac{2}{9}\right)^2 \cdot \left(\frac{1}{9}\right)^1 \cdot \left(\frac{2}{9}\right)^1 \cdot \left(\frac{2}{9}\right)^1 = 6.77 \cdot 10^{-5}.$$

In this case, we see that $\Pr(+|T5) > \Pr(-|T5)$ and the Multinomial Naive Bayes classifier predicts that the new tweet has positive polarity, in contrast to regular Naive Bayes, which predicted negative polarity.

6.3   Decision Trees

Decision trees are a very popular classifier technique since it is very easy to interpret and visualize the tree models. In a decision tree, each internal node corresponds to an attribute that splits into a branch for each attribute value, and leaves correspond to classification predictors, usually majority class classifiers. Figure 6.2 shows an example.

The accuracy of decision trees can be improved using other classifiers at the leaves, such as Naive Bayes, or using ensembles of decision trees, as we will see later on.

The basic method to build a tree is to start by creating a root node at the beginning $node = root$, and then do the following:

Contains "Money"	Domain type	Has attach.	Time received	spam
yes	com	yes	night	yes
yes	edu	no	night	yes
no	com	yes	night	yes
no	edu	no	day	no
no	com	no	day	no
yes	cat	no	day	yes

Figure 6.2
A dataset describing email features for deciding whether the email is spam, and a decision tree for it.

1. If training instances are perfectly classified at the node, then stop. Else:

2. Assign A to be the "best" decision attribute for $node$.

3. For each value of A, create new descendant (leaf) of $node$.

4. Split the training instances according to the value of A, and pass each split to the corresponding leaf.

5. Apply this method recursively to each leaf.

Two common measures are used to select the best decision attribute:

- Information gain, that is, the difference between the entropy of the class before and after splitting by the attribute. Recall that the entropy H of a sample S is $H(S) = -\sum_c p_c \log(p_c)$, where p_c is the probability in S of class label c. The entropy of S after splitting on attribute A is $H(S, A) = \sum_a H(S_a) |S_a|/|S|$, where S_a is the subset of S where A has value a. The information gain of A is then $IG(S, A) = H(S) - H(S, A)$. This measure was made popular after the C4.5 decision tree algorithm.

- Gini impurity reduction, that is, the difference between the Gini index before and after splitting by the attribute. This measure was made popular after the CART decision tree algorithm. The Gini index of a random variable C is another nonlinear measure of the dispersion of C, defined as $G(C) = \sum_c p_c(1 - p_c) = \sum_{c \neq c'} p_c p_{c'}$.

6.3.1 Estimating Split Criteria

The measures above need to be estimated from finite samples, but in a way that generalizes to future examples (that is, whether it is made now or in a month, year, or decade hence, it will still be the same decision, assuming stationarity). This calls for concentration inequalities in the spirit of those presented in section 4.2, which bound the probability that an estimate over a finite sample is far off its expectation.

Hoeffding's inequality has often been used for estimating measures like information gain or the Gini index. Unfortunately, these measures cannot be expressed as a sum of independent random variables, and so Hoeffding's bound is argued in recent work by Rutkowski et al. [218] to be the wrong tool.

A generalization of Hoeffding's inequality called McDiarmid's inequality can, however, be used for making split decisions using these measures as it works explicitly on functions of the data [218]. For information gain IG, the following can be shown for any two attributes A

and B: if $E_S[IG(S, A) - IG(S, B)] > \epsilon$, then with probability $1 - \delta$ we have $IG(S, A) - IG(S, B) > 0$, where $\epsilon = K(n_c, n)\sqrt{\ln(1/\delta)/2n}$, $K(n_c, n) = 6(n_c \log en + \log 2n) + 2 \log n_c$, n is the size of S, and n_c is the number of classes. The formulation for the Gini index is simpler: it suffices to have $\epsilon = \sqrt{8 \ln(1/\delta)/2n}$. Similar bounds are given in [215]. Misclassification error can also be used [217], eventually giving a bound very similar to Hoeffding's bound.

Note that our description of work on decision trees for streaming takes a historical perspective. The use of McDiarmid's bound is cutting-edge for this particular method and represents a relatively new result. Hoeffding trees may, in the future, be proven *incorrect* in the sense of being based on assumptions that do not hold, however, they are still very effective in practice, and so worthy of study.

6.3.2   The Hoeffding Tree

In the data stream setting, where we cannot store all the data, the main problem of building a decision tree is the need to reuse instances to compute the best splitting attributes. Domingos and Hulten [88] proposed the Hoeffding Tree, a very fast decision tree algorithm for streaming data, where instead of reusing instances, we wait for new instances to arrive. The most interesting feature of the Hoeffding Tree is that it builds a tree that provably converges to the tree built by a batch learner with sufficiently large data; a more precise statement of this equivalence is provided later in this section.

The pseudocode of the Hoeffding Tree is shown in figure 6.3. It is based on Hoeffding's bound, discussed in section 4.2. On the basis of the bound, the proposal in [88] was to choose, as a confidence interval for the estimation of the entropy at a node, the value

$$\epsilon = \sqrt{\frac{R^2 \ln 1/\delta}{2n}},$$

where R is the range of the random variable, δ is the desired probability of the estimate *not* being within ϵ of its expected value, and n is the number of examples collected at the node. In the case of information gain, the entropy is in the range $[0, \ldots, \log n_c]$ for n_c class values. Although the use of Hoeffding's bound in this context is formally incorrect, as explained before, it is still used in most implementations; the reasonable results it achieves may be due to the fact that it gives, in most cases, an overestimation of the true probability of error.

HOEFFDINGTREE($Stream, \delta$)

    Input: a stream of labeled examples, confidence parameter δ

1   let *HT be a tree with a single leaf (root)*
2   init counts n_{ijk} at root
3   **for** each example (x, y) in *Stream*
4   **do** HTGROW($(x, y), HT, \delta$)

HTGROW($(x, y), HT, \delta$)

1   sort (x, y) to leaf l using HT
2   update counts n_{ijk} at leaf l
3   **if** examples seen so far at l are not all of the same class
4   **then**
5   compute G for each attribute
6   **if** G(best attribute) - G(second best) $> \sqrt{\frac{R^2 \ln 1/\delta}{2n}}$
7   **then**
8   split leaf on best attribute
9   **for** each branch
10   **do** start new leaf and initialize counts

Figure 6.3

The Hoeffding Tree algorithm.

The Hoeffding Tree algorithm maintains in each node the statistics needed for splitting attributes. For discrete attributes, this is the same information as needed for computing the Naive Bayes predictions: a 3-dimensional table that stores for each triple (x_i, v_j, c) a count $n_{i,j,c}$ of training instances with $x_i = v_j$, together with a 1-dimensional table for the counts of $C = c$. The memory needed depends on the number of leaves of the tree, not on the length of the data stream.

A theoretically appealing feature of the Hoeffding Tree not shared by other incremental decision tree learners is that it has sound guarantees of performance. It was shown in [88] that its output is asymptotically nearly identical to that of a nonincremental learner using infinitely many examples, in the following sense.

The *intensional disagreement* Δ_i between two decision trees DT_1 and DT_2 is the probability that the path of an example through DT_1 will differ from its path through DT_2, in length, or in the attributes tested, or in the class prediction at the leaf. The following result is rigorously proved in [88]: Let HT_δ be the tree produced by the Hoeffding Tree algorithm with parameter δ from an infinite stream of examples, DT be the batch tree built from an infinite batch, and p be the smallest probability of a leaf in DT. Then we have $E[\Delta_i(HT_\delta, DT)] \leq \delta/p$.

Domingos and Hulten [88] improved the Hoeffding Tree algorithm to a more practical method called the very fast decision tree (VFDT), with the following characteristics:

- Ties: When two attributes have similar split gain G, the improved method splits if Hoeffding's bound is lower than a certain threshold parameter τ.

$$G(\text{best attribute}) - G(\text{second best}) < \sqrt{\frac{R^2 \ln 1/\delta}{2n}} < \tau.$$

- To speed up the process, instead of computing the best attributes to split every time a new instance arrives, the VFDT computes them every time a number n_{min} of instances has arrived.

- To reduce the memory used in the mining, the VFDT deactivates the least promising nodes, those with the lowest product $p_l \times e_l$, where

  - p_l is the probability to reach leaf l, and
  - e_l is the error in node l.

- The method can be started from any preexisting decision tree, for example, one built from an available batch of data. Hoeffding trees can grow slowly and performance can be poor initially, so this extension provides an immediate boost to the learning curve.

It is worth noting that there has been very little research on the last point in the VFDT method. Slow initial learning is an issue for these trees, and bootstrapping via an initial decision tree to create a better starting point makes sense.

One way to improve the classification performance of the Hoeffding Tree is to use Naive Bayes learners at the leaves instead of the majority class classifier. Gama and Medas [113] were the first to use Naive Bayes in Hoeffding Tree leaves, replacing the majority class classifier. However, Holmes et al. [135] identified situations where the Naive Bayes method outperforms the standard Hoeffding Tree initially but is eventually overtaken. To solve that, they proposed a hybrid adaptive method that generally outperforms the two original prediction methods for both simple and complex concepts: when performing a prediction on a test instance, the leaf will return the Naive Bayes prediction if it has been more accurate overall than the majority class prediction, otherwise it returns the majority class. The only overhead is keeping the two counts for the number of times each classifier has been correct.

6.3.3   CVFDT

Hulten et al. [138]   presented the concept-adapting very fast decision tree (CVFDT) algorithm as an extension of VFDT to deal with concept drift, maintaining a model that is consistent with the instances stored in a sliding window. Unfortunately, such trees do not have theoretical guarantees like Hoeffding trees. Note that, theoretically, Hoeffding trees can to some extent adapt to concept drift, because leaves that would not grow any more under a stationary distribution may start to grow again if evidence gathers that further splitting would improve accuracy. However, this process is too slow in practice.

Figure 6.4 shows a sketch of the code for the CVFDT algorithm; a fuller description is provided in the reference above. It is similar to the code for the Hoeffding Tree but with the changes listed below. Note that here we use the terms "remove" and "forget" which look the same. They are different, however, as forgetting is a complex procedure that removes an instance from the tree. In contrast, adding and removing instances only applies to the sliding window.

CVFDT($Stream, \delta$)

    Input: a stream of labeled examples, confidence parameter δ

1   let *HT be a tree with a single leaf (root)*
2   init counts n_{ijk} at root
3   **for** each example (x, y) in *Stream*
4   **do** add, remove, and forget Examples
5   CVFDTGROW($(x, y), HT, \delta$)
6   CHECKSPLITVALIDITY(HT, n, δ)

CVFDTGROW($(x, y), HT, \delta$)

1   sort (x, y) to leaf l using HT
2   update counts n_{ijk} at leaf l and nodes traversed in the sort
3   **if** examples seen so far at l are not all of the same class
4   **then**
5   compute G for each attribute
6   **if** G(best attribute)$-G$(second best) $> \sqrt{R^2 \ln(1/\delta)/(2n)}$
7   **then**
8   split leaf on best attribute
9   **for** each branch
10   **do** start new leaf and initialize counts
11   create alternate subtree

CHECKSPLITVALIDITY(HT, n, δ)

1   **for** each node l in HT that it is not a leaf
2   **do for** each tree T_{alt} in ALT(l)
3   **do** CHECKSPLITVALIDITY(T_{alt}, n, δ)
4   **if** there is a new promising attribute at node l
5   **do** start an alternate subtree

Figure 6.4
The CVFDT algorithm.

- The main method maintains a sliding window with the latest instances, so it has to add, remove, and forget instances.

- The main method calls procedure CVFDTGROW to process an example, but also method CHECKSPLITVALIDITY to check whether the chosen splits are still valid.

- CVFDTGROW also updates counts of the nodes traversed in the sort.

- CHECKSPLITVALIDITY creates an alternate subtree if the attributes chosen to split are now different from the ones that were chosen when the split was done.

- Periodically, the algorithm checks whether the alternate branch is performing better than the original branch tree, and if so it replaces the original branch, and if not, it removes the alternate branch.

6.3.4   VFDTc and UFFT

VFDTc and UFFT are two methods that extend the Hoeffding Tree to handle numeric attributes and concept drift. VFDTc, developed by Gama et al. [111], does the following:

1. It keeps Naive Bayes learners at the leaves to make predictions.

2. It handles numeric attributes using binary trees, as explained in section 6.4.2.

3. To handle concept drift, it uses the statistical DDM method explained in section 5.3.4.

The ultra fast forest of trees (UFFT), developed by Gama and Medas [113], generates a forest of binary trees, one for each possible pair of classes. The trees contain a Naive Bayes classifier at each node, like VFDTc. The main difference from VFDTc is in the handling of numeric attributes.

UFFT uses analytical techniques to choose the splitting criteria, and information gain to estimate the merit of each possible splitting test. For multiclass problems, the algorithm builds a binary tree for each possible pair of classes, leading to a forest of trees, that comprises $k(k-1)/2$ classifiers for a k-class problem. The analytical method uses a modified form of quadratic discriminant analysis to include different variances on the two classes.

6.3.5   Hoeffding Adaptive Tree

The *Hoeffding Adaptive Tree* [33] is an adaptive extension to the Hoeffding Tree that uses ADWIN as a change detector and error estimator. It has theoretical guarantees of performance and requires no parameters related to change control. In contrast, CVFDT has no theoretical guarantees, and requires several parameters with default values that can be changed by the user, but which are fixed for a given execution. It requires:

1. W: The example window size.

2. T_0: Every T_0 examples, CVFDT traverses the entire decision tree, and checks at each node whether the splitting attribute is still the best. If there is a better splitting attribute, it starts growing an alternate tree rooted at this node, and it splits on the current best attribute according to the statistics at the node.

3. T_1: After an alternate tree is created, the following T_1 examples are used to build the alternate tree.

4. T_2: After the arrival of T_1 examples, the following T_2 examples are used to test the accuracy of the alternate tree. If the alternate tree is more accurate than the current one, CVFDT replaces it with this alternate tree (we say that the alternate tree is promoted).

The default values are $W = 50,000$, $T_0 = 10,000$, $T_1 = 9,000$, and $T_2 = 1,000$. We can interpret these figures as the assumptions that often the last $50,000$ examples are likely to be relevant, that change is not likely to occur faster than every $10,000$ examples, and that $1,000$ examples will be sufficient to tell the best among current and candidate trees. These assumptions may or may not be correct for a given data source. Moreover, the stream may change differently at different times, so no single set of values may be best for all the stream.

The main differences of the Hoeffding Adaptive Tree with respect to CVFDT are:

- The alternate trees are created as soon as change is detected, without having to wait for a fixed number of examples to arrive after the change. Furthermore, the more abrupt the change, the faster a new alternate tree will be created.

- The Hoeffding Adaptive Tree replaces an old tree with the alternate tree as soon as there is evidence that it is more accurate, rather than waiting for another fixed number of examples.

These two effects can be summarized by saying that the Hoeffding Adaptive Tree adapts to the scale of time change in the data, rather than relying on the a priori guesses made by the user.

6.4 Handling Numeric Attributes

Handling numeric attributes in a data stream classifier is much more difficult than in a nonstreaming setting. In this section we will review the most popular methods used for *discretization* in decision trees and Naive Bayes algorithms in evolving data streams. We need to examine how to manage the statistics of numeric attributes and how to determine the best splitting points in decision trees.

We start by mentioning the methods in the nonstreaming scenario. There, the main discretization strategies are:

- Equal width: The range of the numeric attribute is divided into a fixed quantity of bins of the same size. The maximum and minimum values are needed to compute the upper and lower values in the bins. This is the simplest method as it does not need to sort the data, but it is vulnerable to the existence of outliers and to skewed distributions.

- Equal frequency: This strategy also uses a fixed number of bins, but each bin contains the same number of elements. For n values and k bins, the bin weight will be n/k, up to rounding. It is well suited for outliers and skewed distributions, but it needs more processing time, as it needs to sort the values.

- Fayyad and Irani's method [98]: This is based on computing the best cutpoints using information gain as it is used in decision trees. First, it sorts the data, and then each point between adjacent pairs of values is selected as a split candidate. Using information gain, the best cut-point is selected, and then the procedure continues recursively in each of the parts. A stopping criterion is needed to stop the recursive process. The criterion is based on stopping when intervals become pure, with values of one class only, or when the *minimum description length* principle estimates that dividing the numeric range will not bring any further benefit.

6.4.1 VFML

The very fast machine learning (VFML) package of Hulten and Domingos [137] contains a method for handling numeric attributes in VFDT and CVFDT. Numeric attribute values are summarized by a set of ordered bins. The range of values covered by each bin is fixed at creation time and does not change as more examples are seen. A hidden parameter serves as a limit on the total number of bins allowed—in the VFML implementation this is hard-coded to allow a maximum of 1,000 bins. Initially, for every new unique numeric value seen, a new bin is created. Once the fixed number of bins have been allocated, each subsequent value in the stream updates the counter of the nearest bin.

Essentially, the algorithm summarizes the numeric distribution with a histogram, made up of a maximum of 1,000 bins. The boundaries of the bins are determined by the first 1,000 unique values seen in the stream, and after that the counts of the static bins are incrementally updated.

There are two potential issues with this approach. Clearly, the method is sensitive to data order. If the first 1,000 examples seen in a stream happen to be skewed to one side of the total range of values, then the final summary cannot accurately represent the full range of values.

The other issue is estimating the optimal number of bins. Too few bins will mean the summary is small but inaccurate, whereas too many bins will increase accuracy at the cost of space. In the experimental comparison the maximum number of bins is varied to test this effect.

6.4.2 Exhaustive Binary Tree

Gama et al. [111] present this method in their VFDTc system. It aims at achieving perfect accuracy at the expense of storage space. The decisions made are the same that a batch method would make, because essentially it is a batch method—no information is discarded other than the order of values.

It works by incrementally constructing a binary tree as values are observed. The path a value follows down the tree depends on whether it is less than, equal to, or greater than the value at a particular node in the tree. The values are implicitly sorted as the tree is constructed, and the number of nodes at each time is the number of distinct values seen. Space saving occurs if the number of distinct values is small.

On the other hand, the structure saves search time versus storing the values in an array as long as the tree is reasonably balanced. In particular, if values arrive in order, then the tree degenerates to a list and no search time is saved.

6.4.3   Greenwald and Khanna's Quantile Summaries

The field of database research is also concerned with the problem of summarizing the numeric distribution of a large dataset in a single pass and limited space. The ability to do so can help to optimize queries over massive databases.

Greenwald and Khanna [129] proposed a *quantile summary* method with even stronger accuracy guarantees than previous approaches. The method works by maintaining an ordered set of tuples, each of which records a value from the input stream, along with implicit bounds for the range of each value's true rank. Precisely, a tuple $t_i = (v_i, g_i, \Delta_i)$ consists of three values:

- a value v_i of one of the elements seen so far in the stream,
- a value g_i that equals $r_{min}(v_i) - r_{min}(v_{i-1})$, where $r_{min}(v)$ is the lower bound of the rank of v among all the values seen so far, and
- a value Δ_i that equals $r_{max}(v_i) - r_{min}(v_i)$, where $r_{max}(v)$ is the upper bound of the rank of v among all the values seen so far.

Note that

$$r_{min}(v_i) = \sum_{j \le i} g_j, \quad \text{and} \quad r_{max}(v_i) = r_{min}(v_i) + \Delta_i = \sum_{j \le i} g_j + \Delta_i.$$

The quantile summary is ϵ-approximate in the following sense: after seeing N elements of a sequence, any quantile estimate returned will not differ from the exact value by more than ϵN. An operation for compressing the quantile summary is defined that guarantees $\max(g_i + \Delta_i) \le 2\epsilon N$, so that the error of the summary is kept within 2ϵ.

The worst-case space requirement is shown to be $O(\frac{1}{\epsilon} \log(\epsilon N))$, with empirical evidence showing it to be even better than this in practice.

6.4.4   Gaussian Approximation

This method, presented in [199], approximates a numeric distribution in small constant space, using a Gaussian or normal distribution. Such a distribution can be incrementally maintained by storing only three numbers, in a way that is

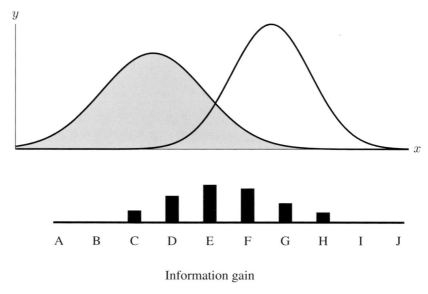

Information gain

Figure 6.5
Gaussian approximation of two classes. Figure based on [199].

insensitive to data order. A similar method to this one was described by Gama and Medas in their UFFT system [113].

For each numeric attribute, the method maintains a separate Gaussian distribution per class label. The possible values are reduced to a set of points spread equally across the range, between the minimum and maximum values observed. The number of evaluation points is determined by a parameter, so the search for split points is *parametric*, even though the underlying Gaussian approximations are not. For each candidate point, the weight of values to either side of the split can be approximated for each class, using their respective Gaussian curves, and the information gain is computed from these weights.

The process is illustrated in figure 6.5. At the top of the figure are two Gaussian curves, each approximating the distribution of values for a numeric attribute and labeled with a particular class. Each curve can be described using three values: the mean, the variance, and the total weight of examples. For instance, in figure 6.5, the class shown to the left has a lower mean, higher variance, and higher example weight (larger area under the curve) than the other class. Below the curves, the range of values has been divided into ten split points, labeled A to J. The vertical bar at the bottom displays the relative amount of information gain calculated for each split. The split point that would be chosen as the best is point E, which the evaluation shows has the highest information gain.

A refinement of this method involves also tracking the minimum and maximum values of each class. This requires storing an extra two counts per class, but they are simple and take little time to maintain. When evaluating split points, the method exploits per-class minimum and maximum information to determine when class values lie completely to one side of a split, eliminating the small uncertainty otherwise present in the tails of the Gaussian curves. From the per-class minimum and maximum, the minimum and maximum of the entire range of values can be established, which helps to determine the position of split points to evaluate.

Approximation by a sum of Gaussians will almost certainly not capture the full detail of an intricate numeric distribution, but the approach is efficient in both computation and memory. Whereas the binary tree method uses extreme memory costs to be as accurate as possible, this method employs the opposite approach—using gross approximation to use as little memory as possible. And in fact, the simplified view of numeric distributions is not necessarily harmful to the accuracy of the trees it produces. There will be further opportunities to refine split decisions on a particular attribute by splitting again further down the tree. Also, the approximation by a few simple parameters can be more robust and resistant to noise and outliers than more complicated methods, which concentrate on finer details.

6.5 Perceptron

The Perceptron, proposed by Rosenblatt in 1957, is a linear classifier and one of the first methods for online learning. Because of its low computational cost, it was shown in [37] to be a useful complement to the Majority Class and Naive Bayes classifiers at the leaves of decision trees.

The algorithm is given a stream of pairs $(\vec{x}_i, y_i)$, where $\vec{x}_i$ is the ith example and y_i is its class. The perceptron keeps at all times a vector of weights $\vec{w}$ that defines the function $h_{\vec{w}}$ used to label examples; in particular, for every example $\vec{x}$ we have $h_w(x) = \sigma(\vec{w}^T \vec{x})$, where $\sigma(x) = 1/(1 + e^{-x})$ is a soft-threshold function whose range is $[0, 1]$. The prediction given to the outside is more likely produced by applying the sign function (i.e., a 0 or 1 value), but using σ is more convenient for the derivation of the update rule. A nonzero decision threshold can be simulated by adding an additional feature in x that is always 1.

The derivation of the update rule can be found in many texts on ML, and is omitted here. In essence, its goal is to update the weights $\vec{w}$ to minimize the number of misclassified examples, and this is achieved by moving each component of $\vec{w}$ in the direction of the gradient that decreases the error. More precisely, the rule is:

$$\vec{w} = \vec{w} + \eta \sum_i (y_i - h_{\vec{w}}(\vec{x}_i)) \, h_{\vec{w}}(\vec{x}_i) \, (1 - h_{\vec{w}}(\vec{x}_i)) \, \vec{x}_i,$$

where η is a parameter called the *learning rate*.

This method is the simplest example of so-called stochastic gradient descent for incremental optimization of a loss function on a set or stream of examples.

6.6   Lazy Learning

Perhaps the most obvious batch method to try in the streaming context is the k-nearest neighbor method, k-NN [209]. The change to streaming is readily achieved by using a sliding window as the search space for determining the k-nearest neighbors to a new unclassified instance, and predicting the majority among their k labels. Votes can optionally be weighted by the inverse of the distance to the point to predict, or some other scheme. The method using a sliding window with the 1,000 most recent instances was found to be remarkably effective in [209].

As the window slides, the method naturally responds to concept drift. Concept drift can be either abrupt or gradual, and responding to these differently makes sense for lazy learners [28].

If implemented naively, the method is generally inefficient at prediction time because of the search for neighbors, but it is possible to index the instances in the sliding window to improve prediction efficiency [257].

More recently, Losing et al. [162] proposed the use of two memories for coping with different concept drift types and drift speeds. A short-term memory, containing data from the most current window, is used to model the current concept, and a long-term memory is used to maintain knowledge of past concepts. By carefully managing these two memories, very competitive results can be achieved in benchmark tests. The authors point out that the method is useful in practice because it does not require any meta-parameters to be tuned.

Some variant of k-NN, even just the simplest one, should always be used when evaluating new classification methods.

6.7   Multi-label Classification

In many real-world applications, particularly those involving text, we are faced with multiclass problems: classifying instances into multiple class labels rather than only one. An example in text categorization is applying *tags* to documents. Imagine that we are tagging news articles, and we have to tag an article about a rugby game between France and New Zealand. That document can be classified as both *France* and *New Zealand*, as well as *rugby* and possibly *sports*. There are many other applications: scene and video classification, medical diagnosis, and applications in microbiology.

The main challenge in multi-label classification is detecting and modeling dependencies between labels, without becoming too complex computationally. A simple baseline method is binary relevance (BR). BR transforms a multi-label problem into multiple binary problems, such that binary models can be employed to learn and predict the relevance of each label. An advantage of the method is that it is quite resistant to labelset overfitting, since it learns on a per-label basis. It has often been overlooked in the literature because it fails to take into account label correlations directly during the classification process [123, 210, 235], although there are several methods that overcome this limitation [68, 123, 211]. For example, in [211] Read et al. introduced ensembles of BR classifiers, and also the concept of *classifier chains*, both of which improve considerably on BR in terms of predictive performance.

A problem for BR methods in data streams is that class-label imbalance may become exacerbated by large numbers of training examples. Countermeasures to this are possible, for example by using per-label thresholding methods or classifier weightings as in [203].

BR can be applied directly to data streams by using streaming binary base models. Additional advantages in the streaming setting are BR's low time complexity and the fact that it can be easily parallelized.

An alternative paradigm to BR is the *label combination* or *label powerset* method (LC). LC transforms a multi-label problem into a single-label (multiclass) problem by treating all label combinations as atomic labels, that is, each labelset in the training set becomes a single class-label within a single-label problem. Thus, the set of single class-labels represents all distinct label subsets in the original multi-label representation, so label correlations are taken into account. Disadvantages of LC include its worst-case computational cost (as there are potentially up to 2^L labelsets on L labels) and a strong tendency to overfit the training data, although this problem has been largely overcome by newer methods [210, 235]; ideas include, for example, taking random label subsets from the labelset to train an ensemble of classifiers, as well as various pruning strategies.

A particular challenge for LC methods in a data stream context is that the label space expands over time due to the emergence of new label combinations. It is possible to adapt probabilistic models to account for the emergence of new labelset combinations over time; however, probabilistic models are not necessarily the best-performing ones. A general "buffering" strategy may be useful [208], where label combinations are learned from an initial number of examples and these are considered sufficient to represent the distribution. During the buffering phase, another model can be employed to adhere to the "ready to predict at any point" requirement.

Another multi-label approach is pairwise classification (PW), where binary models are used for every possible *pair* of labels [109]. PW performs well in some contexts, but the complexity in terms of models—namely, $L \times (L-1)/2$ for L labels—demands new ideas to make it applicable to large problems.

Note that these are all *problem transformation* methods, wherein a multi-label problem is transformed into one or more single-label problems, after which any off-the-shelf multi-class classifier (or binary, in the case of BR and PW) can be used. These methods are interesting generally due to their flexibility and general applicability.

The iSOUP-Tree (incremental structured output prediction) method [188] is a multi-label classifier that performs multi-label classification via multitarget regression. There exist two variants of the iSOUP-Tree method (building regression and model trees), as well as ensembles of iSOUP-Trees.

6.7.1 Multi-label Hoeffding Trees

A Multi-label Hoeffding tree was presented in [208], based on adaptation of the information gain criterion to multi-label problems.

Recall that Hoeffding trees use the information gain criterion to decide the best attribute at each expanding node, and that the information gain of an attribute is the difference between the entropy of the dataset before and after the split. As entropy measures the amount of uncertainty in the dataset, in the case of multi-label examples, we need to add to the entropy the information needed to describe all the classes that an example does not belong to.

Clare and King [72] showed that this can be accomplished by adding to the regular entropy a term that adds, for each label, a quantity related to the class entropy in the examples having that label. From there, they proposed a multi-label version of C4.5. The Multi-label Hoeffding Tree [208] uses this strategy to construct a decision tree. A Majority Labelset Classifier (the multi-label version of Majority Class) is used as the default classifier on the leaves of a Multi-label Hoeffding tree. However, any multi-label classifier at the leaves can be used.

6.8   Active Learning

Classifier methods need labeled training data to build models. Often unlabeled data is abundant but labeling is expensive. Labels can be costly to obtain due to the required human input (labor cost). Consider, for example, textual news arriving as a stream. The goal is to predict whether a news item will be interesting to a given user at a given time, and the interests of the user may change. To obtain training data the historical news needs to be read and labeled as interesting or not interesting. Currently this requires human labor. Labeling can also be costly due to a required expensive, intrusive, or destructive laboratory test. Consider a production process in a chemical plant where the goal is to predict the quality of production output. The relationship between input and output quality might change over time due to constant manual tuning, complementary ingredients, or replacement of physical sensors. In order to know the quality of the output (the true label) a laboratory test needs to be performed, which is costly. Under such conditions it may be unreasonable to require true labels for all incoming instances.

Active learning algorithms ask for labels selectively instead of expecting to receive all the instance labels. This has been extensively studied in pool-based [157] and online settings [77]. In pool-based settings, the decision concerning which instances to label is made from all historical data.

In [261], a framework setting for active learning in evolving data streams was presented. It works as follows: Data arrives in a stream, and predictions need to be made in real time. Concept drift is expected, so learning needs to be adaptive. The true label can be requested immediately or never, as the

ACTIVE LEARNING FRAMEWORK($Stream, B$)

    Input: a stream of unlabeled examples, labeling budget B,
      other strategy parameters
    Output: a stream of predictions

1 **for each** x_t—incoming instance
2   **do if** ACTIVE LEARNING STRATEGY($x_t, B, \ldots$) = **true**
3   **then** request the true label y_t of instance x_t
4   train classifier L with (x_t, y_t)
5   **if** L_n exists **then** train classifier L_n with (x_t, y_t)
6   **if** change warning is signaled
7   **then** start a new classifier L_n
8   **if** change is detected
9   **then** replace classifier L with L_n

Figure 6.6
Active learning framework.

instances are regularly discarded from memory. The goal is to maximize pre-diction accuracy over time, while keeping the labeling costs fixed within an allocated budget. After scanning an instance and outputting the prediction for it, we need a strategy to decide whether or not to query for the true label, so that our model could train itself with this new instance. Regular retraining is needed due to changes in data distribution. Active learning strategies in data streams, in addition to learning an accurate classifier in stationary situations, must be able to

• balance the labeling budget over time,

• notice changes happening anywhere in the instance space, and

• preserve the distribution of the incoming data for detecting changes.

More formally, the setting is as follows: The algorithm receives a stream of unlabeled instances x_t and a budget B, expressing the fraction of past instances that it is allowed to ask for labeling. If it requests the label for x_t, the algo-rithm receives the true label of x_t, denoted y_t. The cost of obtaining a label is assumed to be the same for all instances. $B = 1$ means that all arriving instances can be labeled, whereas $B = 0.2$ means that, at any moment, the algorithm may have requested the labels of at most 20% of the instances seen so far.

Figure 6.6 shows the framework that combines active learning strategies with adaptive learning. This framework uses the change detection technique of [114]: when the accuracy of the classifier begins to decrease, a new classifier is built and trained with new incoming instances. When a change is detected, the old classifier is replaced by the new one.

Next we describe four of the strategies proposed for budget allocation.

6.8.1   Random Strategy

The first (baseline) strategy is naive in the sense that it labels the incoming instances at random instead of actively deciding which label would be most relevant. For every incoming instance the true label is requested with probability B, where B is the budget.

6.8.2   Fixed Uncertainty Strategy

Uncertainty sampling is perhaps the simplest and the most common active learning strategy [224]. The idea is to label the instances for which the current classifier is the least confident. In an online setting, this corresponds to labeling the instances for which the certainty is below some fixed threshold. A simple way to measure uncertainty is to use the posterior probability estimates, output by a classifier.

6.8.3   Variable Uncertainty Strategy

One of the challenges with the fixed uncertainty strategy in a streaming data setting is how to distribute the labeling effort over time. Using a fixed threshold, after some time a classifier will either exhaust its budget or reach the threshold certainty. In both cases it will stop learning and thus fail to adapt to changes.

Instead of labeling the instances that are less certain than the threshold, we want to label the least certain instances within a time interval. Thus we can introduce a variable threshold, which adjusts itself depending on the incoming data to align with the budget. If a classifier becomes more certain (stable situations), the threshold expands to be able to capture the most uncertain instances. If a change happens and suddenly a lot of labeling requests appear, then the threshold is contracted to query only the most uncertain instances.

VARIABLEUNCERTAINTY(x_t, L, B, s)

Input: x_t—incoming instance, L—trained classifier,
B—budget, s—adjusting step
Output: $label \in \{\textbf{true}, \textbf{false}\}$ indicates whether to request
the true label y_t
Starting defaults:
total labeling cost $u = 0$, initial labeling threshold $\theta = 1$

1   **if** $(u/t < B)$
2   **then**   ▷ budget is not exceeded
3                $\hat{y}_t = \arg\max_y P_L(y|x_t)$, where $y \in \{1, \ldots, c\}$
4   is one of the class labels
5   **if** $(P_L(\hat{y}_t|x_t) < \theta)$
6   **then**   ▷ uncertainty below the threshold
7                            $u = u + 1$ ▷ labeling costs increase
8                            $\theta = \theta(1 - s)$ ▷ the threshold decreases
9   **return true**
10   **else**   ▷ certainty is good
11   ▷ make the uncertainty region wider
12                           $\theta = \theta(1 + s)$
13   **return false**
14   **else**   ▷ budget is exceeded
15   **return false**

Figure 6.7
Variable uncertainty strategy, with a dynamic threshold.

It may seem counterintuitive to ask for more labels in quiet periods and fewer labels at change points. But, in fact, this ensures that the algorithm asks for the same fraction of labels in all situations. Since it does not know when or how often changes will be happening, this helps in spending the budget uniformly over time.

The variable uncertainty strategy is described in figure 6.7. More detail and a comparison with the other strategies can be found in [261].

6.8.4   Uncertainty Strategy with Randomization

The uncertainty strategy always labels the instances that are closest to the decision boundary of the classifier. In data streams, changes may happen anywhere in the instance space. When concept drift happens in labels, the classifier will not notice it without the true labels. In order to not miss concept drift we should, from time to time, label some instances about which the classifier is very certain. For that purpose, for every instance, the strategy randomizes the labeling threshold by multiplying by a normally distributed random variable that follows $N(1, \delta)$. This way, it labels the instances that are close to the decision boundary more often, but occasionally also labels some distant instances.

This strategy trades off labeling some very uncertain instances for labeling very certain instances, in order to not miss changes. Thus, in stationary situations this strategy is expected to perform worse than the uncertainty strategy, but in changing situations it is expected to adapt faster.

Table 6.3 summarizes the four strategies with respect to several requirements. The random strategy satisfies all three requirements. Randomized uncertainty satisfies budget and coverage, but it produces biased labeled data. Variable uncertainty satisfies only the budget requirement, and fixed uncertainty satisfies none.

Table 6.3

Summary of budget allocation strategies.

	Controlling budget	Instance space coverage	Labeled data distribution
Random	present	full	IID
Fixed uncertainty	no	fragment	biased
Variable uncertainty	handled	fragment	biased
Randomized uncertainty	handled	full	biased

6.9   Concept Evolution

Concept evolution occurs when new classes appear in evolving data streams. For example, in mining text data from Twitter, new topics can appear in tweets; or in intrusion detection in network data streams, new types of attacks can appear, representing new classes.

Masud et al. [170] were the first to deal with this setting. Their approach consists of training an ensemble of k-NN-based classifiers that contain pseudo-points obtained using a semisupervised k-means clustering. Each member of the ensemble is trained on a different labeled chunk of data. New instances are classified using the majority vote among the classifiers in the ensemble.

Each pseudopoint represents a hypersphere in the feature space with a corresponding centroid and radius. The decision boundary of a model is the union of the feature spaces; and the decision boundary of the ensemble is the union of the decision boundaries of all the models in the ensemble.

Each new instance is first examined by the ensemble of models to see if it is outside the decision boundary of the ensemble. If it is inside the decision boundary, then it is classified normally using the majority vote of the models of the ensemble. Otherwise, it is declared as an F-outlier, or filtered outlier. These F-outliers are potential novel class instances, and they are temporarily stored in a buffer to observe whether they are close to each other. This is done by using a q-neighborhood silhouette coefficient (q-NSC), a unified measure of cohesion and separation that yields a value between -1 and $+1$. A positive value indicates that the point is closer to the F-outlier instances (more cohesion) and farther away from existing class instances (more separation), and vice versa. A new class is declared if there are a sufficient number of F-outliers having positive q-NSC for all classifiers in the ensemble.

The SAND (semisupervised adaptive novel detection) method [133] determines the chunk size dynamically based on changes in the classifier confidence. SAND is thus more efficient and avoids unnecessary training during periods with no changes.

Finally, in [10], a "class-based" ensemble technique is presented that replaces the traditional "chunk-based" approach in order to detect recurring classes. The authors claim that the class-based ensemble methods are superior to the chunk-based techniques.

6.10   Lab Session with MOA

In this session lab you will use MOA through the graphical interface to learn several classifier models and evaluate them in different ways. The initial MOA GUI screen is shown in figure 6.8.

Figure 6.8
MOA graphical user interface.

Exercise 6.1 Click *Configure* to set up a task. Change the task type in the dropdown menu at the top to `LearnModel`. As you can see, the default learner is `NaiveBayes`. You could change it by clicking the *Edit* button and then selecting from the dropdown menu at the top. However, leave it as `NaiveBayes` for now. The default data stream is `RandomTreeGenerator`. Use the corresponding *Edit* button to change it to `WaveformGenerator`, which generates instances from a combination of waveforms. Change the number of instances to generate from $10,000,000$ to $1,000,000$. Finally, specify a `taskResultFile`, say `modelNB.moa`, where MOA will output the model.

Now click *OK, and then* Run *to launch this task. Textual output appears in the center panel: in this case, every* $10,000$ *steps. Various evaluation measures appear in the lower panel, and are continuously updated until the task completes. MOA can run several tasks concurrently, as you will see if you click* Run *twice in quick succession. Clicking on a job in the top panel displays its information in the lower two panels.*

The task you have just run is

```
LearnModel -l bayes.NaiveBayes
   -s generators.WaveformGenerator
   -m 1000000 -O modelNB.moa
```

—you can see this in the line beside the Configure *button—and it has stored the Naive Bayes model in the file* `modelNB.moa`*. (However, parameters that have their default value are not shown in the configuration text.)*

Click Configure *and change the learner to a Hoeffding Tree with output file* `modelHT.moa`*:*

```
LearnModel -l trees.HoeffdingTree
   -s generators.WaveformGenerator
   -m 1000000 -O modelHT.moa
```

and run it. Now we have two models stored on disk, `modelNB.moa` *and* `modelHT.moa`*.*

We will evaluate the Naive Bayes model using $1,000,000$ *new instances generated by the* `WaveformGenerator`*, which is accomplished by the task*

```
EvaluateModel -m file:modelNB.moa
   -s (generators.WaveformGenerator -i 2) -i 1000000
```

The `-i 2` *sets a different random seed for the waveform generator. You can set up most of these in the* Configure *panel: at the top, set the task to* `Eval-uateModel`*, and configure the stream (which has now changed to* `RandomTreeGenerator`*) to* `WaveformGenerator` *with* `instanceRandomSeed` *equal to 2. Frustratingly, though, you cannot specify that the model should be read from a file.*

It is useful to learn how to get around such problems. Click OK to return to the main MOA interface, select Copy configuration to clipboard *from the right-click menu, then select* Enter configuration *and paste the clipboard into the new configuration, where you can edit it, and type* `-m file:modelNB.moa` *into the command line. This gives the* `EvaluateModel` *task the parameters needed to load the Naive Bayes model produced in the previous step, generate a new waveform stream with a random seed of 2, and test on* $1,000,000$ *examples.*

a. *What is the percentage of correct classifications?*

b. *Edit the command line to evaluate the Hoeffding Tree model. What is the percentage of correct classifications?*

c. *Which model performs best according to the Kappa statistic?*

Exercise 6.2 In MOA, you can nest commands. For example, the `LearnModel` and `EvaluateModel` steps can be rolled into one, avoiding the need to create an external file. You cannot do this within the interactive *Configure interface; instead you have to edit the Configure command text.*

`OzaBag` is an incremental bagging technique that we will see in the next chapter. Evaluate it as follows:

```
EvaluateModel -m (LearnModel -l meta.OzaBag
  -s generators.WaveformGenerator -m 1000000)
  -s (generators.WaveformGenerator -i 2) -i 1000000
```

Do this by copying this command and pasting it as the Configure *text using right-click,* Enter configuration.

What is the accuracy of `OzaBag`*?*

Exercise 6.3 The task `EvaluatePeriodicHeldOutTest` trains a model while taking performance snapshots at periodic intervals on a holdout test set.

a. The following command trains the `HoeffdingTree` classifier on $10,000,000$ samples from the `WaveformGenerator` data, after holding out the first $100,000$ samples as a test set; after every $1,000,000$ examples it performs a test on this set:

```
EvaluatePeriodicHeldOutTest -l trees.HoeffdingTree
  -s generators.WaveformGenerator
  -n 100000 -i 10000000 -f 1000000
```

You can copy this configuration and paste it in (cheating!), or set it up in the interactive *Configure* interface (test size $100,000$, train size $10,000,000$, sample frequency $1,000,000$). It outputs a CSV file with 10 rows in the center panel and final statistics in the lower panel. What is the final accuracy?

    b. What is the final Kappa statistic?

Exercise 6.4 Prequential evaluation evaluates first on any instance, then uses it to train. Here is an `EvaluatePrequential` task that trains a `HoeffdingTree` classifier on $1,000,000$ examples of the `WaveformGenerator` data, testing every $10,000$ examples, to create a 100-line CSV file:

```
EvaluatePrequential -l trees.HoeffdingTree
  -s generators.WaveformGenerator
  -i 1000000 -f 10000
```

Set it up in the interactive *Configure* interface and run it. At the bottom, the GUI shows a graphical display of the results—a learning curve. You can compare the results of two different tasks: click around the tasks and you will find that the current one is displayed in red and the previously selected one in blue.

    a. Compare the prequential evaluation of `NaiveBayes` with `HoeffdingTree`. Does the Hoeffding Tree always outperform Naive Bayes in the learning curve display?

    b. What is the final Kappa statistic for the Hoeffding Tree?

    c. What is the final Kappa statistic for Naive Bayes?

Exercise 6.5 By default, prequential evaluation displays performance computed over a window of 1000 instances, which creates a jumpy, jagged learning curve. Look at the evaluator in the *Configure panel: you can see that the WindowClassificationPerformanceEvaluator is used, with a window size of* 1000. *Instead, select the BasicClassificationPerformanceEvaluator, which computes evaluation measures from the beginning of the stream using every example:*

```
EvaluatePrequential -l trees.HoeffdingTree
  -s generators.WaveformGenerator
  -e BasicClassificationPerformanceEvaluator
  -i 1000000 -f 10000
```

As you can see, this ensures a smooth plot over time, because each individual example becomes less and less significant to the overall average.

a. Compare again the prequential evaluations of the Hoeffding Tree and Naive Bayes using the `BasicClassificationPerformanceEvalua-tor`*. Does the Hoeffding tree always outperform Naive Bayes in the learning curve display?*

b. What is the final Kappa statistic for the Hoeffding Tree?

c. What is the final Kappa statistic for Naive Bayes?

7 Ensemble Methods

Ensemble predictors are combinations of smaller models whose individual predictions are combined in some manner (say, averaging or voting) to form a final prediction. In both batch and streaming scenarios, ensembles tend to improve prediction accuracy over any of their constituents, at the cost of more time and memory resources, and they are often easy to parallelize. But in streaming, ensembles of classifiers have additional advantages over single-classifier methods: they are easy to scale; if mining a distributed stream, they do not require the several streams to be centralized toward a single site; and they can be made to adapt to change by pruning underperforming parts of the ensemble and adding new classifiers. A comprehensive and up-to-date discussion of ensembles for streams is [124].

We first discuss general methods for creating ensembles by weighting or voting existing classifiers, such as weighted majority and stacking. We then discuss bagging and boosting, two popular methods that create an ensemble by transforming the input distribution before giving it to a base algorithm that creates classifiers. Next, we discuss a few methods that use Hoeffding Trees as the base classifiers. Finally, we discuss recurrent concepts, that is, scenarios where distributions that have appeared in the past tend to reappear later, and how they can be addressed with ensembles.

7.1 Accuracy-Weighted Ensembles

A simple ensemble scheme takes N predictors $C_1, \ldots, C_N$ and applies some function f to combine their predictions: on every instance x to predict, the ensemble predicts $f(C_1(x), \ldots, C_N(x))$, where $C_i(x)$ denotes the prediction of C_i for x. The predictors may be fixed from the beginning, perhaps trained offline from batch data, or trained online on the same stream.

For classification, f may simply be *voting*, that is, producing the most popular class among the $C_i(x)$. In *weighted voting*, each classifier C_i has a weight w_i attached to its vote. If we have a two-class problem, with classes in $\{0, 1\}$, weighted voting may be expressed as:

$$prediction(x) = \begin{cases} 1 & \text{if } \sum_i w_i C_i(x) > \theta \\ 0 & \text{otherwise} \end{cases}$$

where θ is a suitable threshold. Weights may be fixed for the whole process, determined by an expert or by offline training, or vary over time. We concentrate on the latter, more interesting case.

Accuracy-Weighted Ensembles (AWE) were proposed by Wang et al. [244], and designed to mine evolving data streams using nonstreaming learners. An AWE processes a stream in chunks and builds a new classifier for each new chunk. Each time a classifier is added, the oldest one is removed, allowing the ensemble to adapt to changes. AWEs are implemented in MOA as ACCURA-CYWEIGHTEDENSEMBLE.

It is shown in [244] that the ensemble performs better than the base classifiers if each classifier is given weight proportional to $err_r - err_i$, where err_i is the error of the ith classifier on the test set and err_r is the error of a random classifier, one that predicts class c with the probability of class c in the training set. As a proxy for the test set, AWE computes these errors on the most recent chunk, assumed to be the one that is most similar to the instances that will arrive next.

Advantages of this method are its simplicity and the fact that it can be used with nonstreaming base classifiers and yet work well on both stationary and nonstationary streams. One disadvantage of the method is that the chunk size must be determined externally, by an expert on the domain, taking into account the learning curve of the base classifiers.

Variations of AWE have been presented, among others, in [58, 148]. The one in [58] is implemented in MOA as ACCURACYUPDATEDENSEMBLE.

7.2   Weighted Majority

The Weighted Majority Algorithm, proposed by Littlestone and Warmuth [160], combines N existing predictors called "experts" (in this context), and learns to adjust their weights over time. It is similar to the perceptron algorithm, but its update rule changes the weights multiplicatively rather than additively. Unlike the perceptron, it can be shown to converge to almost the error rate of the best expert, plus a small term depending on N. It is thus useful when the number of experts is large and many of them perform poorly.

The algorithm appears in figure 7.1. The input to the algorithm is a stream of items requiring prediction, each followed by its correct label. Upon receiving item number t, x_t, the algorithm emits a prediction $\hat{y}_t$ for the label of x_t. Then the algorithm receives the correct label y_t for x_t. In the algorithm the $sign$ function returns 0 for negative numbers and 1 for nonnegative ones.

At time t, the algorithm predicts 1 if the sum of the experts' predictions, weighted by the current set of weights, is at least $1/2$. After that, the weight

WEIGHTEDMAJORITY(*Stream*, β)

    Input: a stream of pairs (x, y), parameter $\beta \in (0, 1)$
    Output: a stream of predictions $\hat{y}$ for each x

1   initialize experts $C_1, \ldots, C_N$ with weight $w_i = 1/N$ each
2   **for** each x in *Stream*
3   **do** collect predictions $C_1(x), \ldots, C_N(x)$
4           $p \leftarrow \sum_i w_i \cdot C_i(x)$
5           $\hat{y} \leftarrow sign\left(p - \frac{1}{2}\right)$
6   **for** $i \in 1 \ldots N$
7   **do if** $(C_i(x) \neq y)$ **then** $w_i \leftarrow \beta \cdot w_i$
8           $s \leftarrow \sum_i w_i$
9   **for** $i \in 1 \ldots N$
10   **do** $w_i \leftarrow w_i/s$

Figure 7.1
The Weighted Majority algorithm.

of every classifier that made a mistake is reduced by factor β. The weights are renormalized so that they add up to 1 at all times.

The intuition of the algorithm is that the weight of an expert decreases exponentially with the number of errors it makes. Therefore, if any expert has a somewhat smaller error rate than the others, its weight will decrease much more slowly, and it will soon dominate the linear combination used to make the prediction. Formalizing this argument, it was shown in [160] that no matter the order of the stream elements, at all times t,

$$err_{\text{WM},t} \leq \frac{\log(1/\beta) \min_i err_{i,t} + \log N}{\log(2/(1 + \beta))}$$

where $err_{\text{WM},t}$ is the number of prediction errors (examples where $\hat{y} \neq y$) made by Weighted Majority up to time t, and $err_{i,t}$ is the analogous figure for expert number i (number of examples where $C_i(x) \neq y$). In particular, for $\beta = 0.5$, we have

$$err_{\text{WM},t} \leq 2.41 \left(\min_i err_{i,t} + \log N\right).$$

In words, the number of mistakes of the Weighted Majority algorithm is only a constant factor larger than that of the *best* expert, plus a term that does not grow with t and depends only logarithmically on the number of experts. Observe, however, that the running time on each example is at least linear in N, unless the algorithm is parallelized.

For deterministic algorithms, the constant factor in front of $\min_i err_{i,t}$ cannot be made smaller than 2. A randomized variant is proposed in [160]: rather than predicting $\hat{y} = sign(p)$ in line 5, predict $\hat{y} = 1$ with probability p and 0 with probability $1 - p$. Randomness defeats to some extent the worst adversary choice of labels, and the constants in the bound are improved in expectation to

$$\mathrm{E}[err_{\mathrm{WM},t}] \leq \frac{\ln(1/\beta)\min_i err_{i,t} + \ln N}{1 - \beta}.$$

So, choosing β close enough to 1, the constant in front of $\min_i err_{i,t}$ can be made as close to 1 as desired. In particular, setting $\beta = 0.5$ we get

$$\mathrm{E}[err_{M,t}] \leq 1.39\min_i err_{i,t} + 2\ln N.$$

If we are interested in bounding the errors up to some time horizon T known in advance, we can set $\beta = \exp(-\sqrt{T})$; some calculus shows:

$$\mathrm{E}[err_{M,T}] \lesssim (1 + 1/\sqrt{T})\min_i err_{i,t} + \sqrt{T}\log N,$$

so the coefficient in the first term tends to 1 for large T. Weighted Majority is a special case of the Exponentiated Gradient method [147], which applies when labels and predictions are real values not in $\{0, 1\}$, that is, it applies to regression problems.

7.3   Stacking

Stacking [247] is a generalization of Weighted Majority and, in fact, the most general way of combining experts. Assuming again N experts C_1 to C_N, a meta-learning algorithm is used to train a meta-model on instances of the form $(C_1(x), \ldots, C_N(x))$, that is, the prediction of expert C_i is considered to be feature number i. The instance x can, optionally, also be given to the meta-classifier.

The meta-learner used in stacking is often a relatively simple one such as the perceptron. Weighted Majority and Exponentiated Gradient can be seen as special cases of Stacking where a meta-learner learns a linear classifier using a multiplicative update rule instead of the additive one in the perceptron.

7.4 Bagging

The *bagging* method is due to Breiman [52] for the batch setting, and works in a quite different way. A base learning algorithm is used to infer M different models that are potentially different because they are trained with different *bootstrap samples*. Each sample is created by drawing random samples with replacement from the original training set. The resulting meta-model makes a prediction by taking the simple majority vote of the predictions of the M classifiers created in this way.

The rationale behind bagging is that voting reduces the sample variance of the base algorithm, that is, the difference among classifiers trained from different samples from the same source distribution. In fact, it works better the higher the variance among the bootstrapped classifiers.

7.4.1 Online Bagging Algorithm

In the streaming setting, it seems difficult at first to draw a sample *with replacement* from the stream. Yet the following property allows bootstrapping to be simulated: in a bootstrap replica, the number of copies K of each of the n examples in the training set follows a binomial distribution:

$$P(K = k) = \binom{n}{k} p^k (1 - p)^{n-k} = \binom{n}{k} \frac{1}{n}^k \left(1 - \frac{1}{n}\right)^{n-k}.$$

For large values of n, this binomial distribution tends to a $\text{Poisson}(1)$ distribution, where $\text{Poisson}(1) = \exp(-1)/k!$. Using this property, Oza and Russell proposed Online Bagging [189, 190], which, instead of sampling with replacement, gives each arriving example a weight according to $\text{Poisson}(1)$. Its pseudocode is given in figure 7.2. It is implemented in MOA as OZABAG.

7.4.2 Bagging with a Change Detector

A problem with the approach above is that it is not particularly designed to react to changes in the stream, unless the base classifiers are themselves highly adaptive.

ADWIN Bagging [38], implemented in MOA as OZABAGADWIN, improves on Online Bagging as follows: it uses M instances of ADWIN to monitor the error rates of the base classifiers. When any one detects a change,

ONLINE BAGGING(*Stream*, *M*)

    Input: a stream of pairs (x, y), parameter $M =$ ensemble size
    Output: a stream of predictions $\hat{y}$ for each x

1   initialize base models h_m for all $m \in \{1, 2, \ldots, M\}$
2   **for** each example (x, y) in *Stream*
3   **do** predict $\hat{y} \leftarrow \arg\max_{y \in Y} \sum_{t=1}^{T} I(h_t(x) = y)$
4   **for** $m = 1, 2, \ldots, M$
5   **do** $w \leftarrow Poisson(1)$
6   update h_m with example (x, y) and weight w

Figure 7.2

Online Bagging for M models. The indicator function $I(\text{condition})$ returns 1 if the condition is true, and 0 otherwise.

the worst classifier in the ensemble is removed and a new classifier is added to it. This strategy is sometimes called "replace the loser."

7.4.3   Leveraging Bagging

An experimental observation when using online bagging is that adding more randomness to the input seems to improve performance. Since adding randomness increases the diversity or variance of the base classifiers, this agrees with the intuition that bagging benefits from higher classifier variance.

Additional randomness can be introduced by sampling with distributions other than Poisson(1). For example, Lee and Clyde [155] use the $\Gamma(1, 1)$ distribution to obtain a Bayesian version of bagging. Note that $\Gamma(1, 1)$ equals $Exp(1)$. Bühlmann and Yu [60] propose subbagging, that is, using resampling without replacement.

Leveraging Bagging [36] samples the stream with distribution Poisson(λ), where $\lambda \geq 1$ is a parameter of the algorithm. Since the Poisson distribution has variance (and mean) λ, this does increase the variance in the bootstrap samples with respect to regular Online Bagging. It is implemented in MOA as LEVERAGINGBAG.

Besides adding randomness to the input, Leveraging Bagging also adds randomization at the output of the ensemble using output codes. Dietterich and Bakiri [87] introduced a method based on error-correcting output codes, which handles multiclass problems using only a binary classifier. The classes assigned to each example are modified to create a new binary classification of the data induced by a mapping from the set of classes to $\{0,1\}$. A variation of this method by Schapire [222] presented a form of boosting using output codes. Leveraging Bagging uses random output codes instead of deterministic codes. In standard ensemble methods, all classifiers try to predict the same function. However, using output codes, each classifier will predict a different function. This may reduce the effects of correlations between the classifiers, and increase the diversity of the ensemble.

Leveraging Bagging also incorporates the "replace the loser" strategy in ADWIN Bagging. Experiments in [36] show that Leveraging Bagging improves over regular Online Bagging and over ADWIN Bagging.

7.5   Boosting

Like bagging, boosting algorithms combine multiple base models trained with samples of the input to achieve lower classification error. Unlike bagging, the models are created sequentially rather than in parallel, with the construction of each new model depending on the performance of the previously constructed models. The intuitive idea of boosting is to give more weight to the examples misclassified by the current ensemble of classifiers, so that the next classifier in the sequence pays more attention to these examples. AdaBoost.M1 [108] is the most popular variant of batch boosting.

This sequential nature makes boosting more difficult than bagging to transfer to streaming. For online settings, Oza and Russell [189, 190] proposed *Online Boosting*, an online method that, rather than building new models sequentially each time a new instance arrives, instead updates each model with a weight computed depending on the performance of the previous classifiers. It is implemented in MOA as OZABOOST. Other online boosting-like methods are given in [53, 54, 65, 85, 197, 243, 259].

According to [187], among others, in the batch setting boosting often outperforms bagging, but it is also more sensitive to noise, so bagging gives improvements more consistently. Early studies comparing online boosting and online bagging methods, however, seemed to favor bagging [38, 189, 190]. An exception is [100], which reported the Arc-x4 boosting algorithm [53] performing better than online bagging. Additional studies comparing the more recent variants would be interesting. Also, it is unclear how to make a boosting algorithm deal with concept drift, because a strategy such as "replace the loser" does not seem as justifiable as in bagging.

7.6   Ensembles of Hoeffding Trees

Since Hoeffding Trees are among the most useful and best-studied streaming classifiers, several ways of combining them into ensembles have been proposed.

7.6.1   Hoeffding Option Trees

Hoeffding Option Trees (HOT) [198] represent ensembles of trees implicitly in a single tree structure. A HOT contains, besides regular nodes that test one attribute, *option nodes* that apply no test and simply branch into several subtrees. When an instance reaches an option node, it continues descending through all its children, eventually reaching several leaves. The output of the tree on an instance is then determined by a vote among all the leaf nodes reached.

Option nodes are introduced when the splitting criterion of the Hoeffding Tree algorithm seems to value several attributes similarly after receiving a reasonable number of examples. Rather than waiting arbitrarily long to break a tie, all tied attributes are added as options. In this way, the effects of limited lookahead and instability are mitigated, leading to a more accurate model.

We omit several additional details given in [198] and implemented in the MOA version of HOT, named HOEFFDINGOPTIONTREE. The voting among the leaves is weighted rather than using simple majority voting. Strategies to limit tree growth are required, as option trees have a tendency to grow very rapidly if not controlled. HOTs for regression, with subtle differences in the construction process, were proposed in [140].

7.6.2   Random Forests

Breiman [55] proposed Random Forests in the batch setting as ensembles of trees that use randomization on the input and on the internal construction of the decision trees. The input is randomized by taking bootstrap samples, as in standard bagging. The construction of the trees is randomized by requiring that at each node only a randomly chosen subset of the attributes can be used for splitting. The subset is usually quite small, with a size such as the square root of the total number of attributes. Furthermore, the trees are grown without pruning. Random Forests are usually among the top-performing classifier methods in many batch tasks.

Streaming implementations of random forests have been proposed by, among others, Abdulsalam et al. [2], who did not exactly use Hoeffding Trees but another type of online tree builder. An implementation using Hoeffding Trees that exploits GPU computing power is given in [167]. These and most other implementations of streaming Random Forests use the "replace the loser" strategy for dealing with concept drift.

Unfortunately, none of these Random Forest algorithms have been able to compete effectively with the various bagging- and boosting-based algorithms mentioned before. Recently, however, Gomes et al. [125] presented the Adaptive Random Forest (ARF) algorithm that appears as a strong contender. In contrast to previous attempts at replicating Random Forests for data stream learning [124], ARF includes an effective resampling method and adaptive operators that can cope with different types of concept drift without complex optimizations for different datasets. The parallel implementation of ARF presented in [125] shows no degradation in terms of classification performance compared to a serial implementation, since trees and adaptive operators are independent of one another.

7.6.3   Perceptron Stacking of Restricted Hoeffding Trees

An observation made repeatedly in ML is that, often, complicated models are outperformed by simpler models that do not attempt to model complex interactions among attributes. This possibility was investigated for ensembles of Hoeffding Trees by Bifet et al. [31]. In contrast with Random Forests of full Hoeffding Trees, they proposed to use stacking with the perceptron algorithm using small trees.

More precisely, their algorithm enumerates all the subsets of attributes of size k and learns a Hoeffding Tree on each. These trees are the input to a stacking algorithm that uses the perceptron algorithm as a meta-learner. Growing the trees is fast, as each tree is small, and we expect the meta-learner to end up assigning large weights to the best combination(s) of k attributes.

Since there are $\binom{n}{k}$ sets of size k among n attributes, only small values of k are feasible for most values of n. For $k = 1$ the algorithm becomes the perceptron, but $k = 2$ is found to be practical for medium-size datasets. To deal with concept drift, the method adds an ADWIN change detector to each tree. When the error rate of a tree changes significantly, the tree is reset and a new tree with that attribute combination is learned. The method is shown in [31] to perform better than ADWIN Bagging on simple synthetic datasets, which suggests that it could perform well in cases where the key to prediction is not a complex combination of attributes.

This method is implemented in MOA as LIMATTCLASSIFIER.

7.6.4 Adaptive-Size Hoeffding Trees

The Adaptive-Size Hoeffding Tree (ASHT) method [38], implemented in MOA as OZABAGASHT, creates an ensemble of Hoeffding trees with the following restrictions:

- Each tree in the ensemble has an associated value representing the maximum number of internal nodes it can reach.

- After a node split occurs in a tree, if its size exceeds its associated value, then the tree is reset to a leaf.

If there are N trees in the ensemble, one way to assign the maximum sizes is to choose powers of, say, 2: 2, 4, ... up to 2^k. The intuition behind this method is that smaller trees adapt more quickly to changes, and larger trees perform better during periods with little or no change, simply because they were built using more data. Trees limited to size s will be reset about twice as often as trees limited to size $2s$. This creates a set of different reset speeds for an ensemble of such trees, and therefore a subset of trees that are a good approximation for the current rate of change.

The output of the ensemble can be the majority vote among all trees, although [38] finds experimentally that it is better to weight them in inverse proportion to the square of their errors. The error of each tree is monitored by an EWMA estimator.

It is important to note that resets will happen all the time, even for stationary datasets, but this behavior should not harm the ensemble's predictive performance.

7.7   Recurrent Concepts

In many settings, the stream distribution evolves in such a way that distributions occurring in the past reappear in the future. Streams with clear daily, weekly, or yearly periodicity (such as weather, customer sales, and road traffic) are examples, but reoccurrence may also occur in nonperiodic ways.

Recurring or *recurrent concept* frameworks have been proposed [112, 127, 143, 219] for these scenarios. Proposals differ in detail, but the main idea is to keep a library of classifiers that have been useful in the past but have been removed from the ensemble, for example because at some point they underperformed. Still, their accuracy is rechecked periodically in case they seem to be performing well again, and if so, they are added back to the ensemble.

Far fewer examples are required to estimate the accuracy of a classifier than to build a new one from scratch, so this scheme trades training time for memory. Additional rules are required for discarding classifiers from the library when it grows too large.

The RCD recurrent concept framework by Gonçalves and de Barros [143] is available as a MOA extension.

7.8   Lab Session with MOA

In this lab session we will use MOA through the graphical interface with various ensemble streaming classifiers and evolving streams.

Exercise 7.1   We begin with a non-evolving scenario. The `RandomRBF` data generator creates a random set of centers for each class, each comprising a weight, a central point per attribute, and a standard deviation. It then generates instances by choosing a center at random (taking the weights into consideration), which determines the class, and randomly choosing attribute values and an offset from the center. The overall vector is scaled to a length that is randomly sampled from a Gaussian distribution around the center.

a. What is the accuracy of Naive Bayes on a `RandomRBFGenerator` stream of $1,000,000$ instances with default values, using `Prequential` evaluation and the `BasicClassificationPerformanceEvaluator`?

b. What is the accuracy of the Hoeffding Tree in the same situation?

Exercise 7.2 MOA's Hoeffding Tree algorithm can use different prediction methods at the leaves. The default is an adaptive Naive Bayes method, but a majority class classifier can be used instead by specifying -1 (`trees.HoeffdingTree -1 MC`). You can set this up in MOA's *Configure* interface (you need to scroll down).

a. What is the accuracy of the Hoeffding Tree when a majority class classifier is used at the leaves?

b. What is the accuracy of the `OzaBag` bagging classifier?

Exercise 7.3 Now let us use an evolving data stream. The rate of movement of the centroids of the `RandomRBFGeneratorDrift` generator can be controled using the `speedChange` parameter.

a. Use the Naive Bayes classifier on a `RandomRBFGeneratorDrift` stream of 1,000,000 instances with 0.001 change speed. Use again `BasicClassificationPerformanceEvaluator` for prequential evaluation. What is the accuracy that we obtain?

b. What is the accuracy of a Hoeffding Tree under the same conditions?

c. What is the corresponding accuracy of `OzaBag`?

Exercise 7.4 The Hoeffding Adaptive Tree adapts to changes in the data stream by constructing tentative "alternative branches" as preparation for changes, and switching to them if they become more accurate. A change detector with theoretical guarantees (ADWIN) is used to check whether to substitute alternative subtrees.

a. What is the accuracy of `HoeffdingAdaptiveTree` in the above situation?

b. What is the accuracy for `OzaBagAdwin`, the ADWIN adaptive bagging technique?

c. Finally, what is the accuracy for `LeveragingBag` method?

Exercise 7.5 Besides data streams, MOA can also process ARFF files. We will use the `covtypeNorm.arff` dataset, which can be downloaded from the MOA website. Run the following task, which uses the Naive Bayes classifier:

```
EvaluatePrequential
```

```
-s (ArffFileStream -f covtypeNorm.arff)
-e BasicClassificationPerformanceEvaluator
-i 1000000 -f 10000
```

You will have to copy and paste this into the *Configure* text box, because you cannot specify an `ArffFileStream` in MOA's interactive interface. Also, the default location for files is the top level of the MOA installation folder—you will probably find the model files `modelNB.moa` and `modelHT.moa` that you made in the last session lab there—so you should either copy the ARFF file there or use its full pathname in the command.

a. What is the accuracy of Naive Bayes on this dataset?

b. What is the accuracy of a Hoeffding Tree on the same dataset?

c. Finally, what is the accuracy of Leveraging Bagging?

d. Which method is fastest on this data?

e. Which method is most accurate?

8 Regression

Regression is a learning task whose goal is to predict a numeric value, instead of a categorical attribute as in classification. Some of the techniques that are used in classification can be used in regression, but not all. Decision trees, the Perceptron and lazy learning can be used for regression, with modifications.

8.1 Introduction

Given a *numeric* attribute to be predicted, called the *outcome*, a regression algorithm builds a model that predicts for every unlabeled instance x a numeric prediction y for the outcome of x.

Examples of regression problems are predictions of quantities that cannot be reduced to a discrete label, such as prices in stock markets, product sales, time delays, or the number of visits to a website. It is possible to reduce regression to classification problems by discretizing the values of the outcome into intervals, or the other way around, to use regression algorithms to do classification, transforming the discrete class into a numerical variable. Of course, these transformations need not give optimal results.

The simplest regression algorithm is to return the mean value of the attribute that we want to predict. This is equivalent to the majority class method in classification, a learner that does not use the information in the rest of the attributes. A far more useful method in nonstreaming regression is *linear regression*.

Linear regression builds a linear model f, of the form

$$f(x) = \beta_0 + \sum_{j=1}^{p} \beta_j x_j = \mathbf{X}\beta,$$

that minimizes the residual sum of squares:

$$RSS(\beta) = \sum_{i=1}^{N} (y_i - f(x_i))^2 = (\mathbf{y} - \mathbf{X}\beta)'(\mathbf{y} - \mathbf{X}\beta),$$

where the input is the set of N pairs (x_i, y_i). However, the exact solution is

$$\hat{\beta} = (\mathbf{X}'\mathbf{X})^{-1}\mathbf{X}'\mathbf{y},$$

which is hard to compute incrementally, let alone in the streaming setting. Approximate solutions can be given using random projection sketches (see [73, 248] for example), but their use in practical data mining is still preliminary. So we look for other strategies that are more clearly incremental and adaptive.

8.2   Evaluation

To evaluate regression methods, we can use the same methodologies as in classification, such as holdout, prequential, and Interleaved test-then-train, but the misclassification rate measure is not applicable. The following measures are usually considered in regression:

- **Mean square error (MSE):** This is the most common measure, and gives the error using the mean of the squares of the differences between the actual values and the predictions:

$$MSE = \sum_i (f(x_i) - y_i)^2 / N.$$

- **Root mean square error:** The square root of the mean square error:

$$RMSE = \sqrt{MSE} = \sqrt{\sum_i (f(x_i) - y_i)^2 / N}.$$

- **Relative square error:** The ratio between the MSE of the regression method, and the MSE of the simplest regression method available, the mean regression algorithm:

$$RSE = \sum (f(x_i) - y_i)^2 / \sum_i (\bar{y}_i - y_i)^2.$$

- **Root relative square error:** The square root of the relative square error:

$$RRSE = \sqrt{RSE} = \sqrt{\sum_i (f(x_i) - y_i)^2 / \sum_i (\bar{y}_i - y_i)^2}.$$

- **Mean absolute error:** This measure is similar to the MSE, but considers absolute values of the difference:

$$MAE = \sum_i |f(x_i) - y_i| / N.$$

- **Relative absolute error:** Similar to the relative square error, but considers absolute values of the difference:

$$RAE = \sum_i |f(x_i) - y_i| / \sum_i |\hat{y}_i - y_i|.$$

It is easy to see that all these measures can be computed incrementally by maintaining a constant number of values in memory.

8.3   Perceptron Learning

The Perceptron [37] was presented in section 6.5 as an online classification method. However, it is just as naturally viewed as a regression method.

Given a data stream of pairs $(\vec{x}_i, y_i)$, where $\vec{x}_i$ is an example and y_i is its numeric outcome value, the goal of the perceptron is to minimize MSE on the examples. To do this, the strategy is again to move each weight in the weight vector $\vec{w}$ in the direction of the descending error gradient.

The update rule becomes in this case:

$$\vec{w} = \vec{w} + \eta \sum_i (y_i - h_{\vec{w}}(\vec{x}_i))\vec{x}_i.$$

As in classification, weights can be updated at every single example, as in the weight above, or taken in mini-batches for a single update step per mini-batch. This allows us to fine-tune the trade-off between update time and adaptiveness.

8.4   Lazy Learning

Lazy learning is one of the simplest and most natural models for classification and regression—in particular the k-Nearest Neighbor algorithm. Given a distance function d among instances, the k-NN method in regression finds the k instances closest to the instance to predict, and averages their outcomes. As in classification, the average may be weighted according to the distance to each neighbor.

The performance of the method strongly depends on the distance function used. For dense instances with numeric attributes, the Euclidean distance could be appropriate. For textual data, the cosine similarity measure or the Jaccard coefficient could be more appropriate.

IBLStreams, due to Shaker and Hüllermeier [225], is an implementation of lazy learning for regression on streams. Besides the basic ideas from streaming k-NN, it includes heuristics for removing outlier points from the database, removing instances that are too close to some already in the database (hence, not that useful), and for adaptively choosing the size of the database and of the parameter k.

8.5   Decision Tree Learning

Fast Incremental Model Tree with Drift Detection (FIMT-DD) is a decision tree for streaming regression due to Ikonomovska et al. [139]. It is an extension of the Hoeffding Tree method that differs in the following areas:

- Splitting criterion: Variance reduction is used instead of information gain, that is, the attribute chosen is the one such that the variance $\sum (\bar{y} - y_i)^2 / N$ is maximally reduced if splitting by this attribute.

- Numeric attributes: They are handled using an extension of the exhaustive binary tree method seen in section 6.4.2. At each node of the tree, the method stores a key value and keeps the following information for each of the two ranges $\leq key$, or $> key$:

  - the sum of the values of the numeric outcome,
  - the sum of the square of the values of the outcome, and
  - a count of the number of instances.

- Pruning: Some pruning rules are used to avoid storing every single value of the outcome.

- Linear model at the leaves: Perceptrons are used at the leaves, to adapt to drift.

- Concept drift handling: The Page-Hinkley test is used at the inner nodes of the decision tree to detect changes in the error rate.

- Tree updates: When a subtree is underperforming, an alternate tree is grown with new incoming instances; it replaces the original tree when (and if) it performs better.

FIMT-DD overall behaves similarly to Hoeffding Trees for classification, and is one of the state-of-the-art methods for regression. An option tree for regression was presented later in [140].

8.6   Decision Rules

Decision rules are a formalism that combines high expressive power with high interpretability. Learning sets of decision rules has consequently received intense attention in the batch case. In the streaming case, the AMRules algorithm developed by Almeida, Ferreira, Gama, Duarte, and Bifet [12, 13, 90–92] is the first and still most popular rule-learning system.

AMRules stands for adaptive model rules, and is specifically designed so that rules can be added and removed from the ruleset as the stream evolves. A rule in AMRules is of the form $A \to M$ where:

- The antecedent A is a conjunction of literals and M is a model that emits a prediction.

- A literal is either a condition of the form $A = a$, where A is a discrete attribute and a one of its values, or of the form $A \leq v$ or $A \geq v$, where A is continuous and v a real value. We say that a rule *covers* an example x if x satisfies all the conditions in the rule's antecedent.

- Model M is a regression model. AMRules supports three types of regressors: (1) the mean of the target attribute computed from the examples covered by the rule; (2) a linear combination of the attributes; and (3) an adaptive strategy that chooses between (1) and (2), picking the one with lower MSE on recent examples.

AMRules maintains a set of rules that are neither exclusive nor complete, in the sense that they need not cover all examples and that an example may be covered by several rules. This differentiates it from decision trees, which can naturally be viewed as a set of exclusive and complete rules. A set of rules can be viewed as ordered or unordered; AMRules supports both views. If viewed as ordered, the prediction of an example is that of the first rule that covers it. If the rules are viewed as unordered, all rules that cover an example are evaluated and their predictions are averaged. In addition, AMRules maintains a distinguished *default* rule that has no antecedents and that is applied whenever no rule covers an example.

At the core of the algorithm are the methods for creating new rules, expanding existing rules, and deleting underperforming rules.

Rule expansion. In a way similar to the Hoeffding Tree for trees, for each rule and for each attribute, the algorithm monitors the standard deviation reduction (SDR) that would be introduced if the attribute was added to the rule. If the ratio of the two largest SDR measures among all potential attributes exceeds a threshold, the feature with the largest SDR is added to the rule to expand it. When an example is received, it is used to update the statistics to compute the SDR values of the first rule that covers it, if the ruleset is ordered, or of all the rules that cover it, if the set is unordered. Expansion of a rule is only considered after it has received a certain minimum number of examples N_{min}.

Rule creation. If the default rule is expanded, it will become a normal rule and will be added to the model's ruleset. A new default rule is initialized to replace the expanded one.

Rule deletion. The error rate of every rule on the examples that it covers is monitored with a Page-Hinkley test. If the test indicates that its cumulative error exceeds a threshold, then the rule may be removed.

AMRules is reported in [90, 92] to have better performance on average than IBLStreams and FIMT-DD on a variety of synthetic and real datasets. The unordered version seems to achieve a slightly lower error rate than the ordered version; however, this is at the cost of interpretability, because the prediction for an example is easier to understand if it comes from a single rule than if it is the average of several rules.

8.7   Regression in MOA

MOA currently includes the algorithms discussed in this chapter: the Average (or Majority) algorithm, the Perceptron, IBLStreams (as an extension), and AMRules.

It also includes SGD, a stochastic gradient descent for learning various linear models (binary class SVM, binary class logistic regression and linear regression), and SPegasos, the stochastic variant of the Pegasos (Primal Estimated sub-GrAdient SOlver for SVM) method of Shalev-Shwartz et al. [226].

9 Clustering

Clustering is an *unsupervised* learning task that works on data without labels. It consists of distributing a set of instances into groups according to their commonalities or affinities. The main difference versus classification is that the groups are unknown before starting the learning process, and in fact the task is to create them. Uses of clustering include customer segmentation in marketing and finding communities in social networks, among many others.

Many, but not all, clustering methods are based on the assumption that instances are points in some space on which we can impose a distance function d, and that more similar instances are closer in the distance. In many of these methods, a clustering is determined by a set of centroid points in this space. A more formal definition of centroid-based clustering is the following: given a set of instances P belonging to some space X, a distance function d among elements in X, and optionally a number of clusters k, a clustering algorithm computes a set C of centroids or cluster centers $C \subseteq P$, with $|C| = k$, that (approximately) minimizes the objective function

$$cost(C, P) = \frac{1}{|P|} \sum_{x \in P} d(x, C)$$

where

$$d(x, C) = min_{c \in C} d(x, c),$$

that is, the distance from x to the nearest point in C.

As indicated, some algorithms require the user to specify a value for k, while others determine a number of clusters by themselves. Observe that by taking $k = |P|$ and assigning an instance to a cluster by itself leads to a clustering with 0 cost, so if k is not bound, some form of penalization on the number of clusters will be required to get meaningful results.

We start by discussing the evaluation problem in clustering and review the popular k-means method. We then discuss three incremental methods that are inspired more or less distantly by k-means: Birch, BICO, and CLUSTREAM. After that, we look at two density-based methods, starting with DBSCAN for nonstreaming data, which leads to Den-Stream for the streaming setting. Finally, we describe two more recent and state-of-the-art tree-based streaming methods, ClusTree and StreamKM++. We provide references and brief discussions of other methods in the closing section 9.7.

9.1   Evaluation Measures

Evaluating a clustering is unfortunately not as unambiguous as evaluating a classifier. There are many different measures of clustering quality described in the literature, maybe too many, which formalize different expectations of what a "good clustering" should achieve.

Measures can be categorized into two distinct groups: structural or internal measures, and ground-truth-based ones, called external measures. The first kind are strictly based on the data points and the clustering obtained. An extensive study of thirty internal measures can be found in [178], and other studies of external measures include [57, 231, 250]. Some examples are:

- **Cohesion:** The average distance from a point in the dataset to its assigned cluster centroid. The smaller the better.

- **SSQ:** The sum of squared distances from data points to their assigned centroids. Closely related to cohesion. The smaller the better.

- **Separation:** Average distance from a point to the points assigned to other clusters. The larger the better.

- **Silhouette coefficient:** Roughly speaking, the ratio between cohesion and the average distances from the points to their second-closest centroid. It rewards clusterings where points are very close to their assigned centroids and far from any other centroids, that is clusterings with good cohesion and good separation.

External measures, on the other hand, require knowledge of the "true" clustering of the data points, or ground truth, which by definition is almost always unknown in real scenarios. However, when evaluating new clusterers, one often creates synthetic datasets from a known generator, so it is possible to compare the clustering obtained by the algorithm with the true model. Some measures in these cases are similar to others applied in classification or information retrieval:

- **Accuracy:** Fraction of the points assigned to their "correct" cluster.

- **Recall:** Fraction of the points of a cluster that are in fact assigned to it.

- **Precision:** Fraction of the points assigned to a cluster that truly belong to it.

K-MEANS(P, k)

    Input: a dataset of points $P = \{p_1, \ldots, p_n\}$, a number of clusters k
    Output: centers $\{c_1, \ldots, c_k\}$ implicitly dividing P into k clusters

1   choose k initial centers $C = \{c_1, \ldots, c_k\}$
2   **while** stopping criterion has not been met
3   **do** ▷ assignment step:
4   **for** $i = 1, \ldots, N$
5   **do** find closest center $c_k \in C$ to instance p_i
6   assign instance p_i to set C_k
7   ▷ update step:
8   **for** $i = 1, \ldots, k$
9   **do** set c_i to be the center of mass of all points in C_i

Figure 9.1

The k-means clustering algorithm, or Lloyd's algorithm.

- **Purity:** In a maximally pure clustering, all points in the cluster belong to the same ground-truth class or cluster. Formally, purity is

$$\frac{1}{N} \sum_{c=1}^{k} (\text{number of points in cluster } c \text{ in the majority class for } c).$$

- **Cluster Mapping Measure (CMM):** A measure introduced by Kremer et al. [151], specifically designed for evolving data streams, which takes into account the fact that mergers and splits of clusters over time may create apparent errors.

The measures listed above can be easily maintained incrementally storing a constant number of values, if the centroids remain fixed. When the centroids evolve over time, we can resort to turning these values into EWMA accumulators or to evaluating on a sliding window.

9.2 The k-means Algorithm

The k-means (also called Lloyd's) algorithm is one of the most used methods in clustering, due to its simplicity. Figure 9.1 shows its pseudocode.

The k-means assumes that the set of points P is a subset of $\Re^d$ for some dimension d, so that points can be added and averaged. The algorithm starts selecting k centroids in an unspecified way—for example, at random. After that, two steps are iterated: first, each instance is assigned to the nearest centroid; second, centroids are recomputed as the mean or center of mass of the examples assigned to it. The process typically stops when no point changes centroid, or after a maximum number of iterations has been performed. The k centroids produced determine the k clusters found by the algorithm.

The greedy heuristic implicit in k-means only guarantees convergence to a local minimum, and the quality of the solution found and the speed of convergence of k-means notoriously depend on the initial random assignment step. k-means++ [19] improves the stability of the method over the purely random one, using a new initialization step:

1   choose center c_1 to be p_1
2   **for** $i = 2, \ldots, k$
3   **do** select $c_i = p \in P$ with probability $d(p, C)/cost(C, P)$.

In words, the initial center is selected at random, but all subsequent centers are selected with probability proportional to their distance to already selected centers. Spreading out the k initial cluster centers helps in that it leads to faster convergence to better local minima. The stream clustering method StreamKM++ also employs this strategy.

Converting k-means to the streaming setting is not straightforward, since it iterates repeatedly over the dataset. We will see that most stream clustering methods have two phases, one online and one offline. The online phase updates statistics of the data, producing some form of summary or sketch, usually represented as a reduced number of points called *microclusters*. The offline phase then uses these summaries to compute a final clustering efficiently, either at regular time intervals, or on demand.

9.3   BIRCH, BICO, and CLUSTREAM

These three algorithms are incremental and share a common idea for summarizing the stream in microclusters, in order to cluster them in the offline phase.

Balanced Iterative Reducing and Clustering using Hierarchies (BIRCH) is due to Zhang et al. [258]. It is the first method for incremental clustering that proposes to use so-called *clustering feature* (CF) vectors to represent micro-clusters. Assuming dataset points are vectors of d real numbers, a CF is a triple (N, LS, SS) composed of the following items:

- N: number of data points in the CF
- LS: d-dimensional sum of the N data points
- SS: d-dimensional sum of squares of the N data points.

CFs have the following useful properties:

- They are additive: $CF_1 + CF_2 = (N_1 + N_2, LS_1 + LS_2, SS_1 + SS_2)$.
- The distance from a point to a cluster, the average intercluster distance, and the average intracluster distance are easy to compute from the CF.

Another feature of BIRCH is its use of *CF trees*, a height-balanced tree similar to the classical $B+$ tree data structure. It is defined with two parameters: the branching factor B, or maximum number of children that any given node may have, and the leaf radius threshold R. The algorithm maintains the property that all points represented by a leaf fall in a ball of radius R of the centroid there. Every leaf and also every inner node contains a CF vector.

The BIRCH algorithm comprises up to four phases:

Phase 1: Scan all data and build an initial in-memory CF tree

Phase 2: Condense the CF tree into a smaller one (optional)

Phase 3: Cluster globally

Phase 4: Refine clusters (optional and offline, as it requires more passes).

Phases 2, 3, and 4 are the offline part. Phase 3, in particular, performs batch clustering based on the information collected in the CF tree. Phase 1 is the online process, and the one that actually works on the stream. For every arriving point, the algorithm descends the tree, updating the statistics at the CFs of the inner nodes traversed, to reach a leaf closest to the point. Then it checks whether the leaf can absorb it within radius R. If so, the point is "assigned" to the leaf by updating the leaf statistics. If not, a new leaf is created for the new point. This new leaf may cause the parent node to have more than B children; if so, it has to be split into two, and so recursively up to the root. A further rule, not described here, is applied to merge leaves and nodes that may have become too close in the process.

BICO (an acronym for "BIRCH meets coresets for k-means clustering") is due to Fichtenberger et al. [101]. It combines the data structure of BIRCH with the theoretical concept of coresets for clustering. Coresets are explained in detail in section 9.6. BIRCH decides heuristically how to group the points into subclusters. The goal of BICO is to find a reduced set that is not only small, but also offers guarantees of approximating the original point set.

CLUSTREAM, by Aggarwal et al. [6], is designed as an adaptive extension of BIRCH that can deal with changing streams. In CLUSTREAM, nodes of the CF tree maintain CF vectors of the form (N, LS, SS, LT, ST), which extend BIRCH CFs with two additional temporal features:

- LT: sum of the timestamps
- ST: sum of squares of the timestamps

The offline phase of CLUSTREAM simply applies k-means periodically to the microclusters at the leaves of the CF tree. The online phase is similar to that of BIRCH, but it takes the recency of clusters into account. It keeps a maximum number of microclusters in memory. If a point requires creating a new microcluster (leaf) and there is no more space available, the algorithm either deletes the oldest microcluster or else merges two of the oldest microclusters. The notion of the "oldest" microcluster is defined taking into account whether there has been significant recent activity in the microcluster. More precisely, statistics LT and ST are used to compute average and standard deviation of its timestamps; assuming a normal distribution of the timestamps, the algorithm can use them to decide whether a desired fraction of the points in the microcluster are older than a desired recency threshold.

The fact that the oldest clusters, not the smallest ones, are chosen for deletion gives CLUSTREAM an interesting property: by looking at microclusters of similar timestamp distributions, we can obtain a snapshot of the clustering in a desired time frame, with more resolution for more recent time frames and less resolution as we move further back in time. This is sometimes called a *pyramidal* time frame.

9.4   Density-Based Methods: DBSCAN and Den-Stream

Density-based clusterers are based on the idea that clusters are formed not only by overall proximity in distance, but also by the density of connections. They may thus produce clusters that are not spherical, but rather have shapes that adapt to the specific data being clustered.

The DBSCAN algorithm [96], due to Ester et al., is the best-known density-based, offline algorithm. It is based on the idea that clusters should be built around points with a significant number of points in their neighborhoods. The following definitions formalize this idea:

- The ϵ-neighborhood of p is the set of points at a distance ϵ or less from p.

- A *core point* is one whose ϵ-neighborhood has an overall weight (fraction of dataset points) of at least μ.

- A *density area* is the union of the ϵ-neighborhoods of core points.

- A point q is *directly reachable* from p if q is in the ϵ-neighborhood of p. Point q is *reachable* from p if there is a sequence $p_1, \ldots, p_n$ such that $p_1 = p$, $p_n = q$, and each p_{i+1} is directly reachable from p_i.

- A core point p forms a cluster with all the (core or non-core) points that are reachable from it.

- All points that are not reachable from core points are considered outliers.

Note that a cluster is determined by any of the core points it contains, and that these definitions create a unique clustering for any dataset, for given values of ϵ and μ.

The DBSCAN algorithm has parameters ϵ and μ and uses these properties to find this unique clustering. It visits the points in the dataset in an arbitrary order. For a previously unvisited point p, it finds all the points that are directly ϵ-reachable from p. If p is found to be a μ core point, a new cluster is formed and all points reachable from p are added to the cluster and marked visited; otherwise, if p has weight below μ, it is temporarily marked as "outlier" and the method proceeds to the next unvisited point. An outlier may later be found to be reachable from a true core point, and declared "not outlier" and added to some cluster.

Observe that DBSCAN is strongly nonstreaming, because each point may be repeatedly accessed.

Den-Stream, developed by Cao et al. [61], is a density-based streaming method based on ideas similar to DBSCAN, but using microclusters to compute online statistics quickly. It uses the damped window model, meaning that the weight of each data point decreases exponentially using a fading function $f(t) = 2^{-\lambda t}$ where $\lambda > 0$.

For a microcluster with center c and representing points $p_1, p_2, \ldots, p_n$, with timestamps $T_1, T_2, \ldots, T_n$, Den-Stream maintains the following information at time t:

- Weight: $w = \sum_{i=1}^{n} f(t - T_i)$
- Center: $c = \sum_{i=1}^{n} f(t - T_i) p_i / w$
- Radius: $r = \sum_{i=1}^{n} f(t - T_i) d(p_i, c) / w$ (in fact, the sums of the squares of p_i are kept, from which r can be computed when needed)

There are two types of microcluster: depending on whether the weight is larger or smaller than μ, the microcluster is called a potential core microcluster (p-microcluster) or an outlier microcluster (o-microcluster). So an outlier microcluster is a microcluster that does not (yet) have enough weight to be considered a core.

The DEN-STREAM method has two phases, an online phase and an offline phase. Their pseudocode is shown in figure 9.2. In the online phase, every time a new point arrives, DEN-STREAM first tries to merge it into one of the potential microclusters. If this is not possible, it then tries to merge the point with an outlier microcluster. If the weight of the outlier microcluster has increased enough to be a potential microcluster, the microcluster is promoted. Otherwise, DEN-STREAM starts a new outlier microcluster. The offline phase consists of removing the microclusters that have not reached a sufficient weight, and performing a batch DBSCAN clustering.

9.5 CLUSTREE

The streaming clustering algorithms presented up to now require an application of an offline phase in order to produce a cluster when requested. In contrast, CLUSTREE (Kranen et al. [150]) is an anytime clustering method, that is, it can deliver a clustering at any point in time. It is a parameter-free algorithm that automatically adapts to the speed of the stream and is capable of detecting concept drift, novelty, and outliers in the stream.

CLUSTREE uses a compact and self-adaptive index structure for maintaining stream summaries with a logarithmic insertion time. The structure is a balanced tree where each node contains a CF of a number of points, as in CLUSTREAM. This tree contains a hierarchy of microclusters at different levels of granularity. The balanced condition guarantees logarithmic access time for all microclusters.

DEN-STREAM(*Stream*, λ, μ, β)

    Input: a stream of points, decaying factor λ,
          core weight threshold μ, tolerance factor β

1   ▷ Online phase
2    $T_p \leftarrow \lceil \frac{1}{\lambda} \log(\frac{\beta\mu}{\beta\mu-1}) \rceil$
3   **for** each new point that arrives
4   **do** try to merge to a p-microcluster; if not possible,
5   merge to nearest o-microcluster
6   **if** o-microcluster weight $> \beta\mu$
7   **then** convert the o-microcluster to p-microcluster
8   **else** create a new o-microcluster

9   ▷ Offline phase
10   **if** ($t \bmod T_p = 0$)
11   **then for** each p-microcluster c_p
12   **do if** $w_p < \beta\mu$
13   **then** remove c_p
14   **for** each o-microcluster c_o
15   **do if** $w_o < (2^{-\lambda(t-t_o+T_p)} - 1)/(2^{-\lambda T_p} - 1)$
16   **then** remove c_o
17   apply DBSCAN using microclusters as points

Figure 9.2
The DEN-STREAM algorithm.

When a new point arrives, the CLUSTREE method descends the tree to find the microcluster that is most similar to the new point. If the microcluster at the leaf reached is similar enough, then the statistics of the microcluster are updated, otherwise a new microcluster is created. But, unlike other algorithms, this process is interruptible: if new points are arriving before the leaf is reached, the point being processed is stored temporarily in an aggregate in the current inner node, and insertion is interrupted. When a new point passes later through that node, the buffered local aggregate is taken along as a "hitchhiker" and pushed further down the tree. This way, CLUSTREE can prevent the loss of points at burst times in variable-speed streams.

9.6   StreamKM++: Coresets

Given a problem and a set of input instances P, a *coreset* is a small weighted subset that can be used to approximate the solution to the problem. In other words, solving the problem for the coreset provides an approximate solution for the problem on P. In clustering, we can define a (k, ϵ)-coreset as a pair (S, w) where S is a subset of P and function w assigns a nonnegative real value, the weight, to each point, in a way that the following is satisfied for each size-k subset C of P:

$$(1 - \epsilon)\, cost(P, C) \leq cost_w(S, C) \leq (1 + \epsilon)\, cost(P, C),$$

where $cost_w$ denotes the cost function where each point s of S is weighted by $w(s)$. That is, any possible clustering chosen on P is almost equally good in S weighted by w, and vice versa. So indeed, solving the clustering problem on S and on P is approximately the same.

StreamKM++, due to Ackermann et al. [3], is based on this coreset idea. It uses the randomized k-means++ algorithm, explained in section 9.2, to create an initial set of seeds $S = \{s_1, \ldots, s_m\}$. It then defines $w(s_i)$ to be the number of points in P that are closer to s_i than to any other seed in S. One of the main results in [3] is that (S, w) defined in this way is a (k, ϵ)-coreset with probability $1 - \delta$, if m is, roughly speaking, of the form $k \log n / (\delta^{d/2} \epsilon^d)$. Here, d is the dimension of the points in P and n is the cardinality of P. The dependence on n is very good; not so the dependence on d, although experimental results seem to indicate that this bound is far from tight concerning d.

Furthermore, StreamKM++ places the points in a *coreset tree*, a binary tree that is designed to speed up the sampling according to d. The tree describes a hierarchical structure for the clusters, in the sense that the root represents the whole set of points P and the children of each node p in the tree represent a partition of the examples in p.

StreamKM++ performs an online and an offline phase. The online phase maintains a coreset of size m using coreset tree buckets. For a stream of n points, the method maintains $L = \lceil \log_2(\frac{n}{m}) + 2 \rceil$ buckets $B_0, B_1, \ldots, B_{L-1}$. Bucket B_0 can store less than m numbers, and the rest of the buckets are empty or maintain m points. Each bucket maintains a coreset of size m that represents $2^{i-1}m$ points. Each time a point arrives, it is inserted in the first bucket. If this first bucket is full, then a new bucket is computed, merging B_0 and B_1 into a new coreset tree bucket, and moved into B_2. If B_2 is not empty, this merge-and-move process is repeated until an empty bucket is reached.

At any point of time the offline phase consists of applying k-means++ to a coreset of size m. The coreset of size m is obtained from the union of the buckets $B_0, B_1, \ldots, B_{L-1}$.

Note that StreamKM++ does not handle evolving data streams, as it has no forgetting or time-decaying mechanism.

9.7 Additional Material

Clustering is possibly the most studied task in stream mining after classification, so many other methods have been proposed besides the ones described here, including some that can be considered state-of-the-art as well. Recent comprehensive surveys are [84, 185] and [7, chapter 10]. See also chapter 2 of [4] for an earlier survey perspective.

Streaming clustering methods were classified in [84] in five categories: partitioning methods, hierarchical methods, density-based methods, grid-based methods, and model-based methods. Among partitioning methods, DGClust and ODAC are among those with best performance. Among the hierarchical ones, improving on CLUSTREAM, are HPstream, SWClustream (which unlike CLUSTREAM can split microclusters), EStream (which explicitly models cluster dynamics by appearance, disappearance, merging, and splitting operations), and REPSTREAM (inspired by CHAMELEON). The STREAM-LEADER method by Andrés-Merino and Belanche [15] was implemented on MOA and performed very competitively versus CLUSTREAM, Den-Stream, and ClusTree, both in metrics and in scalability. Among the grid-based, besides

D-Stream, we can mention MR-Stream and CellTree. We refer to the surveys above for references and more details.

Given the emphasis we placed on Hoeffding Trees in the classification chapter, we mention very fast k-means (VFKM), by Domingos and Hulten [89]. It continues the philosophy of the Hoeffding Tree in that, rather than performing several passes over the same data, fresh stream data is used to simulate the further passes, and that Hoeffding's bound is used to determine when the algorithm has seen enough data to make statistically sound choices. Like the Hoeffding Tree, VFKM has a formal guarantee that it converges to the same clustering as k-means if both work on infinite data.

9.8   Lab Session with MOA

In this lab session you will use MOA through the graphical interface to compare two clustering algorithms and evaluate them in different ways.

Exercise 9.1   Switch to the *Clustering* tab to set up a clustering experiment. In this tab, we have two sub-tabs, one for setup and one for visualization. This is shown in figure 9.3. The *Setup* tab is selected by default. In this tab, we can specify the data stream, and the two clustering algorithms that we want to compare.

By default, the `RandomRBFGeneratorEvents` will be used. It generates data points with class labels and weights that reflect the age of a point, depending on the chosen horizon. Since clusters move, a larger horizon yields more tail-like clusters; a small horizon yields more sphere-like clusters. Technically, the data points are obtained by generating clusters, which have a center and a maximal radius and which move through a unit cube in a random direction. At the cube boundaries, the clusters bounce off. At specific intervals, all cluster centers are shifted by 0.01 in their respective direction and points are drawn equally from each generating cluster. All clusters have the same expected number of points. This stream generator has the following parameters: the number of clusters moving through the data space, the number of generated points, the shift interval, the cluster radius, the dimensionality, and the noise rate.

The clustering algorithms that can be selected are mainly the ones we have discussed in this chapter. On the right side of the tab we can find the evaluation measures that are going to be used in the experiments.

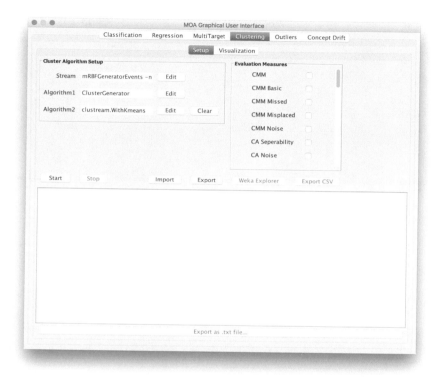

Figure 9.3
The MOA *Clustering* GUI tab.

Start by selecting clustering methods `denstream.WithDBSCAN` and `clustream.WithKmeans`. Now we are going to run and visualize our experiments. Switch to the *Visualization* tab.

Click *Start* to launch the experiment. The GUI will look like in figure 9.4. The upper part of this tab offers options to pause and resume the stream, adjust the visualization speed, and choose the dimensions for x and y as well as the components to be displayed (points, micro and macro clustering, and ground truth). The lower part of the GUI displays the measured values for both settings as numbers (left side, including mean values) and the currently selected measure as a plot over the examples seen. Textual output appears in the bottom panel of the *Setup* tab.

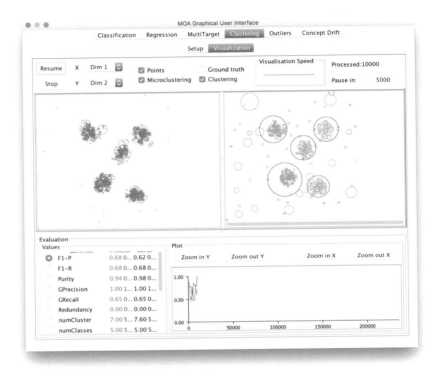

Figure 9.4
Evolving clusters in the GUI *Clustering* tab.

Click *Resume* to continue running the experiment.
a. What is the purity for both algorithms after 5,000 instances?
b. What is the purity for both algorithms after 10,000 instances?

Exercise 9.2   In MOA, we can easily change the parameters of the data stream generator and clustering methods.
a. Add more noise to the data, changing the noise level from 0.1 to 0.3. Which method is performing better in terms of purity after 50,000 instances?
b. Change the epsilon parameter in the Den-Stream algorithm to 0.01. Does this improve the purity results of the algorithm? Why?

Exercise 9.3 Let us compare CLUSTREAM and CLUSTREE using the default parameters. Change the methods to use in the *Setup* tab.

    a. Which method performs better in terms of purity?

    b. And in terms of CMM?

Exercise 9.4 Let us compare the performance of CLUSTREAM and CLUSTREE in the presence of noise.

    a. What is the CMM of each method when there is no noise on the data stream?

    b. What happens when the noise in the data stream is 5%, 10%, 15%, and 20%?

10 Frequent Pattern Mining

Frequent pattern mining is an important unsupervised learning task in data mining, with multiple applications. It can be used purely as an unsupervised, exploratory approach to data, and as the basis for finding association rules. It can also be used to find discriminative features for classification or clustering.

In this chapter we describe techniques for building stream pattern mining algorithms. We start (section 10.1) by presenting the main concepts related to pattern mining, the fundamental techniques used in the batch setting, and the concept of a *closed* pattern, particularly relevant in the stream setting. We then show (section 10.2) in general how to use batch miners to build stream miners and how to use *coresets* for efficiency. We then concentrate on two instances of the notion of pattern—itemsets and graphs—with algorithms that use the general approach with various optimizations. In section 10.3 we describe several algorithms for frequent itemset mining, and particularly the IncMine algorithm implemented in MOA. In section 10.4 we describe algorithms for frequent subgraph mining, including the AdaGraphMiner implemented in MOA. Section 10.5 provides references for additional reading.

10.1 An Introduction to Pattern Mining

10.1.1 Patterns: Definitions and Examples

In a very broad sense, *patterns* are entities whose presence or absence, or frequency, indicate ways in which data deviates from randomness. Combinatorial structures such as itemsets, sequences, trees, and graphs, presented next, are widely used to embody this idea. Patterns in this sense can all be viewed as subclasses of graphs [255]. Our presentation, based on the idea of *pattern relation*, follows the lines of [34]; we believe that this allows a more unified presentation of many algorithmic ideas.

Itemsets are subsets of a set of items $I = \{i_1, \cdots, i_n\}$. In itemsets, the notions of subpattern and superpattern correspond to the notions of subset and superset. The most cited example of itemset mining is the case in which I is the set of products for sale at a supermarket and an itemset is the set of products in one particular purchase. Mining frequent itemsets means finding the sets of products that customers often buy together.

Sequences in their most basic form are ordered lists of items, such as $\langle i_3, i_7, i_2, i_{10}, i_6 \rangle$; both $\langle i_7, i_{10} \rangle$ and $\langle i_3, i_7, i_6 \rangle$ are subsequences of this sequence. An example of usage would be finding sequences of commands frequently issued by the users of some software. A generalization makes every element of the ordered list an itemset, such as $S = \langle I_1, I_2, \ldots, I_n \rangle$, where each I_i is a subset of I. The notion of subsequence is correspondingly more difficult: $S' = \langle I'_1, I'_2, \ldots I'_m \rangle$ is a subsequence of S if there exist integers $1 \leq j_1 < j_2 < \ldots < j_n \leq n$ such that $I'_1 \subseteq I_{j_1}, I'_2 \subseteq I_{j_2}, \ldots$, and $I'_m \subseteq I_{j_m}$.

Trees are a special case of acyclic graphs; trees may or may not be rooted, and nodes and edges may or may not be labeled. There are several possible notions of *subtree* or tree subpattern. An *induced subtree* of a tree t is any tree rooted at some node v of t whose vertices and edges are subsets of those of t. A *top-down subtree* of a tree t is an induced subtree of t that contains the root of t. An *embedded subtree* of a tree t is any tree rooted at some node v of t. See [69, 142] for examples and discussions. A practical application of frequent tree mining is related to servers of XML queries, as XML queries are essentially labeled rooted trees. Detecting the frequent subtrees or subqueries may be useful, for example, to classify queries or to optimize, precompute, or cache their answers.

A *graph* G is a pair formed by a set of nodes V and a set of edges E among nodes. One may add labels to nodes and edges. A common definition of $G = (V, E)$ being a subgraph, or graph subpattern, of $G' = (V', E')$ is that $V \subseteq V'$ and $E \subseteq (V \times V) \cap E'$. In complex network analysis, *motifs* are subnetworks that appear recurrently in larger networks, and typically can be used to predict or explain behaviors in the larger network. Finding significant motifs in a network is closely related to mining frequent subgraphs.

Let us now generalize these definitions to a single one. A class of patterns is a set $\mathcal{P}$ with a relation $\preceq$ that is a partial order: reflexive, antisymmetric, and transitive, possibly with pairs of patterns that are incomparable by $\preceq$. For patterns $p, p' \in \mathcal{P}$, if $p \preceq p'$, we say that p is a subpattern of p' and p' is a superpattern of p. Also, we write $p \prec p'$ if p is a proper subpattern of p', that is, $p \preceq p'$ and $p \neq p'$.

The input to our data mining process is a dataset (or stream, in the stream setting) D of transactions, where each transaction $s \in D$ consists of a transaction identifier and a pattern. We will often ignore the transaction identifiers and view D as a multiset of patterns, or equivalently a set of pairs (p, i) where p occurs i times in D.

We say that a transaction t *supports* a pattern p if p is a subpattern of the pattern in transaction t. The *absolute support* of pattern p in dataset D, denoted $supp(p)$, is the number of transactions in dataset D that support p. The *relative support* of p is $\sigma(p) = supp(p)/|D|$, where $|D|$ is the cardinality of D. The σ-*frequent patterns* in a database are those with relative support at

ID	Transaction
t1	abce
t2	cde
t3	abce
t4	acde
t5	abcde
t6	bcd

Figure 10.1

Example of an itemset dataset.

	Support	**Frequent**	**Gen**	**Closed**	**Max**
6	t1, t2, t3, t4, t5, t6	c	c	c	
5	t1, t2, t3, t4, t5	e, ce	e	ce	
4	t1, t3, t4, t5	a, ac, ae, ace	a	ace	
4	t1, t3, t5, t6	b, bc	b	bc	
4	t2, t4, t5, t6	d, cd	d	cd	
3	t1, t3, t5	ab, abc, abe	ab		
		be, bce, abce	be	abce	abce
3	t2, t4, t5	de, cde	de	cde	cde

Figure 10.2

Frequent, closed, and maximal itemsets with minimum absolute support 3, or relative support 0.5, for the dataset in figure 10.1.

least σ in it. Note that the σ-frequent itemsets of size 1 were called σ-heavy hitters in section 4.6.

The *frequent pattern mining problem* is defined as follows: given a dataset D and a threshold σ in $[0, 1]$, find all σ-frequent patterns in D.

Figure 10.1 presents a dataset of itemsets, and Figure 10.2 shows the frequent, closed, and maximal itemsets of that dataset (closed and maximal patterns will be defined later). For example, patterns *de* and *cde* appear in transactions *t2, t4, t5*, and no other, and therefore have support 3.

In most cases of interest there is a notion of *size*, a natural number, associated with each pattern. We assume that size is compatible with the pattern relation, in the sense that if $p \prec p'$ then p is smaller in size than p'. The size of an itemset is its cardinality, the size of a sequence is the number of items it contains, and the size of a tree or graph is its number of edges. Typically the number of possible patterns of a given size n is exponential in n.

10.1.2   Batch Algorithms for Frequent Pattern Mining

In principle, one way to find all frequent patterns is to perform one pass over the dataset, keep track of every pattern that appears as a subpattern in the dataset together with its support, and at the end report those whose support is larger than the required minimum support. However, the number of sub-patterns in the dataset typically grows too fast with dataset size to make this feasible. Therefore, more efficient approaches are required.

A most useful property is *antimonotonicity*, also known as *Apriori property*: any subpattern of a frequent pattern is also frequent; equivalently, any super-pattern of an infrequent pattern is also infrequent. This suggests the following approach, embodied in the groundbreaking Apriori algorithm for frequent itemset mining [9]:

1. Compute the set F_1 of frequent patterns of size 1, with one pass over the dataset.

2. For $k > 1$, given the set F_{k-1},

    2.1. compute the set C_k of candidate patterns, those patterns of size k all of whose subpatterns of size $k - 1$ are in F_{k-1};

    2.2. with one pass over the dataset, compute the support of every pattern in C_k; let F_k be the subset of patterns in C_k that are frequent.

3. Stop when F_k is empty.

Observe that by the antimonotonicity property we are not losing any truly frequent pattern in step 2.1 when restricting the search to C_k. Furthermore, in practice, the number of frequent patterns in F_k decreases quickly with k, so step 2.1 becomes progressively faster and the number of passes is moderate. In other words, Apriori [9] performs a *breadth-first* exploration of the set of all frequent patterns. It also incorporates other strategies to make the candidate generation phase 2.1 efficient, in particular representing itemsets in lexicographical order.

Other approaches to batch itemset mining differ in the exploration strategy and on the data structures added for efficiency. For example, the FP-growth algorithm [131] uses a clever data structure called FP-Trees to store the dataset in a compact form using two passes, and then retrieve the frequent itemsets from the FP-tree directly, thus avoiding the expensive candidate generation phase. The Eclat algorithm [256] can be seen as performing a depth-first search: it associates to each itemset observed a list of the transaction identifiers that support it, then recursively intersects these sets to obtain the lists for larger itemsets.

These and similar ideas have been applied to mining frequent sequences, trees, and graphs. See the surveys cited in section 10.5 for references.

The algorithms sketched above are very clearly batch-oriented: Apriori performs several passes over the dataset; Eclat and FP-growth perform one and two passes, respectively, but it is unclear how they can return results in an anytime way, and they store too many patterns for streaming settings. Before describing approaches that work in streaming, we introduce additional notions that help in reducing memory requirements, in both the batch and stream cases.

10.1.3   Closed and Maximal Patterns

A major problem of frequent pattern mining in practice is that often the algorithm obtains far more patterns than can be later analyzed or used; not only that, the patterns are often redundant or uninteresting in ways that are sometimes obvious and sometimes subtle. See [119] for proposals of *interest measures* in pattern mining.

One form of redundancy is to have two frequent patterns p and q such that $p \prec q$ but p and q have the same or almost the same support. Knowing that p is frequent does not add much when we know that q is frequent. The notions of *closed* and *maximal* pattern help reduce redundancy in the output as well as time and memory usage, in both batch and stream miners.

DEFINITION 10.1   A pattern is *closed* for a dataset D if it has higher support in D than every one of its superpatterns. A pattern is *maximal* if it is frequent and none of its superpatterns are frequent.

Figure 10.2 shows the frequent closed and frequent maximal itemsets of the dataset in figure 10.1. For example, ce is closed because it has higher support than its supersets ace, bce, and cde, but e is not, because it has the same support as its superset ce. Pattern ce is frequent but not maximal because its superset cde is also frequent.

Observe that every maximal pattern is closed. It is easy to see (exercise 10.1) that, given all frequent closed patterns, we can retrieve all frequent patterns. If we know moreover the frequency of all closed patterns, we can deduce the frequency of every pattern. There are often far fewer frequent closed patterns than frequent patterns in a dataset. Therefore, algorithms that look for frequent closed patterns without computing all frequent patterns might be much more efficient in time and memory, while providing the same information and less redundant output. This has been verified repeatedly in practice. Maximal patterns only inform us about the border between frequency and infrequency.

CHARM, CLAIM, and FPClose are batch algorithms for mining frequent closed itemsets. BIDE+, ClaSP, and CloSPan are batch miners for frequent closed sequences. CloseGraph finds frequent closed subgraphs. The references can be found in the surveys cited in section 10.5.

10.2   Frequent Pattern Mining in Streams: Approaches

Algorithms for extracting frequent patterns from data streams can be classified according to a number of criteria, including:

- Whether they mine all frequent patterns or only the closed or maximal ones.

- Whether they consider the pattern frequency from the beginning of the stream, or give more importance to recent items, either via sliding windows or some importance decay scheme.

- Whether they update the set of frequent items after each item arrives, or perform batch updates: that is, collect a batch of stream items, then update the data structure that represents frequent patterns using the batch. The choice of *batch size* is key to performance.

- Whether they are exact or approximate, that is, whether they return exactly the set of patterns that satisfy the frequency condition, or just some approximation of the set. Approximate algorithms may have false positives (infrequent patterns reported as frequent), false negatives (frequent patterns not reported), or both.

We will focus mostly on closed pattern mining using approximate algorithms that perform batch updates. This is because closed pattern mining has a large advantage because of the memory and time reduction it implies. Approximate answers are acceptable in many applications, especially if that saves the high computational cost of exact algorithms. Finally, per-item updates are too slow in most cases and make little difference in the result compared to batch updates.

BATCHUPDATEPATTERNMINER(*Stream*, b, w, σ)

    Input: a stream of patterns, a batch size b,
                 a window size w, a relative minimum support σ
    Output: at every moment C contains (approximately) the set of
                   σ-frequent closed patterns in the last bw stream elements

```
1   C ← an empty summary representing the empty set of patterns
2   Q ← the empty queue of summaries
3   repeat
4           collect the next b elements in Stream into a batch B
5           if Q has size w      ▷ queue is full
6             then let C1 be the oldest summary in Q
7                       C ← remove(C, C1)
8                       delete C1 from Q
9             add B to Q
10            using a batch miner, obtain a summary C2 representing
11                  the patterns in B with support ≥ σ
12            C ← add(C, C2)
```

Figure 10.3
A general stream pattern miner with batch updates and sliding window.

Algorithms that perform batch updates typically behave as in figure 10.3. A specific algorithm fixes a summary data structure to remember the current set of patterns being monitored. The summary type will depend on whether the algorithm mines all patterns, or closed ones, or maximal ones. Of course, the summary is also designed from efficiency considerations. The key operations are *add*(C, C') and *remove*(C, C'). Here, C and C' are summary structures representing two pattern datasets D and D'. The operations should return the summaries corresponding to $D \cup D'$ and $D \setminus D'$, or approximations thereof. Here $D \setminus D'$ denotes multiset difference, the multiset that contains $\max\{0, supp_D(p) - supp_{D'}(p)\}$ copies of each pattern p. As mentioned already, exact algorithms pay a high computational price for exactness, so *add* and *remove* operations that are not exact but do not introduce many false positives or false negatives may be of interest.

The most obvious summary of a dataset D simply forgets the order of transactions in D and keeps the multiset of patterns they contain, or more compactly the set of pairs $(p, supp_D(p))$. Then, *add* and *remove* are simply multiset union and multiset difference, and are exact. A more sophisticated summary is to keep the pairs $(p, supp_D(p))$ for all patterns that are closed in D, even if they do not appear literally in D. This is still exact because the support of all nonclosed patterns can be recovered from the summary. Efficient rules for implementing exact *add* and *remove* operations on this representation are given, for example, in [34].

Example 10.1   Suppose $D = \{ab, ac, ab\}$. Its summary in terms of closed patterns is $C = \{(ab, 2), (ac, 1), (a, 3)\}$, because a is closed in D. If the new batch is $D' = \{ac, bd\}$, its summary is $C' = \{(ac, 1), (bd, 1)\}$, and $add(C, C')$ ideally should return the summary of $D \cup D'$, which is $\{(ab, 2), (ac, 2), (bd, 1), (a, 4), (b, 3)\}$. Observe that *add* must somehow include $(b, 3)$, even though b is neither in C nor in C'.

Since every pattern that occurs literally in a transaction is closed, this summary contains even more *distinct* patterns than the stream, which seems inefficient. However, if we keep in the summary only the σ-frequent closed patterns, the number of patterns stored decreases drastically, at the cost of losing exactness. In particular, we may introduce false negatives over time, as we may be dropping from a batch summary occurrences of p that are critical to making p σ-frequent in the stream. These false negatives may be reduced by using, in line 15 of the algorithm, some support value $\sigma' < \sigma$. Assuming a stationary distribution of the patterns, this makes it less likely that a truly σ-frequent pattern is dropped from a batch because it is not even σ'-frequent there by statistical fluctuations. Hoeffding's bound or the normal approximation can be used to bound the rate of false negatives introduced by this approach in terms of σ, σ' and batch size (see, for example [35]).

10.2.1   Coresets of Closed Patterns

Recall from section 9.6 that a *coreset* of a set C with respect to some problem is a small subset of C such that solving the problem on the coreset provides an approximate solution for the problem on C. We describe an application of the notion of coreset to speed up frequent pattern mining, at the cost of some approximation error. It was proposed for graphs in [35] as a generalization of closed graphs, but can be applied to other pattern types.

Recall that $supp(p)$ and $\sigma(p)$ denote the absolute and relative supports of p. We say that p is δ-closed in D if every superpattern of p has support less than $(1 - \delta)\, supp_D(p)$. Closed patterns are the 0-closed patterns and maximal patterns are the 1-closed patterns. This notion is related to others used in the literature, such as the *relaxed support* in the CLAIM algorithm [230].

Now define a (σ, δ)-*coreset* of D to be any dataset $D' \subseteq D$ such that, for every pattern p,

- every pattern p occurring in D' is σ-frequent and δ-closed in D,
- and furthermore, if $p \in D'$ then p occurs as many times in D' as in D.

A (σ, δ)-coreset is a lossy, compressed summary of a dataset. This compression is two-dimensional:

- Minimum support σ excludes infrequent patterns, and
- δ-closure excludes patterns whose support is very similar to that of some subpattern.

Example 10.2 Suppose $D = \{(ab, 10), (ac, 5), (a, 8), (b, 2)\}$. A $(0, 0.4)$-coreset of D is $\{(ab, 10), (ac, 5), (a, 8)\}$. a is in the coreset because it has support 23 in D, and the supports of both ab and ac are below $0.6 \cdot 23$. On the other hand, b is not, because it has support 12 in D and the support of ab is above $0.6 \cdot 12$. From the coreset we can only say that the support of b in D is at least 10 and at most 16.

We can build a (σ, δ)-coreset by greedily choosing a subset of the σ-frequent, δ-closed patterns in D and then putting all their occurrences in D'. If we do this until it is no longer possible, we obtain a maximal coreset, that is, one that cannot be extended by adding more patterns from D and remain a coreset. See exercise 10.2. For $\delta = 0$, the set of all σ-frequent closed patterns is the unique maximal $(\sigma, 0)$-coreset. If $0 < \delta < 1$, however, there may be several maximal (σ, δ)-coresets of D.

A strategy for reducing computation time and memory in the generic algorithm is to keep only summaries of (σ, δ)-coresets of the batches. Of course, the summaries do not exactly represent the full dataset, not even the σ-frequent patterns in the dataset, so the output will only be approximate.

10.3   Frequent Itemset Mining on Streams

10.3.1   Reduction to Heavy Hitters

In chapter 4 we described a number of sketches for maintaining the heavy hitters of a stream, that is, the elements with relative frequency above a threshold ϵ. Such sketches can often be used to maintain the set of frequent patterns in a stream. The extensions need to take into account that it is no longer true that there are at most $1/\epsilon$ frequent elements, because each stream element may generate updates for many patterns.

For example, the paper that presents the Lossy Counting algorithm [165] also presents an extension to count frequent itemsets. The stream is divided in batches, each batch is mined for frequent itemsets, and the sketch is updated with the result. The error in the frequency estimates of Lossy Counting translates to rates of false positives and negatives in the set of frequent patterns. A similar idea can be developed for the SPACESAVING sketch (exercise 10.3).

This approach has two disadvantages in some settings: one, it tracks all frequent itemsets rather than frequent closed ones, so it may require large memory. Second, Lossy Counting and Space Saving do not allow removals, so it is not possible to simulate the forgetting effect of a sliding window.

10.3.2   Moment

Moment, by Chi et al. [70], is a closed frequent itemset miner on a sliding window. It is an *exact* algorithm: at every moment, it reports exactly the set of frequent closed itemsets in the sliding window.

The method uses a tree structure called a *Closed Enumeration Tree* to store all the itemsets that are needed at any given moment, where the root is at the top and corresponds to the smallest (empty) itemset. Nodes in the tree belong to one of four types, two on the boundary of frequent and infrequent itemsets, and two on the boundary of closed and nonclosed frequent itemsets:

- Infrequent gateway node: Contains an itemset x that is not frequent, but whose parent node contains an itemset y that is frequent and has a frequent sibling z such that $x = y \cup z$.

- Unpromising gateway node: Contains an itemset x that is frequent and such that there is a closed frequent itemset y that is a superset of x, has the same support, and is lexicographically before x.

- Intermediate node: A node that is not an unpromising gateway and contains a frequent itemset that is nonclosed, but has a child node that contains an itemset with the same support.

- Closed node: Contains a closed frequent itemset.

These definitions imply the following properties of Closed Enumeration Trees:

1. All supersets of itemsets in infrequent gateway nodes are infrequent.

2. All itemsets in unpromising gateway nodes, and all their descendants, are nonclosed.

3. All itemsets in intermediate nodes are nonclosed but have some closed descendant.

4. When adding a transaction, closed itemsets remain closed.

5. When removing a transaction, infrequent items remain infrequent and non-closed itemsets remain nonclosed.

The core of Moment is a set of rules for adding and removing a transaction from the tree while maintaining these five properties.

10.3.3 FP-STREAM

FP-STREAM, by Giannella et al. [121], is an algorithm for mining frequent itemsets at multiple time granularities from streams. It uses a FP-Tree structure as in FP-growth to store the set of frequent patterns, and a tilted-time window. There are two types of tilted-time window:

- Natural tilted-time window: Maintains the most recent 4 quarters of an hour, the last 24 hours, and the last 31 days. It needs only 59 counters to keep this information.

- Logarithmic tilted-time window: Maintains slots with the last quarter of an hour, the next 2 quarters, 4 quarters, 8 quarters, 16 quarters, and so on. As in Exponential Histograms, the memory required is logarithmic in the length of time being monitored.

FP-STREAM maintains a global FP-Tree structure and processes transactions in batches. Every time a new batch is collected, it computes a new FP-Tree and adds it to the global FP-Tree.

If only the frequent itemsets in each batch are kept, or only frequent itemsets are maintained in the global FP-Tree structure, many itemsets will be lost, because many nonzero counts that do not reach the minimum required threshold σ will not be included, therefore they are considered effectively zero. It is convenient to keep also some infrequent ones, in case they become frequent in the future. For that purpose, FP-STREAM uses the notion of subfrequent pattern. A pattern is *subfrequent* if its support is more than σ' but less than σ, for a value $\sigma' < \sigma$. FP-STREAM computes frequent and subfrequent patterns. Pattern occurrences in a batch whose frequency is below σ' will not be added to the global FP-Tree, so they will be undercounted and may become false negatives later on. This, however, drops from consideration a large amount of truly infrequent patterns, saving memory and time. A reinforcement of this idea is crucial to the next algorithm we will present.

In summary, FP-STREAM allows us to answer time-sensitive queries approximately and keeps more detailed information on recent data. It does however consider all frequent itemsets instead of closed ones.

10.3.4   IncMine

The IncMine algorithm for mining frequent closed sets was proposed by Cheng et al. in [66]. It is approximate and exhibits a controllable, usually small, amount of false negatives, but it is much faster than Moment and FP-STREAM. Its implementation in MOA, including some details not explicit in [66], is described in [202].

At a high level, IncMine maintains a sliding window with batches of the most recent transactions. IncMine aims at reporting the frequent closed itemsets (FCIs) in the window. But it actually stores a superset of those, including some that are not frequent in the current window but may become frequent in the future; we call this set the *semi-FCI*. Its definition is more restrictive than that of subfrequent patterns in FP-STREAM.

Stream elements are collected in batches B of some size b. Let w be the number of batches stored in the window, which therefore represents wb transactions.

Let C denote the set of semi-FCIs mined at any given time from the current window. When a new batch of transactions b arrives, C must be updated to reflect the transactions in B and forget the effect of the oldest batch of transactions in the window. Roughly speaking, IncMine performs this by first mining the set $C2$ of FCIs in B, and then updating C with the contents of $C2$, according to a set of rules that also implements the forgetting of expired transactions. We omit this part of the description, but note that it is crucial for the efficiency of IncMine. Note also that it is specific to itemsets, unlike the following ideas, which are applicable to other types of patterns such as sequences and graphs.

However, a direct implementation of this idea is costly. The number of itemsets that have to be stored in order to perform this task exactly can grow to be very large, because even itemsets that seem very infrequent at this time have to be kept in C, just in case they start appearing more often later and become frequent in the window within the next wb time units or w batches.

IncMine adopts the following heuristic to cut down on memory and computation. Suppose that our minimum support for frequency is σ. If pattern p is frequent in a window of wb batches, by definition it appears at least σwb times in it. Naively, we might expect that it would appear σib times in the first i batches. But it is too much to expect that patterns are so uniformly distributed among batches. However, if p appears *far less* than σib times in the first i batches, it becomes less likely that the required occurrences appear later in the window, and we might decide to drop pattern p from the window, at the risk that it becomes a false negative some time later. This risk becomes smaller and smaller as i approaches w.

More generally, if σ is the desired minimum support for an FCI, IncMine sets up a schedule of augmented supports $r(i)$ for $i = 1 \ldots b$, such that $r(1) < r(2) < \cdots < r(w-1) < r(w) = 1$. When a pattern in the ith batch in the window has frequency below $r(i)\sigma i b$, it is considered unlikely that it will reach frequency σwb after adding $w - i$ batches more, and it is dropped from the current set C.

Therefore, the set C kept by IncMine at a given time is, precisely speaking, the set of σ-frequent closed itemsets in the window plus the set of infrequent closed itemsets that have not been dropped as unpromising in the last w batches. If $r(w) = 1$, this implies that all itemsets that have lived through w batches are σ-frequent in the window, and can be reported as true FCIs. Thus, IncMine may have false negatives, but not false positives, because an itemset reported as frequent is guaranteed to be frequent.

Cheng et al. [66] propose the linear schedule $r(i) = (i-1) \cdot (1-r)/(w-1) + r$ for some value $r < 1$. Observe that $r(1) = r$ and $r(w) = 1$. An analysis in [202] yields another schedule, based on Hoeffding's bound, that cuts unpromising itemsets much more aggressively while still guaranteeing that at most a desired rate of false negatives is produced, assuming a stationary distribution in the stream.

Let us note also that the implementation in MOA described in [202] uses CHARM [254] as the batch miner, partly because of the superior performance reported in [254] and partly because it can use the well-tested implementation in the Sequential Pattern Mining Framework, SPMF [106]. The implementation is experimentally shown in [202] to perform orders of magnitude faster than Moment, with far less memory and with a very small, often negligible, number of false negatives.

10.4   Frequent Subgraph Mining on Streams

Note first that the term *graph mining* has been used to describe several tasks. A common meaning, which we do not cover here, is the task of mining information such as communities, shortest paths, and centrality measures, from a single large graph such as a social network; the graph arrives an edge at a time, often with edge insertions and deletions. Here we are consistent with the rest of the chapter: each element of the stream is in itself a graph, and the task is to mine the subgraphs of these incoming graphs that are frequent (and, perhaps, closed).

We present two coreset-based algorithms described in [35], one that implements the general idea for mining patterns over a fixed-size sliding window described in section 10.2, and another one that adapts to change by reporting the approximate set of closed frequent graphs for the recent graphs, those in an adaptive-size sliding window over the stream where the distribution seems to be stationary.

Note that [35] represents sets of closed graphs in a form equivalent to, but more convenient than, the one implicitly assumed in section 10.2, which was a set of pairs (closed pattern, frequency). The Δ-*support* of a pattern is its support minus the sum of the absolute supports of all its closed, proper super-patterns; it is called the relative support in [35], a term we already use with another meaning here.

An interesting property of Δ-support is that, conversely, the absolute support of a closed pattern equals the sum of the Δ-supports of all its closed superpatterns (including itself). This makes adding patterns to a summary much faster. Suppose we have computed the set of closed patterns of a dataset and associated to each its absolute support. To add one occurrence of a pattern p to the summary, we need to increment by 1 the absolute support of p *and of all its closed subpatterns.* If we instead have kept the Δ-supports of each closed pattern, simply adding 1 to the Δ-support of p implicitly adds 1 to the regular support of all its subpatterns, by the property above. The same argument can be made for removals. Regular supports have to be computed only when the algorithm is asked to output the set of frequent closed graphs, which should happen far more rarely than additions and removals.

If all closed patterns of D are kept in the summary, the Δ-support of p is the number of transactions in D whose pattern is precisely p. However, if the summary is based on a (σ, δ)-coreset, the missing occurrences of p from the omitted patterns may lead to *negative* Δ-supports.

10.4.1   WINGRAPHMINER

The WINGRAPHMINER algorithm maintains the frequent closed graphs in a sliding window of fixed size, implementing the coreset idea described in section 10.2. Its pseudocode is shown in figure 10.4. Note that, for brevity, in line 8 we have used set operations in $(G \cup C) \setminus R$ to denote what really is an application of operation *add* and an application of operation *remove*.

Every batch of graphs arriving from the stream is mined for closed frequent graphs using some batch miner, and transformed to the relative support representation. Procedure CORESET implements this idea using the CloseGraph algorithm [252]. The coreset maintained by the algorithm is updated by adding to it the coreset of the incoming batch. Also, after the first w batches, the window is full, so the algorithm subtracts the coreset of the batch that falls from the sliding window. The subtraction operation can be performed by changing the signs of all the Δ-supports in the subtracted dataset and then adding the coreset summaries.

10.4.2   ADAGRAPHMINER

ADAGRAPHMINER is an extension of the previous method that is able to adapt to changes in the stream, reporting the graphs that are frequent and closed in the current distribution.

There are two versions of this method. One monitors some simple statistic of the global distribution, and shrinks the window when change is detected; in the implementation presented, ADWIN is used as a change detector, and the statistic monitored is the total number of closed graphs. Another version uses

WINGRAPHMINER(*Stream*, b, w, σ)

    Input: a stream of graphs, batch size b,
            window size w, minimum support σ
    Output: at all times, the summary G contains the (approximate) set of
            frequent closed subgraphs of the last wb graphs in the stream

1 $G \leftarrow \emptyset$
2 **for** every batch B of graphs in *Stream*
3   **do** $C \leftarrow$ CORESET(B, σ)
4   store C in sliding window
5   **if** sliding window is full
6   **then** $R \leftarrow$ oldest batch in sliding window
7   **else** $R \leftarrow \emptyset$
8          $G \leftarrow$ CORESET$((G \cup C) \setminus R, \sigma)$
9 **return** G

CORESET(B, σ)

    Input: Graph dataset B and minimum support σ
    Output: A coreset C of B

1 $C \leftarrow$ CLOSEGRAPH(B, σ)
2 $C \leftarrow$ COMPUTE_Δ_SUPPORT(C)
3 **return** C

Figure 10.4
The WINGRAPHMINER algorithm and procedure CORESET.

a separate ADWIN instance for monitoring the support of each frequent closed subgraph. This version has two advantages: first, it is sensitive to changes in individual graphs that are too small to be noticed in the global distribution. Second, it does not need to keep all the batches in a sliding window in memory, so each graph is stored once, with its ADWIN instance, rather than w times. Although an ADWIN is stored for every graph, this experimentally requires less memory for moderate values of w.

    Figure 10.5 shows the pseudocode of ADAGRAPHMINER, where the parameter *mode* chooses among both versions.

ADAGRAPHMINER(*Stream*, *mode*, *b*, σ)

     Input: a stream of graphs, boolean flag *mode*,
          batch size *b*, minimum support σ
     Output: at all times, the summary G contains the (approximate) set of
          frequent closed subgraphs of the graphs in the current window

1   Init ADWIN
2   **for** every batch B of graphs in *Stream*
3   **do** $C \leftarrow$ CORESET(B, σ)
4         $R \leftarrow \emptyset$
5   **if** *mode* is **true**   ▷ indicating Sliding Window mode
6   **then** store C in sliding window
7   **if** ADWIN detected change
8   **then** $R \leftarrow$ batches to remove from sliding window
9         $G \leftarrow$ CORESET($(G \cup C) \setminus R, \sigma$)
10   **if** *mode* is true   ▷ indicating Sliding Window mode
11   **then** insert number of closed graphs into ADWIN
12   **else** For every g in G, update g's ADWIN
13   **return** G

Figure 10.5
The ADAGRAPHMINER algorithm.

10.5   Additional Material

The literature on frequent pattern mining, both batch and in streams, is vast.
We prioritize surveys if available, from which many other references can be
found. The survey [5] is most comprehensive on pattern mining; see in particular [156], chapter 4, on pattern mining in data streams.

Regarding itemsets, [67] focuses on mining frequent itemsets on streams,
and [202] includes a comparison of the pros and cons of several itemset mining algorithms on streams, besides describing the MOA implementation of
IncMine.

For sequence patterns, [180] is a recent survey, mostly for the batch context.
[174, 204] are two approaches to sequence mining on data streams.

For frequent subtree mining, [24, 69, 142] present in detail the various
notions of "subtree" and survey associated batch algorithms. [158] presents

FQT-Stream, an online algorithm for mining all frequent tree patterns on an XML data stream. [34] describes the generic approach to stream pattern mining that we have used in this chapter, and applies it in particular to subtree mining.

For subgraph mining, two surveys dealing with the batch case are [142, 206]. Two algorithms for mining frequent subgraphs from graphs of streams are gspan [251] and its extension for closed graphs, CloseGraph [252]. [35] proposes the notion of coreset for subgraph mining in graph streams and the algorithms in section 10.2.1. [207] investigates finding frequent subgraphs in a single large dynamic (streaming) graph.

We have omitted the discussion on *association rules*, as typically they are obtained by first mining frequent itemsets from the dataset (or stream), then determining the frequent rules from the mined itemset; that is, there is nothing essentially specific to the streaming setting beyond mining frequent itemsets. Association rules, or probabilistic implications, for trees are discussed in [23], and shown to behave differently from those on sets in several nontrivial ways.

The Sequential Pattern Mining Framework (SPMF) [106] contains many implementations of pattern mining algorithms, mostly for the batch setting, and mostly in Java. Implementations of IncMine, AdaGraphMiner, and Moment are available from the *Extensions* section in the MOA website.

10.6   Exercises

Exercise 10.1   Show that: 1. The set of all frequent patterns in a dataset can be derived from its set of closed frequent patterns. 2. If, additionally, we know the support of each frequent closed pattern, we can compute the support of every frequent pattern.

Exercise 10.2   1. Formalize the greedy algorithm sketched in section 10.2.1 to compute a maximal (σ, δ)-coreset.

2. Consider the dataset $D = \{(a, 100), (ab, 80), (abc, 60), (abcd, 50)\}$ of itemsets. Find two different maximal $(0.1, 0.3)$-coresets of D.

Exercise 10.3 If you have studied the SPACESAVING sketch in chapter 4, think how to adapt it for maintaining the σ-frequent itemsets, counting frequency from the start of the stream. How much memory would it require? Does it have false positives or false negatives, and if so, what bounds can you prove for the error rates?

Exercise 10.4 Without looking at the original paper, give pseudocode for the IncMine algorithm based on the ideas given in this chapter.

Exercise 10.5 Prove that the absolute support of a closed pattern equals the sum of the Δ-supports of all its closed superpatterns (including itself). *Hint:* Use induction from the maximal patterns down.

III THE MOA SOFTWARE

11 Introduction to MOA and Its Ecosystem

Massive Online Analysis (MOA) is an open-source software framework that allows users to build and run ML and data mining experiments on evolving data streams. It is being developed at the University of Waikato in New Zealand and named after the large, extinct, flightless moa bird that used to live only in New Zealand.

The distinctive feature of MOA is that it can learn and mine from large datasets or streams by performing only one pass over the data, with a small time per data item. As it scans the data, it only stores summaries and statistics rather than the instances themselves, so memory use is usually small too.

MOA is written in Java and distributed under the terms of the GNU General Public License. It includes a set of learners, stream generators, and evaluators that can be used from the graphical user interface (GUI), the command-line interface (CLI), and the Java API. Advantages of being Java-based are the portability and the strong and well-developed support libraries. Use of the language is widespread, and features such as automatic garbage collection help reduce programming burden and errors. MOA runs on any platform with an appropriate Java virtual machine, such as Linux, Mac, Windows, and Android.

One intended design goal of MOA is to be easy to use and simple to extend.

There are several open-source software libraries related to MOA. Some of them, such as ADAMS, MEKA, and OpenML, use MOA to perform data stream analytics inside their systems. StreamDM contains an implementation in C++ of some of the most popular methods in MOA, and Apache SAMOA is a new platform that performs stream mining in a distributed environment using Hadoop hardware.

In this part of the book, we show how to use the GUI, the CLI, and the Java API, and how to master MOA algorithms, generators, and evaluators.

In this chapter, we first discuss briefly the architecture of MOA, and how to install the software. After that we look at recent developments in MOA and the extensions available in MOA, and finally we present some of the open-source frameworks that can be used with MOA, or as an alternative to it. The intention is not to make readers proficient in all these other packages, but to make them aware of their possibilities.

11.1   MOA Architecture

MOA is built around the idea of the *task*. All experiments run in MOA are defined as tasks. There are simple tasks, such as writing streams to files or computing the speed of a stream, but the most important tasks are the evaluation tasks. For example, in classification, there are two main types of evaluation methods, described in section 6.1: holdout and prequential.

MOA contains methods for classification, regression, clustering, outlier detection, recommendation, and frequent pattern mining. Tasks are usually composed of stream sources, learners, and the parameters of the evaluation, such as number of instances to use, periodicity of the output result, and name of the file to output the predictions. Also, different task types require different evaluation strategies.

Tasks can be run from the GUI or from the CLI.

11.2   Installation

MOA is available from `https://moa.cms.waikato.ac.nz`, where the latest release can always be downloaded as a compressed zip file. The release contains a `moa.jar` file, an executable Java jar file that can be run as a Java application or called from the command line. It also contains the `sizeofag.jar` file, used to measure the memory used by experiments. The scripts `bin\moa.bat` in Windows and `bin/moa.sh` in Linux and Mac are the easiest way to start MOA's GUI.

11.3   Recent Developments in MOA

Some of the recent developments in MOA, not covered in detail in this book, are:

- **Multitarget learning:** A tab for multitarget learning [91, 188, 232], where the goal is to predict several related target attributes simultaneously. Examples of multitarget learning are the prediction of temperatures in the same building, traces in the same road network, or stock prices.

- **Outlier detection**: A tab for detection of distance-based outliers [20, 120]. This tab uses the most widely employed criteria for determining whether an element is an outlier, based on the number of neighboring elements within a fixed distance, against a fixed threshold.

- **Recommender system**: MOA has a task to use online recommender algorithms. The `EvaluateOnlineRecommender` task in MOA takes a rating predictor and a dataset (each training instance being a [user, item, rating] triplet) and evaluates how well the model predicts the ratings, given the user and item, as more and more instances are processed. This is similar to the online scenario of a recommender system, where new ratings of items by users arrive constantly, and the system has to make predictions of unrated items for the user in order to know which ones to recommend. There are two online recommender algorithms available: `BaselinePredictor` and `BRISMFPredictor`. The first is a very simple rating predictor, and the second implements a factorization algorithm described in [234].

11.4   Extensions to MOA

The following useful extensions to MOA are available from its website:

- **IBLStreams:** IBLStreams [225], described in section 8.4, is an instance-based learning algorithm for classification and regression problems on data streams.

- **MOA-IncMine:** IncMine, proposed in [66] and described in section 10.3.4, computes frequent closed itemsets from evolving data streams. The implementation in MOA is described in [202] and uses the implementation of the CHARM batch miner from [106].

- **MOA-AdaGraphMiner:** AdaGraphMiner [35] (see section 10.4) is a framework for mining frequent subgraphs in time-varying streams. It contains three new methods for mining frequent closed subgraphs. All methods work on coresets of closed subgraphs, compressed representations of graph sets, and maintain these sets in a batch-incremental manner, but use different approaches to address potential concept drift.

- **MOA-Moment:** Moment [70] is a closed frequent itemset miner over a stream sliding window. This version was implemented by M. Jarka (www. admire-project.eu).

- **MOA-TweetReader:** This extension reads and converts tweets from the Twitter Streaming API to MOA instances, to facilitate streaming analysis of tweets.

- **Classifiers & DDMs:** This extension provides several published ensemble classifiers (DWM, RCD, Learn++.NSE, EB), concept drift detectors (ECDD, PHT, Paired Learners), and artificial datasets (Sine and Mixed).

- **MODL split criterion and GK class summary:** This new split criterion for numeric attributes is based on the MODL approach [48]. The GK class summary is based on Greenwald and Khanna's quantile summary (see section 6.4.3) but in this version class counts are included in each tuple in the summary.

- **Incrementally Optimized Very Fast Decision Tree (iOVFDT):** A new extension of the Hoeffding tree (section 6.3.2) proposed in [132].

- **Anytime Nearest Neighbor**: Implementation by Liu and Bell of the anytime classifier presented in [227].

- **Social Adaptive Ensemble 2 (SAE2)**: Social-based algorithms, Scale-Free Network Classifier (SFNClassifier) [25, 126], and the Social Network Clusterer Stream (SNCStream) [26].

- **Framework for Sentiment Analysis of a Stream of Texts**: This project's goal was to build an online, real-time system able to analyze an incoming stream of text and visualize its main characteristics using a minimal desktop application [18].

- **MOAReduction**: An extension for MOA that allows users to perform data reduction techniques on streams without drift. It includes several reduction methods for different tasks, such as discretization, instance selection, and feature selection, as presented in [205].

- **MOA for Android**: Contains software to make MOA usable as part of an Android application.

11.5   ADAMS

WEKA and MOA are powerful tools to perform data mining analysis tasks. Usually, in real applications and professional settings, the data mining processes are complex and consist of several steps. These steps can be seen as a workflow. Instead of implementing a program in Java, a professional data miner will build a solution using a workflow, so that it will be much easier to understand and maintain for nonprogrammer users. The Advanced Data mining And Machine learning System (ADAMS) [213, 214] is a flexible workflow engine aimed at quickly building and maintaining real-world, complex workflows. It integrates data mining applications such as MOA, WEKA, and MEKA, support for the R language, image and video processing and feature generation capabilities, spreadsheet and database access, visualizations, GIS, web services, and fast prototyping of new functionalities using scripting languages (Groovy/Jython).

Figure 11.1
The ADAMS flow editor.

The core of ADAMS is the workflow engine, which follows the philosophy of less is more. Instead of letting the user place operators (or actors, in ADAMS terms) on a canvas and then manually connect inputs and outputs, ADAMS uses a treelike structure. This structure and the control actors define how the data flows in the workflow; no explicit connections are necessary. The treelike structure stems from the internal object representation and the nesting of subactors within actor handlers.

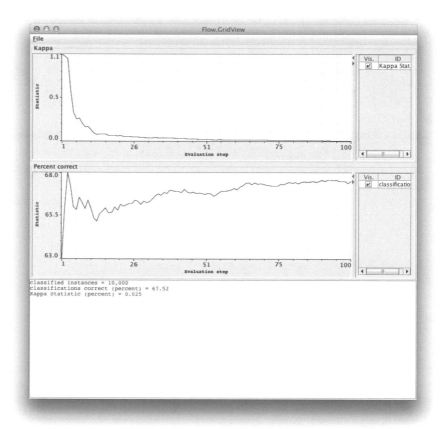

Figure 11.2
The ADAMS flow example.

Figure 11.1 shows the ADAMS flow editor loaded with the *adams-moa-classifier-evaluation* flow. It uses the Kappa statistic and a decision stump, a decision tree with only one internal node. Figure 11.2 shows the result of running the workflow.

ADAMS can also perform tweet analysis. Tweets and their associated meta-data can be recorded using the public Twitter API, storing them for future replay. This tweet stream replay functionality allows the same experiment to be performed as often as required, using the same stream of tweets each time, and applying different filters (e.g., checking for metadata) and algorithms. Tweets with geotagging information can be displayed using the OpenStreetMap GIS functionality, allowing for visualization of geographical phenomena.

ADAMS is also able to process videos in near real time, with frames being obtained at specific intervals. Apart from tracking objects, it is also possible to use the image processing and feature generation functionality to generate input for ML platforms such as MOA or WEKA.

11.6   MEKA

MEKA [212] is an open-source project started at the University of Waikato to perform and evaluate multi-label classification. It uses the so-called problem transformation methods to make WEKA single-label (binary or multiclass) methods available as base classifiers for multi-label classification; see Section 6.7.

MEKA contains all the basic problem transformation methods, advanced methods including varieties of classifier chains that have often been used as a benchmark in the recent multi-label literature, and also algorithm adaptations such as multi-label neural networks and deep neural networks. It includes two strategies for automatic threshold calibration, and a variety of evaluation metrics from the literature. MEKA is easy to use from either the CLI or the GUI (figure 11.3) . Thus no programming is required to parameterize, run, and evaluate classifiers, making it suitable for practitioners unfamiliar with Java. However, it is straightforward to extend MEKA with new classifiers and integrate it into other frameworks. Those familiar with WEKA will have almost no learning curve—much of WEKA's documentation and modus operandi is directly applicable. Any new MEKA classifier can also be combined within any of MEKA's existing ensemble schemes and any WEKA base classifier without writing extra code, and may be compared easily with benchmark and state-of-the-art methods. MEKA also supports semisupervised and streaming classification in the multi-label context, as discussed in section 6.7.

Figure 11.3
The MEKA GUI.

11.7   OpenML

OpenML [238, 239] is an online platform where scientists can automatically log and share machine learning datasets, code, and experiments, organize them online, and build directly on the work of others. It helps automate many tedious aspects of research, it is readily integrated into several ML tools, and it offers easy-to-use APIs. It also enables large-scale and real-time collaboration, allowing researchers to share their very latest results, while keeping track of their impact and reuse. The combined and linked results provide a wealth of information to speed up research, assist people while they analyze data, or automate the experiments altogether.

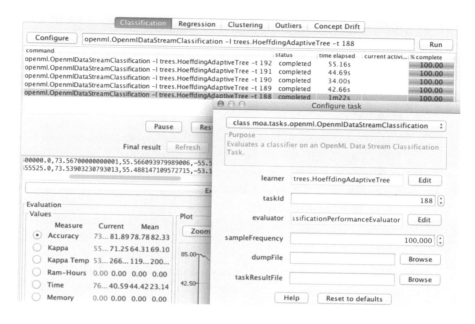

Figure 11.4

Integration of OpenML with MOA.

OpenML features an extensive REST API to search, download, and upload datasets, tasks, flows, and runs. Moreover, programming APIs are offered in Java, R, and Python to allow easy integration into existing software tools. Using these APIs, OpenML is already integrated into MOA, as shown in figure 11.4. In addition, R and Python libraries are provided to search and download datasets and tasks, and upload the results of ML experiments in just a few lines of code.

11.8 StreamDM

StreamDM-C++ [43] is an open-source project started at the Huawei Noah's Ark Lab. It implements Hoeffding adaptive trees (section 6.3.5) for data streams in C++ and has been used extensively at Huawei. Hoeffding adaptive trees adapt to changes in streams, a huge advantage since standard decision trees are built using a snapshot of data and cannot evolve over time.

StreamDM for Spark Streaming [39] is an open-source project for mining big data streams using Spark Streaming [253], an extension of the core Spark API that enables scalable stream processing of data streams.

11.9   Streams

The `streams` [46] framework is a Java implementation of a simple stream processing environment. It aims at providing a clean and easy-to-use Java-based platform to process streaming data. The core module of the streams library is a thin API layer of interfaces and classes that reflect a high-level view of streaming processes. This API serves as a basis for implementing custom processors and providing services with the streams library.

The `stream-analysis` modules of the `streams` library provide implementations for online methods for analysis, such as different approximative counting algorithms and computation of online statistics (e.g., quantile summaries). As `streams` incorporates MOA, the methods from MOA are available inside the framework.

11.10   Apache SAMOA

Apache Scalable Advanced Massive Online Analysis (SAMOA) [181] is a framework that provides distributed ML for big data streams, with an interface to plug in different stream processing platforms that run in the Hadoop ecosystem.

SAMOA can be used in two different modes: it can be used as a running platform to which new algorithms can be added, or developers can implement their own algorithms and run them within their own production system. Another feature of SAMOA is the stream processing platform abstraction, where developers can also add new platforms by using the available API. With this separation of roles, the SAMOA project is divided into the SAMOA API layer and the DSPE-adapter layer. The SAMOA API layer allows developers to develop for SAMOA without worrying about which distributed stream processing engine (SPE) will be used. When new SPEs are released or there is interest in integrating with another platform, a new DSPE-adapter layer module can be added. Currently, SAMOA supports four SPEs that are currently state-of-the-art: Apache Flink, Storm, Samza, and Apex.

The SAMOA modular components are *processor, stream, content event, topology,* and *task.*

- A *processor* in SAMOA is a unit-of-computation element that executes some part of the algorithm on *a specific SPE.* Processors contain the actual logic of the algorithms. *Processing* Items (PIs) are the different internal, concrete implementations of processors for each SPE.

  The SPE-adapter layer handles the instantiation of PIs. There are two types of PI, an *entrance PI* and a *normal PI.* An entrance PI converts data from an external source into instances, or independently generates instances. Then it sends the instances to the destination PI via the corresponding stream using the correct type of content event. A normal PI consumes *content events* from an incoming stream, processes the content events, and may send the same content events or new content events to outgoing streams. Developers can specify the *parallelism hint,* which is the number of *runtime PIs* during SAMOA execution, as shown in figure 11.5. A runtime PI is an actual PI that is created by the underlying SPE during execution. SAMOA dynamically instantiates the concrete class implementation of the PI based on the underlying SPE.

  A PI uses composition to contain its corresponding processor and streams. A processor is reusable, which allows developers to use the same implementation of processors in more than one ML algorithm implementation. The separation between PIs and processors allows developers to focus on developing their algorithms without worrying about the SPE-specific implementation of PIs.

- A *stream* is a connection from a PI into its corresponding destination PIs. Developers view streams as connectors between PIs and as mediums to send content events between PIs. A content event wraps the data transmitted from a PI to another via a stream. Moreover, in a way similar to processors, content events are reusable. Developers can use a content event in more than one algorithm.

- A *source PI* is a PI that sends content events through a stream. A *destination PI* is a PI that receives content events via a stream. Developers instantiate a stream by associating it with exactly one source PI. When destination PIs want to connect to a stream, they need to specify the *grouping* mechanism, which determines how the stream routes the transported content events.

- A *topology* is a collection of connected processing items and streams. It represents a network of components that process incoming data streams. A

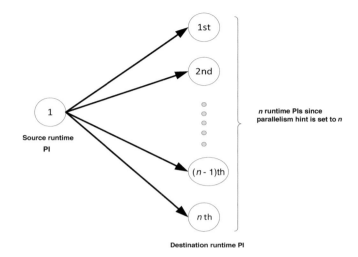

Figure 11.5
Parallelism hint in SAMOA.

distributed streaming algorithm implemented on top of SAMOA corresponds to a topology.

- A *task* is an ML-related activity such as performing a specific evaluation for a classifier. An example of a task is a prequential evaluation task, that is, a task that uses each instance for testing the model performance and then uses the same instance to train the model using specific algorithms. A task also corresponds to a topology in SAMOA.

Platform users esentially call SAMOA tasks. They specify what kind of task they want to perform, and SAMOA automatically constructs a topology based on the task. Next, platform users need to identify the SPE cluster that is available for deployment and configure SAMOA to execute on that cluster. Once the configuration is correct, SAMOA deploys the topology seamlessly into the configured cluster, and platform users can observe the execution results through dedicated log files of the execution.

The ML-adapter layer in SAMOA consists of classes that wrap ML algorithm implementations from other ML frameworks. Currently SAMOA has a wrapper class for MOA algorithms or learners, which means SAMOA can easily use MOA learners to perform some tasks. SAMOA does not change the underlying implementation of the MOA learners, so the learners still execute in a sequential manner on top of the SAMOA underlying SPE.

Developers design and implement distributed streaming ML algorithms with the abstraction of processors, content events, streams, and processing items. Using these modular components, they have flexibility in implementing new algorithms by reusing existing processors and content events, or writing new ones from scratch. They have also flexibility in reusing existing algorithms and learners from existing ML frameworks using the ML-adapter layer.

Developers can also implement tasks with the same abstractions. Since processors and content events are reusable; the topologies and their corresponding algorithms are also reusable. This means they also have flexibility in implementing new tasks by reusing existing algorithms and components, or by writing new algorithms and components from scratch.

Currently, SAMOA contains these algorithms:

- **Vertical Hoeffding tree [149]:** A vertical parallelism approach partitions instances in terms of attributes for parallel processing. Decision tree inducers with vertical parallelism process the partitioned instances (which consist of subsets of attributes) to compute splitting criteria in parallel. For example, if we have instances with 100 attributes and we partition the instances into 5 portions, we will have 20 attributes per portion. In each portion, the algorithm processes the 20 attributes in parallel to determine the locally best attribute to split, and combines the parallel computation results to determine the globally best attribute to split and grow the tree.

- **AMRules [241]:** SAMOA uses a hybrid of vertical and horizontal parallelism to distribute AMRules on a cluster. The decision rules built by AMRules are comprehensible models, where the antecedent of a rule is a conjunction of conditions on the attribute values, and the consequent is a linear combination of the attributes.

- **Adaptive bagging:** This is an easy method to parallelize. Each bagging replica is given to a different processor.

- **Distributed clustering:** Clustering in SAMOA has two levels: a first level that performs clustering on the split data, and a second level that performs a meta-clustering with the microclusters of the output of the first level.

12 The Graphical User Interface

The MOA Graphical User Interface (GUI) allows using MOA via menu selection and form filling. It contains several tabs on the top, for four learning tasks: Classification, regression, clustering, and outlier detection. In this chapter we describe the main options for evaluation, classification, and clustering; readers are encouraged to explore more, and read the MOA documentation for more detail on, for example, the parameters available for each method.

12.1 Getting Started with the GUI

The GUI for configuring and running tasks is invoked with the command:

```
bin/moa.sh
```

in Linux or Mac, and

```
bin\moa.bat
```

in Windows. These commands call the GUI using

```
java -Xmx1G ... moa.gui.GUI
```

There are several tabs, for classification, regression, clustering, and outlier detection. In the following sections we are going to describe how to use them.

12.2 Classification and Regression

The classification and regression tabs in MOA contain four different components as seen in Figure 12.1:

- Configure Current Task
- List of Tasks
- Output Panel
- Evaluation Measure and Chart Output Panel.

To use the classification GUI, first we need to configure a task, then run it, and finally see the results in the output panels.

We can click *Configure* to set up a task, modify the parameters of the task (see Figure 12.2), and when ready we can launch a task clicking *Run*. Several tasks can be run concurrently. We can click on different tasks in the list and

Figure 12.1
The MOA Graphical User Interface.

control them using the buttons below. If textual output of a task is available it will be displayed in the bottom half of the GUI, and can be saved to disk. If graphical output is available it will be displayed in the bottom chart display.

Note that the command line text box displayed at the top of the window represents textual commands that can be used to run tasks on the command line as described in the next chapter. The text can be selected then copied onto the clipboard. At the bottom of the GUI there is a graphical display of the results. It is possible to compare the results of two different tasks: The current task is displayed in red, and the previously executed one is in blue.

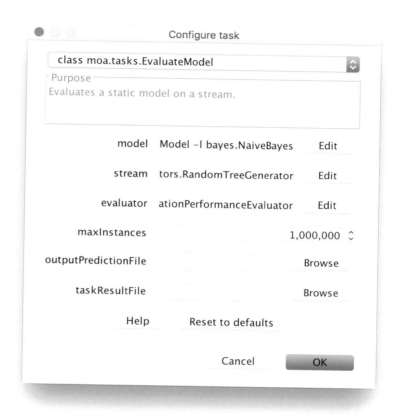

Figure 12.2
Options to set up a task in MOA.

12.2.1 Tasks

The main tasks in MOA are the following:

- **WriteStreamToARFFFile** Outputs a stream to an ARFF file. ARFF is a convenient data format used by the WEKA project [107] that extends the CSV format with a header specifying attribute types, names, and values.

- **MeasureStreamSpeed** Measures the speed of a stream.
- **LearnModel** Learns a predictive model from a stream.
- **EvaluateModel** Evaluates a static predictive model on a stream.
- **EvaluatePeriodicHeldOutTest** Evaluates a classifier on a stream by periodically testing on a holdout set.
- **EvaluateInterleavedTestThenTrain** Evaluates a classifier on a stream by testing then training with each instance in sequence. There is no forgetting mechanism so all instances are equally important in the evaluation.
- **EvaluatePrequential** Evaluates a classifier on a stream by testing then training with each example in sequence. It may optionally use a sliding window or a fading factor as forgetting mechanisms.
- **EvaluatePrequentialCV** Evaluates a classifier on a stream by doing k-fold distributed cross-validation; each time a new instance arrives, it is used for testing in one classifier selected randomly, and trained using the others. It may optionally use a sliding window or a fading factor as forgetting mechanisms.
- **EvaluateInterleavedChunks** Evaluates a classifier on a stream by testing then training with chunks of data in sequence.

Evaluation methods were defined in Section 6.1.

12.2.2 Data Feeds and Data Generators

MOA streams are built using generators, reading ARFF files, joining several streams, or filtering streams. They allow to simulate a potentially infinite sequence of data. The following ones are implemented:

- **ArffFileStream** Reads a stream from an ARFF file.
- **ConceptDriftStream** Creates a stream with concept drift by smoothly merging two streams that have the same attributes and classes.
  MOA models concept drift in a data stream as a weighted mixture of two existing streams that describe the data distributions before and after the drift. MOA uses the sigmoid function as a simple and practical solution to define the merging of two streams to simulate drift.
  We see from Figure 3.5 in Section 3.2.1 that the sigmoid function

$$f(t) = 1/(1 + e^{-s(t-p)})$$

has a derivative at the point p such that $f'(p) = s/4$. The tangent of angle α is equal to this derivative, $\tan \alpha = s/4$. We observe that $\tan \alpha = 1/w$, and as $s = 4\tan\alpha$ then $s = 4/w$. So the parameter s in the sigmoid gives the length of w and the angle α. In this sigmoid model we only need to specify two parameters : the point of change p, and the length of change w. Note that for any positive real number β

$$f(p + \beta \cdot w) = 1 - f(p - \beta \cdot w),$$

and that $f(p + \beta \cdot w)$ and $f(p - \beta \cdot w)$ are constant values that do not depend on p and w. We have, for example,

$$f(p + w/2) = 1 - f(p - w/2) = 1/(1 + e^{-2}) \approx 88.08\%,$$
$$f(p + w) = 1 - f(p - w) = 1/(1 + e^{-4}) \approx 98.20\%,$$
$$f(p + 2w) = 1 - f(p - 2w) = 1/(1 + e^{-8}) \approx 99.97\%.$$

Given two data streams a, b, $c = a \oplus_p^w b$ is defined as the data stream built joining the two data streams a and b, where p is the point of change, w is the length of change and

$$c(t) = \begin{cases} a(t) & \text{with probability } 1 - 1/(1 + e^{-4(t-p)/w}) \\ b(t) & \text{with probability } 1/(1 + e^{-4(t-p)/w}). \end{cases}$$

We observe the following properties, if $a \neq b$:

- $a \oplus_p^w b \neq b \oplus_p^w a$
- $a \oplus_p^w a = a$
- $a \oplus_0^0 b = b$
- $a \oplus_p^w (b \oplus_p^w c) \neq (a \oplus_p^w b) \oplus_p^w c$
- $a \oplus_{p_1}^w (b \oplus_{p_2}^w c) \approx (a \oplus_{p_1}^w b) \oplus_{p_2}^w c$ if $p_1 < p_2$ and $w \ll p_2 - p_1$.

In order to create a data stream with multiple concept changes, we can build new data streams joining different concept drifts:

$$(((a \oplus_{p_1}^{w_1} b) \oplus_{p_2}^{w_2} c) \oplus_{p_3}^{w_3} d) \ldots.$$

- **ConceptDriftRealStream** Generator that creates a stream with concept drift by merging two streams that have different attributes and classes. The new stream contains the attributes and classes of both streams.
- **FilteredStream** A stream that is obtained from a stream filtered by a filter, for example *AddNoiseFilter*.

- **AddNoiseFilter** Adds random noise to examples in a stream. To be used with *FilteredStream* only.

- **generators.AgrawalGenerator** Generates one of ten different pre-defined loan functions.

  This generator was introduced by Agrawal et al. in [8]. It was a common source of data for early work on scaling up decision tree learners. The generator produces a stream containing nine attributes, six numeric ones and three categorical ones. Although not explicitly stated by the authors, a sensible guess is that these attributes describe hypothetical loan applications. There are ten functions defined for generating binary class labels from the attributes. Presumably these determine whether the loan should be approved or not.

  A source code in C is publicly available. The built-in functions are based on the cited paper (page 924), which turn out to be functions pred20 thru pred29 in the public C implementation. The perturbation function works as in the C implementation rather than the description in paper.

- **generators.HyperplaneGenerator** Generates a problem of predicting class of a rotating hyperplane.

  The problem was used as testbed for CVFDT versus VFDT in [138]. A hyperplane in d-dimensional space is the set of points $x \in \Re^d$ that satisfy $\sum_{i=1}^{d} w_i x_i = w_0$, where x_i is the ith coordinate of point x. Point examples for which $\sum_{i=1}^{d} w_i x_i \geq w_0$ are labeled positive, and point examples for which $\sum_{i=1}^{d} w_i x_i < w_0$ are labeled negative. Hyperplanes are useful for simulating time-changing concepts, because we can change the orientation and position of the hyperplane in a smooth manner by changing the relative values of the weights. We add change to this dataset adding drift to each weight attribute, $w_i = w_i + d\sigma$, where σ is the probability that the direction of change is reversed and d is the speed of change.

- **generators.LEDGenerator** Generates a problem of predicting the digit displayed on a 7-segment LED display.

  This data source originates from the CART book [56]. The goal is to predict the digit displayed on a seven-segment LED display, where each attribute has a 10% chance of being inverted. It has an optimal Bayes classification rate (rate of the best possible classifier) of 74%. The particular configuration of the generator used for experiments (led) produces 24 binary attributes, 17 of which are irrelevant.

- **generators.LEDGeneratorDrift** Generates a problem of predicting the digit displayed on a 7-segment LED display with drift.

- **generators.RandomRBFGenerator** Generates a random radial basis function stream.

  This generator was devised to offer an alternate complex concept type that is not straightforward to approximate with decision trees. The RBF (Radial Basis Function) generator works as follows: A fixed number of random clusters are generated. Each cluster has a random center, a standard deviation, a class label and a weight. New examples are generated by selecting a cluster with probability proportional to its weight, then generating a point from a Gaussian distribution with the center at the cluster's center and the cluster's standard deviation along every axis. This effectively creates a normally distributed hypersphere of examples surrounding each center, with varying densities. Only numeric attributes are generated. The chosen cluster also determines the class label of the example.

- **generators.RandomRBFGeneratorDrift** Generates a random radial basis function stream with drift. Drift is introduced by moving the centers at constant speed.

- **generators.RandomTreeGenerator** Generates a stream based on a randomly generated tree.

  This generator is based on that proposed in [88] and produces concepts that should favor decision tree learners. It builds a decision tree by choosing attributes to split at random and assigning a random class label to each leaf. Once the tree is built, examples in the stream are generated by assigning uniformly distributed random values to attributes, which then determine the class label via the tree. The generator has parameters to control the number of classes, attributes, nominal attribute labels, and the depth of the tree.

  Noise can be introduced in the examples after generation. In the case of discrete attributes and the class label, a probability of noise parameter determines the chance that any particular value is switched to something other than the original value. For numeric attributes, a degree of random noise is added to all values, drawn from a random Gaussian distribution with standard deviation equal to the standard deviation of the original values multiplied by noise probability.

- **generators.SEAGenerator** Generates SEA concepts functions.

  This generator was proposed in [233] to study reaction to abrupt concept drift. The stream is generated using three attributes, and only the first two are relevant. All three attributes have values between 0 and 10. The points in the stream are divided into four blocks with different concepts. In each block, the 0/1 class is determined by the inequality $f_1 + f_2 \leq \theta$, where f_1 and f_2 represent the first two attributes and θ is a threshold value. The most usual threshold values for the four classes are 9, 8, 7 and 9.5.

- **generators.STAGGERGenerator** Generates STAGGER concept functions, introduced by Schlimmer and Granger in [223].

  The STAGGER concepts are boolean functions of three attributes encoding objects: size (small, medium, large), shape (circle, triangle, rectangle), and color (red, blue, green). A concept is a conjunction or disjunction of two attributes, such as *(color=red and size=small)* or *(color=green or shape=circle)*.

- **generators.WaveformGenerator** Generates a problem of predicting one of three waveform types.

  It shares its origin with the LED dataset. The goal of the task is to differentiate between three different classes of waveform, each of which is generated from a combination of two or three base waves. The optimal Bayes classification rate is known to be 86%. There are two versions of the problem, wave21 which has 21 numeric attributes, all of which include noise, and wave40, which introduces 19 additional irrelevant attributes.

- **generators.WaveformGeneratorDrift** Generates a problem of predicting one of three waveform types, with drift.

12.2.3   Bayesian Classifiers

- **NaiveBayes** Performs classic bayesian prediction making the naive assumption that all attributes are independent. It has been described in Section 6.2.3.

- **NaiveBayesMultinomial** The Multinomial Naive Bayes classifier is described in 6.2.4.

12.2.4   Decision Trees

- **HoeffdingTree** Decision tree inducer for data streams without change, described in Section 6.3.2. To use majority class learners at the leaves, use `HoeffdingTree -l MC`.

- **DecisionStump** Decision tree with a single inner node, so that only one attribute is tested to predict an instance.

- **HoeffdingOptionTree** Hoeffding Option Trees, described in Section 7.6.1. It is possible to choose the type of classifier placed at the leaves: Majority class, Naive Bayes, or Naive Bayes Adaptive. By default, the option selected is Naive Bayes Adaptive, since it tends to give best results; it monitors the error rate of the majority class and Naive Bayes predictors, and switches from one to the other tracking the one with better rate on recent instances. To run experiments using a majority class learner at leaves, use `HoeffdingOptionTree -l MC`.

- **HoeffdingAdaptiveTree** Decision tree inducer for evolving data streams, described in Section 6.3.5.

- **AdaHoeffdingOptionTree** Adaptive Hoeffding Option Tree for streaming data with Naive Bayes Adaptive classifiers at the leaves [38]. An *Adaptive Hoeffding Option Tree* is a Hoeffding Option Tree with the following improvement: Each leaf stores an estimation of the current error, estimated using an EWMA counter with $\alpha = 0.2$. The weight of each node in the voting process is proportional to the square of the inverse of the error.

12.2.5   Meta Classifiers (Ensembles)

- **OzaBag** Incremental online bagging by Oza and Russell, described in Section 7.4.1.

- **OzaBoost** Incremental online boosting by Oza and Russell [190].

- **OCBoost** Online Coordinate Boosting by Pelossof et al. [197]. An online boosting algorithm for adapting the weights of a boosted classifier, which yields a closer approximation to Freund and Schapire's AdaBoost algorithm. The weight update procedure is derived by minimizing AdaBoost's loss when viewed in an incremental form. This boosting method may be reduced to a form similar to Oza and Russell's algorithm.

- **OzaBagASHT** Bagging using Hoeffding trees, each with a maximum size value, and described in Section 7.6.4. The base learner must be ASHoeffdingTree, a Hoeffding Tree with a maximum size value.

- **OzaBagADWIN** Bagging using ADWIN, described in Section 7.4.2.

- **AccuracyWeightedEnsemble**, described in Section 7.1.

- **AccuracyUpdatedEnsemble**, a variant by Brzezinski and Stefanowski [58] of the method described in Section 7.1.

- **LimAttClassifier**, ensemble combining Restricted Hoeffding Trees using Stacking with a Perceptron, described in Section 7.6.3.

- **LeveragingBag** Leveraging Bagging for evolving data streams using ADWIN, described in Section 7.4.3. There are four different versions of this algorithm:

  - Leveraging Bagging ME, using weight 1 if misclassified, otherwise error/(1-error).
  - Leveraging Bagging Half, using resampling without replacement half of the instances.
  - Leveraging Bagging WT, without taking out all instances.
  - Leveraging Subagging, using resampling without replacement.

  The "-o" option can be used to use Random Output codes.

- **TemporallyAugmentedClassifier** Wrapper that includes labels of previous instances into the training data. This enables a classifier to exploit potential label auto-correlation. See Section 6.2.2.

12.2.6 Function Classifiers

- **MajorityClass** always predicts the class that has been observed most frequently in the training data.

- **NoChange** It predicts the class that has been observed in the last instance used to train the model.

- **Perceptron**, single perceptron classifier. Performs the classic multiclass perceptron learning, incrementally.

- **SGD** Implements stochastic gradient descent for learning various linear models: binary class SVM, binary class logistic regression, and linear regression.

- **SPegasos** Implements the stochastic variant of the Pegasos (Primal Estimated sub-GrAdient SOlver for SVM) method of Shalev-Shwartz et al. [226].

12.2.7 Drift Classifiers

- **SingleClassifierDrift** classifier for handling concept drift data streams, based on using a change detector to monitor the error of the classifier. When the change detector raises a warning signal, a new classifier is created; and when a change signal is raised, the current classifier is replaced by the new one. It is the strategy in the DDM method of Gama et al. [114], described in Section 5.3.4. There are several drift detection methods that can be used:

- **CusumDM** and **PageHinkleyDM**, as seen in Section 5.3.2.
- **DDM**, seen in Section 5.3.4.
- **EDDM**, based on using the estimated distribution. of the distances between classification errors, presented in [22].
- **ADWINChangeDetector**, as seen in Section 5.3.5.
- **EWMAChartDM**, based on using an exponentially weighted moving average (EWMA) chart [216], mentioned in Section 5.3.4.
- **GeometricMovingAverageDM**, based in the use of a geometric moving average estimation.
- **HDDM_A_Test** and **HDDM_W_Test**, based on using Hoeffding's bounds presented in [44].
- **SEEDChangeDetector**, based on detecting volatility shift, presented in [136].
- **SeqDrift1ChangeDetector** and **SeqDrift2ChangeDetector**, the first one based on comparing data in a sliding window and data in a repository, and the second one based in comparing data in a reservoir and data in a repository, presented in [196, 220].
- **STEPD**, based on using a statistical test of equal proportions, presented in [186].

12.2.8   Active Learning Classifiers

- **ActiveClassifier** Classifier for active learning that aims at learning an accurate model while not requesting more labels than allowed by its budget. This classifier can use several active learning strategies that explicitly handle concept drift, described in Section 6.8.

12.3   Clustering

The Clustering tab in MOA has the following main components:

- Data generators for stream clustering on evolving streams (including events like novelty, merge, etc.),
- a set of state-of-the-art stream clustering algorithms,
- evaluation measures for stream clustering, and
- visualization tools for analyzing results and comparing different settings.

12.3.1 Data Feeds and Data Generators

Figure 12.3 shows a screenshot of the configuration dialog for the RBF data generator with events. Generally the dimension, number, and size of clusters can be set as well as the drift speed, decay horizon (aging), and noise rate. Events constitute changes in the underlying data model such as cluster growth, cluster merging, or creation of a new cluster. Using the event frequency and the individual event weights, one can study the behavior and performance of different approaches on various settings. Finally, the settings for the data generators can be stored and loaded, which offers the opportunity of sharing settings and thereby providing benchmark streaming datasets for repeatability and comparison.

12.3.2 Stream Clustering Algorithms

Currently MOA contains several stream clustering methods, including:

- StreamKM++, described in Section 9.2.
- CluStream, described in Section 9.3.
- ClusTree, described in Section 9.5.
- Den-Stream, described in Section 9.5.
- CobWeb. A hierarchical clusterer, and one of the first incremental methods for clustering data, due to Fisher [102].

12.3.3 Visualization and Analysis

After the evaluation process is started, several options for analyzing the outputs are possible:

- The stream can be stopped and the current (micro)clustering result can be passed as a dataset to the WEKA explorer for further analysis or mining;

- the evaluation measures, which are evaluated at configurable time intervals, can be stored as a CSV file to obtain graphs and charts offline using a program of choice;

- finally, both the clustering results and the corresponding measures can be visualized online within MOA.

MOA allows the simultaneous configuration and evaluation of two different setups for direct comparison, for example of two different algorithms on the same stream or the same algorithm on streams with different noise levels, and so on.

The visualization component allows to visualize the stream as well as the clustering results, choose dimensions for multidimensional data, and compare experiments with different settings in parallel. Figure 12.4 shows a screenshot of the visualization tab. In this screenshot, two different settings of the CluStream algorithm are compared on the same stream setting, including merge/split events every 50000 examples, and four measures were chosen for online evaluation (F1, Precision, Recall, and SSQ).

The upper part of the GUI offers options to pause and resume the stream, adjust the visualization speed, choose the dimensions for x and y as well as the components to be displayed (points, micro- and macro- clustering and ground truth). The lower part of the GUI displays the measured values for both settings as numbers (left side, including mean values) and the currently selected measure as a plot over the processed examples (right, SSQ measure in this example).

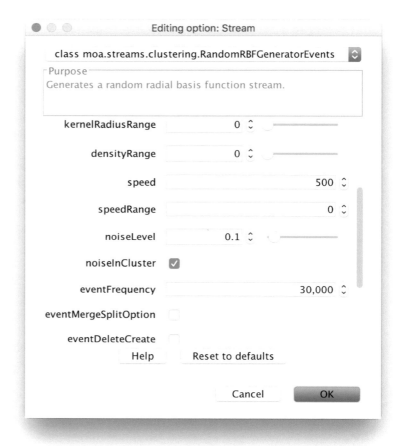

Figure 12.3

Option dialog for the RBF data generator. By storing and loading settings, streaming datasets can be shared for benchmarking, repeatability and comparison.

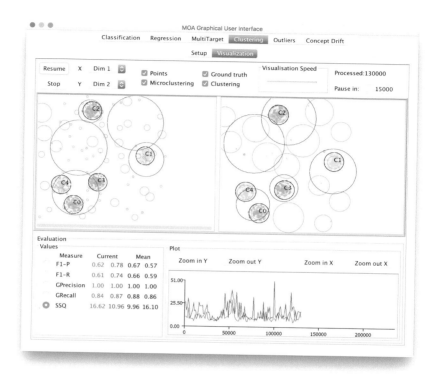

Figure 12.4

Visualization tab of the MOA clustering GUI.

13 Using the Command Line

MOA methods and tasks can be used from the GUI as explained in the previous chapter, or using the CLI. For classification and regression, the task commands used in the GUI can be used in the CLI directly. In this chapter we will show how to run these and other tasks from the command line.

Running tasks is as easy as calling the `moa.DoTask` command from the command line. For example, to run the `LearnModel` task, simply type

```
java -cp moa.jar -javaagent:sizeofag.jar moa.DoTask LearnModel
    ...parameters...
```

In the next sections, we will see specific examples of this use.

13.1 Learning Task for Classification and Regression

The first example will command MOA to train the `HoeffdingTree` classifier and create a model. The `moa.DoTask` class is the main class for running tasks on the command line. It will accept the name of a task followed by any appropriate parameters. The first task we will use is the `LearnModel` task. The `-l` parameter specifies the learner, in this case the `HoeffdingTree` class. The `-s` parameter specifies the data stream to learn from, in this case `generators.WaveformGenerator`, generating a three-class learning problem. The `-m` option specifies the maximum number of examples to train the learner with, in this case 1,000,000 examples. The `-O` option specifies a file to output the resulting model to:

```
java -cp moa.jar -javaagent:sizeofag.jar moa.DoTask
  LearnModel -l trees.HoeffdingTree
  -s generators.WaveformGenerator -m 1000000 -O model1.moa
```

This will create a file named `model1.moa` containing the tree model induced during training.

13.2 Evaluation Tasks for Classification and Regression

The next example will evaluate the model to compute its accuracy on a set of examples generated using a different random seed. The `EvaluateModel` task is given the parameters needed to load the model produced in the previous step, generate a new waveform stream with random seed 2, and test on another 1,000,000 examples:

```
java -cp moa.jar -javaagent:sizeofag.jar moa.DoTask
  "EvaluateModel -m file:model1.moa
  -s (generators.WaveformGenerator -i 2) -i 1000000"
```

Observe the use of nested parameters using parentheses. Quotes have been added around the description of the task, otherwise the operating system might be confused by the parentheses.

After evaluation the following statistics are output:

```
classified instances = 1,000,000
classifications correct (percent) = 84.474
Kappa Statistic (percent) = 76.711
```

Note that the two steps above can be rolled into one, avoiding the need to create an external file, as follows:

```
java -cp moa.jar -javaagent:sizeofag.jar moa.DoTask
  "EvaluateModel -m (LearnModel -l trees.HoeffdingTree
  -s generators.WaveformGenerator -m 1000000)
  -s (generators.WaveformGenerator -i 2) -i 1000000"
```

MOA will create and use the classifier in memory, without storing it in a file.

13.3   Learning and Evaluation Tasks for Classification and Regression

The `EvaluatePeriodicHeldOutTest` task will train a model while taking snapshots of performance using a holdout test set at periodic intervals. The following command creates a CSV file, trains the `HoeffdingTree` classifier on the `WaveformGenerator` data, keeps the first 100,000 examples for testing, trains on a total of 100,000,000 examples, and tests on the holdout set every 1,000,000 examples:

```
java -cp moa.jar -javaagent:sizeofag.jar moa.DoTask
  "EvaluatePeriodicHeldOutTest -l trees.HoeffdingTree
  -s generators.WaveformGenerator
  -n 100000 -i 100000000 -f 1000000" > dsresult.csv
```

For the purposes of comparison, a bagging learner using 10 decision trees can be trained on the same problem:

```
java -cp moa.jar -javaagent:sizeofag.jar moa.DoTask
  "EvaluatePeriodicHeldOutTest -l (OzaBag -l trees.HoeffdingTree
  -s 10) -s generators.WaveformGenerator
  -n 100000 -i 100000000 -f 1000000" > htresult.csv
```

Another evaluation method implemented in MOA is the interleaved test-then-train. It produces smoother plots of accuracy over time, as each individual example becomes less and less significant to the overall average. Here is an example of an `EvaluateInterleavedTestThenTrain` task that creates a CSV file, trains the `HoeffdingTree` classifier on `WaveformGenerator` data, trains and tests on a total of 100,000,000 examples, and records accuracy every 1,000,000 examples:

```
java -cp moa.jar -javaagent:sizeofag.jar moa.DoTask
  "EvaluateInterleavedTestThenTrain -l trees.HoeffdingTree
  -s generators.WaveformGenerator
  -i 100000000 -f 1000000" > htresult.csv
```

13.4   Comparing Two Classifiers

Suppose we want to compare the learning curves of two classifiers, a decision stump and a Hoeffding Tree. First, we have to execute the `EvaluatePeriodicHeldOutTest` task to train a model while taking snapshots of performance with a holdout test set at periodic intervals. The following commands create CSV files and train the `DecisionStump` and the `HoeffdingTree` classifiers on `WaveformGenerator` data, using 1,000 examples for holdout testing, training on a total of 100,000 examples, and testing every 10,000 examples:

```
java -cp moa.jar -javaagent:sizeofag.jar moa.DoTask
  "EvaluatePeriodicHeldOutTest -l trees.DecisionStump
  -s generators.WaveformGenerator
  -n 1000 -i 100000 -f 10000" > dsresult.csv

java -cp moa.jar -javaagent:sizeofag.jar moa.DoTask
  "EvaluatePeriodicHeldOutTest -l (trees.HoeffdingTree -l MC)
  -s generators.WaveformGenerator
  -n 1000 -i 100000 -f 10000" > htresult.csv
```

Assuming that `gnuplot` is installed on the system, the learning curves can be plotted with the following commands:

```
gnuplot> set datafile separator ","
gnuplot> set ylabel "% correct"
gnuplot> set xlabel "examples processed"
gnuplot> plot [][0:100] \
  "dsresult.csv" using 1:9 with linespoints \
  title "DecisionStump", \
  "htresult.csv" using 1:9 with linespoints \
```

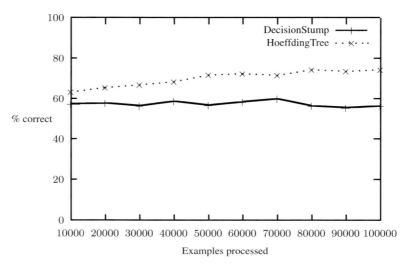

Figure 13.1
Rendering of learning curves of two classifiers using `gnuplot`.

```
title "HoeffdingTree"
```

This results in the graph shown in figure 13.1.

For this problem it is obvious that a full tree can achieve higher accuracy than a single stump. The stump has an almost constant accuracy (around 58%) that does not improve with further training, while that of the full tree increases by 10% on the first 100,000 examples.

14 Using the API

MOA can be used from external Java code by calling its API. It is very easy to use the generators, methods, and tasks of MOA inside your Java applications. In this chapter we show how to use the MOA API and include stream ML capabilities inside your programs. We assume basic knowledge of Java and object-oriented programming.

14.1 MOA Objects

The basic objects available from the MOA API are:

- `Task`: All tasks in MOA follow this interface. All tasks that write their result to a file must extend `MainTask` and implement the `doMainTask` method.
- `InstanceStream`: Streams used in MOA use this interface. To use a stream, call `prepareForUse` to prepare it and then `nextInstance` to get each new instance from the stream.
- `Classifier`: Classifiers should extend `AbstractClassifier`. To use a classifier, first call `prepareForUse` to prepare it, and then use `trainOnInstance` to train the model with a new instance, or `getVotesForInstance` to get the classification predictions for an instance.

14.2 Options

MOA classes that have parameters or options have to extend the class `AbstractOptionHandler`. These options can be of the following types:

- Integer: `IntOption (name, char, purpose, default Value, min Value, max Value)`
- Float: `FloatOption (name, char, purpose, default Value, min Value, max Value)`
- Flag: `FlagOption (name, char, purpose)`
- File: `FileOption (name, char, purpose, default File name, default File extension, Output)`
- String: `StringOption (name, char, purpose, default Value)`

- Multichoice: MultichoiceOption (name, char, purpose, option labels, option descriptions, default option index)
- Class: ClassOption (name, char, purpose, required type, default CLI string)
- List: ListOption (name, char, purpose, expected option type, default list, separator char)

These are some examples of options defined as Java classes:

Listing 14.1: Definition of option classes with default values.

```
public IntOption gracePeriodOption = new
   IntOption(
        "gracePeriod",
        'g',
        "The number of instances a leaf should
           observe between split attempts.",
        200, 0, Integer.MAX_VALUE);

public ClassOption splitCriterionOption = new
   ClassOption("splitCriterion",
        's', "Split criterion to use.",
           SplitCriterion.class,
        "InfoGainSplitCriterion");

public FloatOption splitConfidenceOption = new
   FloatOption(
        "splitConfidence",
        'c',
        "The allowable error in split decision,
           values closer to 0 will take longer
           to decide.",
        0.0000001, 0.0, 1.0);

public FlagOption binarySplitsOption = new
   FlagOption("binarySplits", 'b',
        "Only allow binary splits.");
```

```
public FileOption dumpFileOption = new
    FileOption("dumpFile", 'd',
        "File to append intermediate csv
            results to.", null, "csv", true);

public StringOption xTitleOption = new
    StringOption("xTitle", 'm',
        "Title of the plots' x-axis.",
            "Processed instances");
```

To change the values of these options from your Java source code via API, there are two possibilities:

- `setValueViaCLIString(String s)`: Sets the value for this option via text that can contain several nested parameters, similar to the CLI text.
- Each option has a particular method to change its value:
  - Integer: `setValue(int v)`
  - Float: `setValue(double v)`
  - Flag: `setValue(boolean v)`
  - File: `setValue(String v)`
  - String: `setValue(String v)`
  - Multichoice: `setChosenIndex(int index)`
  - Class: `setCurrentObject(Object obj)`
  - List: `setList(Option[] optList)`

There are also two ways to get the values of these options:

- `getValueAsCLIString()`: Gets the text that describes the nested parameters of this option.
- Each option has a particular method to get its value:
  - Integer: `getValue()`
  - Float: `getValue()`
  - Flag: `isSet()`
  - File: `getFile()`

- String: `getValue()`
- Multichoice: `getChosenIndex()`
- Class: `getPreparedClassOption(ClassOption classOption)`
- List: `getList()`

14.3   Prequential Evaluation Example

As an example, we will write Java code to perform prequential evaluation.

We start by initializing the data stream from which we will read instances. In this example we will use the RandomRBFGenerator, explained in section 12.2.2.

Listing 14.2: Java code for stream initialization.

```
RandomRBFGenerator stream = new
    RandomRBFGenerator();
stream.prepareForUse();
```

Now we have to build an empty learner. We create a Hoeffding Tree, and tell it the information about instance attributes using `setModelContext`.

Listing 14.3: Java code for learner initialization.

```
Classifier learner = new HoeffdingTree();
learner.setModelContext(stream.getHeader());
learner.prepareForUse();
```

To perform prequential evaluation, we have to first test and then train on each one of the instances in the stream. At the same time, we keep some accuracy statistics to be able to compute the final accuracy value.

Listing 14.4: Java code for prequential evaluation.

```
int numInstances=10000;
int numberSamplesCorrect=0;
int numberSamples=0;
boolean isTesting = true;
```

```
while(stream.hasMoreInstances() &&
    numberSamples < numInstances){
    Instance inst =
        stream.nextInstance().getData();
    if(isTesting){
        if(learner.correctlyClassifies(inst)){
            numberSamplesCorrect++;
        }
    }
    numberSamples++;
    learner.trainOnInstance(inst);
}
```

Finally, we output the results of the evaluation. In our case, we are interested in accuracy, so we print the final prequential accuracy of the HoeffdingTree in this setting.

Listing 14.5: Java code to output result.

```
double accuracy = 100.0*(double)
    numberSamplesCorrect /
    (double)numberSamples;
System.out.println(numberSamples+" instances
    processed with "+accuracy+"% accuracy");
```

The complete Java code of our evaluation method is:

Listing 14.6: Complete Java code.

```
RandomRBFGenerator stream = new
    RandomRBFGenerator();
stream.prepareForUse();

Classifier learner = new HoeffdingTree();
learner.setModelContext(stream.getHeader());
learner.prepareForUse();

int numInstances=10000;
```

```
int numberSamplesCorrect=0;
int numberSamples=0;
boolean isTesting = true;
while(stream.hasMoreInstances() &&
    numberSamples < numInstances){
    Instance inst =
        stream.nextInstance().getData();
    if(isTesting){
        if(learner.correctlyClassifies(inst)){
            numberSamplesCorrect++;
        }
    }
    numberSamples++;
    learner.trainOnInstance(inst);
}
double accuracy = 100.0*(double)
    numberSamplesCorrect /
    (double)numberSamples;
System.out.println(numberSamples+" instances
    processed with "+accuracy+"% accuracy");
```

15 Developing New Methods in MOA

In some cases, it is useful to develop new methods that extend MOA capabilities. In this chapter, we present the structure of some of the most popular objects in MOA, and show how to implement new ones. This chapter requires a good understanding of data structures in Java.

15.1 Main Classes in MOA

All objects in MOA should implement the `MOAObject` interface and extend the `AbstractMOAObject` abstract class. To create a new class in Java that needs to configure options, one needs to extend the `AbstractOptionHandler` abstract class. MOA options are very flexible and, since they can be recursive, it is possible to define, as options, objects that have options themselves. For example, this is the specification of a Hoeffding Tree classifier with options different from the default ones:

```
moa.classifiers.trees.HoeffdingTree
    -n (VFMLNumericAttributeClassObserver -n 20)
     -g 300 -s GiniSplitCriterion -t 0.04 -l MC
```

In this example, we are selecting as a numeric attribute class observer a `VFMLNumericAttributeClassObserver` object that has 20 bins. We pass the number 20 as an option to this class. Notice that the options are recursive, and can contain a large number of Java classes.

The main learner interfaces in MOA are:

- **Classifier:** This interface is used by classifiers and regressors. Classifiers usually extend the `AbstractClassifier` abstract class, and implement the following three methods:

  - `resetLearningImpl` to reset or initialize the classifier
  - `trainOnInstanceImpl` to update the learner with a new instance
  - `getVotesForInstance` to obtain a prediction from the learner

  The `AbstractClassifier` abstract class contains the following two methods, used in the API:

  - `prepareForUse`, which calls `resetLearningImpl` to prepare the classifier

- `trainOnInstance`, which uses `trainOnInstanceImpl` to train the learner with a new instance

- **Regressor:** Regression methods implement this interface and extend the `AbstractClassifier` abstract class. The difference between classification and regression is that, for classification, `getVotesForInstance` returns an array with estimated prediction values for each class, while, for regression, `getVotesForInstance` returns an array of length 1 with the predicted outcome.

- **Clusterer:** This interface is used by clusterers and outlier detectors. Clusterers extend the `AbstractClusterer` abstract class, and implement the following methods:

  - `resetLearningImpl` to reset or initialize the clusterer
  - `trainOnInstanceImpl` to update the clusterer with a new instance
  - `getClustering` to obtain the clustering points computed by the clusterer

- **OutlierDetector:** Similar to clusterers, but specifically designed for outlier detection.

15.2   Creating a New Classifier

To demonstrate the implementation and use of learning algorithms in the system, we show and explain the Java code of a simple decision stump classifier. The classifier monitors the information gain on the class when splitting on each attribute and chooses the attribute that maximizes this value. The decision is revisited many times, so the stump has potential to change over time as more examples are seen. In practice it is unlikely to change after sufficient training, if there is no change in the stream distribution.

To describe the implementation, relevant code fragments are discussed in turn, with the entire code listed at the end (listing 15.7). The line numbers from the fragments refer to the final listing.

A simple approach to writing a classifier is to extend the class `moa.classifiers.AbstractClassifier` (line 10), which will take care of certain details to ease the task.

Listing 15.1: Option handling

```
public IntOption gracePeriodOption = new
    IntOption("gracePeriod", 'g',
            "The number of instances to observe between
            model changes.",
            1000, 0, Integer.MAX_VALUE);

public FlagOption binarySplitsOption = new
    FlagOption("binarySplits", 'b',
            "Only allow binary splits.");

public ClassOption splitCriterionOption = new
    ClassOption("splitCriterion",
            'c', "Split criterion to use.",
            SplitCriterion.class,
            "InfoGainSplitCriterion");
```

To set up the public interface to the classifier, you must specify the options available to the user. For the system to automatically take care of option handling, the options need to be public members of the class and extend the `moa.options.Option` type, as seen in listing 15.1.

The example classifier–the decision stump–has three options, each of a different type. The meanings of the first three parameters used to build options are consistent between different option types. The first parameter is a short name used to identify the option. The second is a character intended to be used on the command line. It should be unique– a command-line character cannot be repeated for different options, otherwise an exception will be thrown. The third standard parameter is a string describing the purpose of the option. Additional parameters to option constructors allow you tp specify additional information, such as default values, or valid ranges for values.

The first option specified for the decision stump classifier is the "grace period." The option is expressed with an integer, so the option has the type `IntOption`. The parameter will control how frequently the best stump is reconsidered when learning from a stream of examples. This increases the efficiency of the classifier—evaluating after every single example is expensive, and it is unlikely that a single example will change the choice of the currently best stump. The default value of 1,000 means that the choice of stump will be re-evaluated only every 1,000 examples. The last two parameters specify the range of values that are allowed for the option—it makes no sense to have a negative grace period, so the range is restricted to integers 0 or greater.

The second option is a flag, or a binary switch, represented by a
FlagOption. By default all flags are turned off, and will be turned on only
when the user requests so. This flag controls whether the decision stumps are
only allowed to split two ways. By default the stumps are allowed to have more
than two branches.

The third option determines the split criterion that is used to decide which
stumps are the best. This is a ClassOption that requires a particular Java
class of type SplitCriterion. If the required class happens to be an
OptionHandler, then those options will be used to configure the object
that is passed in.

Listing 15.2: Miscellaneous fields.

```
protected  AttributeSplitSuggestion  bestSplit;

protected  DoubleVector  observedClassDistribution;

protected  AutoExpandVector<AttributeClassObserver>
    attributeObservers;

protected  double  weightSeenAtLastSplit;

public  boolean  isRandomizable() {
    return  false;
}
```

In listing 15.2 four global variables are used to maintain the state of the
classifier:

- The bestSplit field maintains the stump that is currently chosen by the
  classifier. It is of type AttributeSplitSuggestion, a class used to
  split instances into different subsets.

- The observedClassDistribution field remembers the overall distribution of class labels that have been observed by the classifier. It is of
  type DoubleVector, a handy class for maintaining a vector of floating-
  point values without having to manage its size.

- The attributeObservers field stores a collection of
  AttributeClassObservers, one for each attribute. This is the information needed to decide which attribute is best to base the stump on.

- The `weightSeenAtLastSplit` field records the last time an evaluation was performed, so that the classifier can determine when another evaluation is due, depending on the grace period parameter.

The `isRandomizable()` function needs to be implemented to specify whether the classifier has an element of randomness. If it does, it will automatically be set up to accept a random seed. This classifier does not, so `false` is returned.

Listing 15.3: Preparing for learning.

```
1  @Override
   public void resetLearningImpl() {
3      this.bestSplit = null;
       this.observedClassDistribution = new DoubleVector();
5      this.attributeObservers = new
           AutoExpandVector<AttributeClassObserver>();
       this.weightSeenAtLastSplit = 0.0;
7  }
```

The `resetLearningImpl` function in listing 15.3 is called before any learning begins, so it should set the default state when no information has been supplied, and no training examples have been seen. In this case, the four global fields are set to sensible defaults.

Listing 15.4: Training on examples.

```
1  @Override
   public void trainOnInstanceImpl(Instance inst) {
3      this.observedClassDistribution.addToValue((int)
           inst.classValue(), inst
               .weight());
5      for (int i = 0; i < inst.numAttributes() - 1; i++) {
           int instAttIndex =
               modelAttIndexToInstanceAttIndex(i, inst);
7          AttributeClassObserver obs =
               this.attributeObservers.get(i);
           if (obs == null) {
9              obs =
                   inst.attribute(instAttIndex).isNominal()
                   ?
                       newNominalClassObserver() :
                           newNumericClassObserver();
11             this.attributeObservers.set(i, obs);
           }
```

```
13              obs.observeAttributeClass(inst.value(instAttIndex),
                    (int) inst
                              .classValue(), inst.weight());
15        }
         if (this.trainingWeightSeenByModel −
             this.weightSeenAtLastSplit >=
17                      this.gracePeriodOption.getValue()) {
             this.bestSplit =
                     findBestSplit((SplitCriterion)
19           getPreparedClassOption(this.splitCriterionOption));
             this.weightSeenAtLastSplit =
                     this.trainingWeightSeenByModel;
21        }
      }
```

Function `trainOnInstanceImpl` in listing 15.4 is the main function
of the learning algorithm, called for every training example in a stream. The
first step, lines 47–48, updates the overall recorded distribution of classes. The
loop on lines 49–59 repeats for every attribute in the data. If no observations
for a particular attribute have been seen before, then lines 53–55 create a new
observing object. Lines 57–58 update the observations with the values from
the new example. Lines 60–61 check whether the grace period has expired. If
so, the best split is reevaluated.

Listing 15.5: Functions used during training.

```
   protected AttributeClassObserver newNominalClassObserver() {
2          return new NominalAttributeClassObserver();
   }

4

   protected AttributeClassObserver newNumericClassObserver() {
6          return new GaussianNumericAttributeClassObserver();
   }

8

   protected AttributeSplitSuggestion
       findBestSplit(SplitCriterion criterion) {
10         AttributeSplitSuggestion bestFound = null;
           double bestMerit = Double.NEGATIVE_INFINITY;
12         double[] preSplitDist =
               this.observedClassDistribution.getArrayCopy();
           for (int i = 0; i < this.attributeObservers.size();
               i++) {
14             AttributeClassObserver obs =
                   this.attributeObservers.get(i);
               if (obs != null) {
```

```
16              AttributeSplitSuggestion suggestion
                    =
                    obs.getBestEvaluatedSplitSuggestion(
18                      criterion ,
                        preSplitDist ,
20                      i ,
                        this.binarySplitsOption.isSet());
22              if (suggestion.merit > bestMerit) {
                    bestMerit =
                        suggestion.merit;
24                  bestFound = suggestion;
                }
26          }
        }
28      return bestFound;
    }
```

Functions in listing 15.5 assist the training algorithm. Classes `newNominalClassObserver` and `newNumericClassObserver` are responsible for creating new observer objects for nominal and numeric attributes, respectively. The `findBestSplit()` function will iterate through the possible stumps and return the one with the highest "merit" score.

Listing 15.6: Predicting the class of unknown examples.

```
1   public double[] getVotesForInstance(Instance inst) {
        if (this.bestSplit != null) {
3           int branch =
                this.bestSplit.splitTest.branchForInstance(inst);
            if (branch >= 0) {
5               return this.bestSplit
                    .resultingClassDistributionFromSplit(branch);
7           }
        }
9       return this.observedClassDistribution.getArrayCopy();
    }
```

Function `getVotesForInstance` in listing 15.6 is the other important function of the classifier besides training—using the model that has been induced to predict the class of new examples. For the decision stump, this involves calling the functions `branchForInstance()` and `resultingClassDistributionFromSplit()`, which are implemented by the `AttributeSplitSuggestion` class.

Putting all of the elements together, the full listing of the tutorial class is given below.

Listing 15.7: Full listing.

```
package moa.classifiers;

import moa.core.AutoExpandVector;
import moa.core.DoubleVector;
import moa.options.ClassOption;
import moa.options.FlagOption;
import moa.options.IntOption;
import weka.core.Instance;

public class DecisionStumpTutorial extends
    AbstractClassifier {

    private static final long serialVersionUID = 1L;

    public IntOption gracePeriodOption = new
        IntOption("gracePeriod", 'g',
            "The number of instances to observe between model
                changes.",
            1000, 0, Integer.MAX_VALUE);

    public FlagOption binarySplitsOption = new
        FlagOption("binarySplits", 'b',
            "Only allow binary splits.");

    public ClassOption splitCriterionOption = new
        ClassOption("splitCriterion",
            'c', "Split criterion to use.",
                SplitCriterion.class,
            "InfoGainSplitCriterion");

    protected AttributeSplitSuggestion bestSplit;

    protected DoubleVector observedClassDistribution;

    protected AutoExpandVector<AttributeClassObserver>
        attributeObservers;

    protected double weightSeenAtLastSplit;

    public boolean isRandomizable() {
        return false;
    }
```

```
     @Override
38   public void resetLearningImpl() {
         this.bestSplit = null;
40       this.observedClassDistribution = new DoubleVector();
         this.attributeObservers = new
             AutoExpandVector<AttributeClassObserver>();
42       this.weightSeenAtLastSplit = 0.0;
     }

44
     @Override
46   public void trainOnInstanceImpl(Instance inst) {
         this.observedClassDistribution.addToValue((int)
             inst.classValue(), inst
48           .weight());
         for (int i = 0; i < inst.numAttributes() - 1; i++) {
50           int instAttIndex =
                 modelAttIndexToInstanceAttIndex(i, inst);
             AttributeClassObserver obs =
                 this.attributeObservers.get(i);
52           if (obs == null) {
                 obs = inst.attribute(instAttIndex).isNominal() ?
54                   newNominalClassObserver() :
                         newNumericClassObserver();
                 this.attributeObservers.set(i, obs);
56           }
             obs.observeAttributeClass(inst.value(instAttIndex),
                 (int) inst
58               .classValue(), inst.weight());
         }
60       if (this.trainingWeightSeenByModel -
             this.weightSeenAtLastSplit >=
                 this.gracePeriodOption.getValue()) {
62           this.bestSplit = findBestSplit((SplitCriterion)
                 getPreparedClassOption(this.splitCriterionOption));
64           this.weightSeenAtLastSplit =
                 this.trainingWeightSeenByModel;
         }
66   }

68   public double[] getVotesForInstance(Instance inst) {
         if (this.bestSplit != null) {
70           int branch =
                 this.bestSplit.splitTest.branchForInstance(inst);
             if (branch >= 0) {
72               return this.bestSplit
                     .resultingClassDistributionFromSplit(branch);
74           }
         }
76       return this.observedClassDistribution.getArrayCopy();
```

```
        }
78
        protected AttributeClassObserver
            newNominalClassObserver() {
80          return new NominalAttributeClassObserver();
        }
82
        protected AttributeClassObserver
            newNumericClassObserver() {
84          return new GaussianNumericAttributeClassObserver();
        }
86
        protected AttributeSplitSuggestion
            findBestSplit(SplitCriterion criterion) {
88          AttributeSplitSuggestion bestFound = null;
            double bestMerit = Double.NEGATIVE_INFINITY;
90          double[] preSplitDist =
                this.observedClassDistribution.getArrayCopy();
            for (int i = 0; i < this.attributeObservers.size();
                i++) {
92              AttributeClassObserver obs =
                    this.attributeObservers.get(i);
                if (obs != null) {
94                  AttributeSplitSuggestion suggestion =
                        obs.getBestEvaluatedSplitSuggestion(
96                          criterion,
                            preSplitDist,
98                          i,
                            this.binarySplitsOption.isSet());
100                 if (suggestion.merit > bestMerit) {
                        bestMerit = suggestion.merit;
102                     bestFound = suggestion;
                    }
104             }
            }
106         return bestFound;
        }
108
        public void getModelDescription(StringBuilder out, int
            indent) {
110     }
112     protected moa.core.Measurement[]
            getModelMeasurementsImpl() {
            return null;
114     }
116 }
```

15.3   Compiling a Classifier

The following files are assumed to be in the current working directory:

```
DecisionStumpTutorial.java
moa.jar
sizeofag.jar
```

The example source code can be compiled with the following command:

```
javac -cp moa.jar DecisionStumpTutorial.java
```

This command produces a compiled Java class file named
`DecisionStumpTutorial.class`.

Before continuing, note that the commands below set up a directory structure
to reflect the package structure:

```
mkdir moa
mkdir moa/classifiers
cp DecisionStumpTutorial.class moa/classifiers/
```

The class is now ready to use.

15.4   Good Programming Practices in MOA

We recommend the following good practices in Java programming when developing methods in MOA:

- When building new learners or tasks, to add new strategies or behavior, add them using class options. Follow these steps:

  1. Create a new interface for the strategy.
  2. Create different strategy classes that implement that new interface.
  3. Add a class option, so that users can choose what strategy to use from the GUI or command line.

- Minimize the scope of variables.
- Favor composition over inheritance.
- Favor static member classes over nonstatic ones.

- Minimize the accessibility of classes and members.
- Refer to objects by their interfaces.
- Use builders instead of constructors with many parameters.

The book *Effective Java* by Bloch [45] is a good reference for mastering the best practices in Java programming.

Bibliography

[1] Martín Abadi, Paul Barham, Jianmin Chen, Zhifeng Chen, Andy Davis, Jeffrey Dean, Matthieu Devin, Sanjay Ghemawat, Geoffrey Irving, Michael Isard, Manjunath Kudlur, Josh Levenberg, Rajat Monga, Sherry Moore, Derek Gordon Murray, Benoit Steiner, Paul A. Tucker, Vijay Vasudevan, Pete Warden, Martin Wicke, Yuan Yu, and Xiaoqiang Zheng. Tensorflow: A system for large-scale machine learning. In *12th USENIX Symposium on Operating Systems Design and Implementation, OSDI 2016, Savannah, GA, USA, November 2–4, 2016.*, pages 265–283, 2016.

[2] Hanady Abdulsalam, David B. Skillicorn, and Patrick Martin. Streaming random forests. In *Eleventh International Database Engineering and Applications Symposium (IDEAS 2007), September 6–8, 2007, Banff, Alberta, Canada*, pages 225–232, 2007.

[3] Marcel R. Ackermann, Marcus Märtens, Christoph Raupach, Kamil Swierkot, Christiane Lammersen, and Christian Sohler. Streamkm++: A clustering algorithm for data streams. *ACM Journal of Experimental Algorithmics*, 17(1), 2012.

[4] Charu C. Aggarwal, editor. *Data Streams – Models and Algorithms*, volume 31 of *Advances in Database Systems*. Springer, 2007.

[5] Charu C. Aggarwal and Jiawei Han, editors. *Frequent Pattern Mining*. Springer, 2014.

[6] Charu C. Aggarwal, Jiawei Han, Jianyong Wang, and Philip S. Yu. A framework for clustering evolving data streams. In *VLDB 2003, Proceedings of 29th International Conference on Very Large Data Bases, September 9–12, 2003, Berlin, Germany*, pages 81–92, 2003.

[7] Charu C. Aggarwal and Chandan K. Reddy, editors. *Data Clustering: Algorithms and Applications*. CRC Press, 2014.

[8] Rakesh Agrawal, Tomasz Imielinski, and Arun N. Swami. Database mining: A performance perspective. *IEEE Trans. Knowl. Data Eng.*, 5(6):914–925, 1993.

[9] Rakesh Agrawal and Ramakrishnan Srikant. Fast algorithms for mining association rules in large databases. In *VLDB'94, Proceedings of 20th International Conference on Very Large Data Bases, September 12–15, 1994, Santiago de Chile, Chile*, pages 487–499, 1994.

[10] Tahseen Al-Khateeb, Mohammad M. Masud, Khaled Al-Naami, Sadi Evren Seker, Ahmad M. Mustafa, Latifur Khan, Zouheir Trabelsi, Charu C. Aggarwal, and Jiawei Han. Recurring and novel class detection using class-based ensemble for evolving data stream. *IEEE Trans. Knowl. Data Eng.*, 28(10):2752–2764, 2016.

[11] Khaled Al-Naami, Swarup Chandra, Ahmad M. Mustafa, Latifur Khan, Zhiqiang Lin, Kevin W. Hamlen, and Bhavani M. Thuraisingham. Adaptive encrypted traffic fingerprinting with bi-directional dependence. In *Proceedings of the 32nd Annual Conference on Computer Security Applications, ACSAC 2016, Los Angeles, CA, USA, December 5–9, 2016*, pages 177–188, 2016.

[12] Ezilda Almeida, Carlos Abreu Ferreira, and João Gama. Adaptive model rules from data streams. In *Machine Learning and Knowledge Discovery in Databases - European Conference, ECML PKDD 2013, Prague, Czech Republic, September 23–27, 2013, Proceedings, Part I*, pages 480–492, 2013.

[13] Ezilda Almeida, Carlos Abreu Ferreira, and João Gama. Learning model rules from high-speed data streams. In *Proceedings of the 3rd Workshop on Ubiquitous Data Mining co-located with the 23rd International Joint Conference on Artificial Intelligence (IJCAI 2013), Beijing, China, August 3, 2013*, page 10, 2013.

[14] Noga Alon, Yossi Matias, and Mario Szegedy. The space complexity of approximating the frequency moments. In *Proceedings of the Twenty-Eighth Annual ACM Symposium on the Theory of Computing, Philadelphia, Pennsylvania, USA, May 22–24, 1996*, pages 20–29, 1996.

[15] Jaime Andrés-Merino and Lluís Belanche. Streamleader: A new stream clustering algorithm not based in conventional clustering. In *Artificial Neural Networks and Machine*

Learning, ICANN 2016, 25th International Conference on Artificial Neural Networks, Barcelona, Spain, September 6–9, 2016, Proceedings, Part II, pages 208–215, 2016.

[16] Apache Hadoop. `http://hadoop.apache.org`, accessed May 21st, 2017.

[17] Apache Mahout. `http://mahout.apache.org`, accessed May 21st, 2017.

[18] Marta Arias, Albert Bifet, and Alberto Lumbreras. Framework for sentiment analysis of a stream of texts (a 2012 PASCAL Harvest Project). `http://www.cs.upc.edu/~marias/harvest/`, accessed May 28th, 2017.

[19] David Arthur and Sergei Vassilvitskii. k-means++: The advantages of careful seeding. In *Proceedings of the Eighteenth Annual ACM-SIAM Symposium on Discrete Algorithms, SODA 2007, New Orleans, Louisiana, USA, January 7–9, 2007*, pages 1027–1035, 2007.

[20] Ira Assent, Philipp Kranen, Corinna Baldauf, and Thomas Seidl. Anyout: Anytime outlier detection on streaming data. In *Database Systems for Advanced Applications - 17th International Conference, DASFAA 2012, Busan, South Korea, April 15–19, 2012, Proceedings, Part I*, pages 228–242, 2012.

[21] Lars Backstrom, Paolo Boldi, Marco Rosa, Johan Ugander, and Sebastiano Vigna. Four degrees of separation. In *Web Science 2012, WebSci '12, Evanston, IL, USA, June 22–24, 2012*, pages 33–42, 2012.

[22] Manuel Baena-García, José del Campo-Ávila, Raúl Fidalgo, Albert Bifet, Ricard Gavaldà, and Rafael Morales-Bueno. Early drift detection method. In *Fourth International Workshop on Knowledge Discovery from Data Streams, ECML PKDD*, 2006.

[23] José L. Balcázar, Albert Bifet, and Antoni Lozano. Mining implications from lattices of closed trees. In *Extraction et gestion des connaissances (EGC'2008), Actes des 8èmes journées Extraction et Gestion des Connaissances, Sophia-Antipolis, France, 29 janvier au 1er février 2008, 2 Volumes*, pages 373–384, 2008.

[24] José L. Balcázar, Albert Bifet, and Antoni Lozano. Mining frequent closed rooted trees. *Machine Learning*, 78(1–2):1–33, 2010.

[25] Jean Paul Barddal, Heitor Murilo Gomes, and Fabrício Enembreck. SFNClassifier: A scale-free social network method to handle concept drift. In *Symposium on Applied Computing, SAC 2014, Gyeongju, Republic of Korea, March 24–28, 2014*, pages 786–791, 2014.

[26] Jean Paul Barddal, Heitor Murilo Gomes, and Fabrício Enembreck. SNCStream: A social network-based data stream clustering algorithm. In *Proceedings of the 30th Annual ACM Symposium on Applied Computing, Salamanca, Spain, April 13–17, 2015*, pages 935–940, 2015.

[27] Michèle Basseville and Igor V. Nikiforov. *Detection of abrupt changes: Theory and application*. Prentice-Hall, Inc., Upper Saddle River, NJ, USA, 1993. `http://people.irisa.fr/Michele.Basseville/kniga/`, accessed May 21st, 2017.

[28] Jürgen Beringer and Eyke Hüllermeier. Efficient instance-based learning on data streams. *Intell. Data Anal.*, 11(6):627–650, 2007.

[29] Daniel Berrar. Confidence curves: An alternative to null hypothesis significance testing for the comparison of classifiers. *Machine Learning*, 106(6):911–949, 2017.

[30] Albert Bifet. *Adaptive Stream Mining: Pattern Learning and Mining from Evolving Data Streams*, volume 207 of *Frontiers in Artificial Intelligence and Applications*. IOS Press, 2010.

[31] Albert Bifet, Eibe Frank, Geoff Holmes, and Bernhard Pfahringer. Ensembles of restricted Hoeffding trees. *ACM TIST*, 3(2):30:1–30:20, 2012.

[32] Albert Bifet and Ricard Gavaldà. Learning from time-changing data with adaptive windowing. In *Proceedings of the Seventh SIAM International Conference on Data Mining, April 26–28, 2007, Minneapolis, Minnesota, USA*, pages 443–448, 2007.

[33] Albert Bifet and Ricard Gavaldà. Adaptive learning from evolving data streams. In *Advances in Intelligent Data Analysis VIII, 8th International Symposium on Intelligent Data Analysis, IDA 2009, Lyon, France, August 31 – September 2, 2009. Proceedings*, pages 249–260, 2009.

[34] Albert Bifet and Ricard Gavaldà. Mining frequent closed trees in evolving data streams. *Intell. Data Anal.*, 15(1):29–48, 2011.

[35] Albert Bifet, Geoff Holmes, Bernhard Pfahringer, and Ricard Gavaldà. Mining frequent closed graphs on evolving data streams. In *Proceedings of the 17th ACM SIGKDD International Conference on Knowledge Discovery and Data Mining (KDD 11), San Diego, CA, USA, August 21–24, 2011*, pages 591–599, 2011.

[36] Albert Bifet, Geoffrey Holmes, and Bernhard Pfahringer. Leveraging bagging for evolving data streams. In *Machine Learning and Knowledge Discovery in Databases, European Conference, ECML PKDD 2010, Barcelona, Spain, September 20–24, 2010, Proceedings, Part I*, pages 135–150, 2010.

[37] Albert Bifet, Geoffrey Holmes, Bernhard Pfahringer, and Eibe Frank. Fast perceptron decision tree learning from evolving data streams. In *Advances in Knowledge Discovery and Data Mining, 14th Pacific-Asia Conference, PAKDD 2010, Hyderabad, India, June 21–24, 2010. Proceedings. Part II*, pages 299–310, 2010.

[38] Albert Bifet, Geoffrey Holmes, Bernhard Pfahringer, Richard Kirkby, and Ricard Gavaldà. New ensemble methods for evolving data streams. In *Proceedings of the 15th ACM SIGKDD International Conference on Knowledge Discovery and Data Mining (KDD 09), Paris, France, June 28 – July 1, 2009*, pages 139–148, 2009.

[39] Albert Bifet, Silviu Maniu, Jianfeng Qian, Guangjian Tian, Cheng He, and Wei Fan. StreamDM: Advanced data mining in Spark streaming. In *IEEE International Conference on Data Mining Workshop, ICDMW 2015, Atlantic City, NJ, USA, November 14–17, 2015*, pages 1608–1611, 2015.

[40] Albert Bifet, Gianmarco De Francisci Morales, Jesse Read, Geoff Holmes, and Bernhard Pfahringer. Efficient online evaluation of big data stream classifiers. In *Proceedings of the 21th ACM SIGKDD International Conference on Knowledge Discovery and Data Mining (KDD 15), Sydney, NSW, Australia, August 10–13, 2015*, pages 59–68, 2015.

[41] Albert Bifet, Jesse Read, Bernhard Pfahringer, Geoff Holmes, and Indrė Žliobaitė. CD-MOA: Change detection framework for massive online analysis. In *Advances in Intelligent Data Analysis XII - 12th International Symposium, IDA 2013, London, UK, October 17–19, 2013. Proceedings*, pages 92–103, 2013.

[42] Albert Bifet, Jesse Read, Indrė Žliobaitė, Bernhard Pfahringer, and Geoff Holmes. Pitfalls in benchmarking data stream classification and how to avoid them. In *Machine Learning and Knowledge Discovery in Databases, European Conference, ECML PKDD 2013, Prague, Czech Republic, September 23–27, 2013, Proceedings, Part I*, pages 465–479, 2013.

[43] Albert Bifet, Jiajin Zhang, Wei Fan, Cheng He, Jianfeng Zhang, Jianfeng Qian, Geoff Holmes, and Bernhard Pfahringer. Extremely fast decision tree mining for evolving data streams. In *Proceedings of the 23rd ACM SIGKDD International Conference on Knowledge Discovery and Data Mining (KDD 17), Halifax, Canada, August 14-18, 2017*, 2017, to appear.

[44] Isvani Inocencio Frías Blanco, José del Campo-Ávila, Gonzalo Ramos-Jiménez, Rafael Morales Bueno, Agustín Alejandro Ortiz Díaz, and Yailé Caballero Mota. Online and non-parametric drift detection methods based on Hoeffding's bounds. *IEEE Trans. Knowl. Data Eng.*, 27(3):810–823, 2015.

[45] Joshua Bloch. *Effective Java (2nd Edition) (The Java Series)*. Prentice Hall PTR, Upper Saddle River, NJ, USA, 2 edition, 2008.

[46] Christian Bockermann and Hendrik Blom. The streams Framework. Technical Report 5, TU Dortmund University, 12 2012. http://kissen.cs.uni-dortmund.de: 8080/PublicPublicationFiles/bockermann_blom_2012c.pdf, accessed May 21st, 2017.

[47] Paolo Boldi, Marco Rosa, and Sebastiano Vigna. HyperANF: Approximating the neighbourhood function of very large graphs on a budget. In *Proceedings of the 20th International Conference on World Wide Web, WWW 2011, Hyderabad, India, March 28 – April 1, 2011*, pages 625–634, 2011.

[48] Marc Boullé. MODL: A Bayes optimal discretization method for continuous attributes. *Machine Learning*, 65(1):131–165, 2006.

[49] Christos Boutsidis, Dan Garber, Zohar Shay Karnin, and Edo Liberty. Online principal components analysis. In *Proceedings of the Twenty-Sixth Annual ACM-SIAM Symposium on Discrete Algorithms, SODA 2015, San Diego, CA, USA, January 4–6, 2015*, pages 887–901, 2015.

[50] Robert S. Boyer and J. Strother Moore. MJRTY: A fast majority vote algorithm. In *Automated Reasoning: Essays in Honor of Woody Bledsoe*, pages 105–118, 1991.

[51] Vladimir Braverman, Stephen R. Chestnut, Nikita Ivkin, and David P. Woodruff. Beating CountSketch for heavy hitters in insertion streams. In *Proceedings of the 48th Annual ACM SIGACT Symposium on Theory of Computing, STOC 2016, Cambridge, MA, USA, June 18–21, 2016*, pages 740–753, 2016.

[52] Leo Breiman. Bagging predictors. *Machine Learning*, 24(2):123–140, 1996.

[53] Leo Breiman. Arcing classifiers. *The Annals of Statistics*, 26(3):801–824, 1998.

[54] Leo Breiman. Pasting small votes for classification in large databases and on-line. *Machine Learning*, 36(1–2):85–103, 1999.

[55] Leo Breiman. Random forests. *Machine Learning*, 45(1):5–32, 2001.

[56] Leo Breiman, J. H. Friedman, R. A. Olshen, and C. J. Stone. *Classification and Regression Trees*. The Wadsworth statistics/probability series. Chapman and Hall/CRC, 1984.

[57] Marcel Brun, Chao Sima, Jianping Hua, James Lowey, Brent Carroll, Edward Suh, and Edward R. Dougherty. Model-based evaluation of clustering validation measures. *Pattern Recognition*, 40(3):807–824, 2007.

[58] Dariusz Brzezinski and Jerzy Stefanowski. Reacting to different types of concept drift: The accuracy updated ensemble algorithm. *IEEE Trans. Neural Netw. Learning Syst.*, 25(1):81–94, 2014.

[59] Dariusz Brzezinski and Jerzy Stefanowski. Prequential AUC: Properties of the area under the ROC curve for data streams with concept drift. *Knowledge and Information Systems*, 52(2):531–562, 2017.

[60] P. Bühlmann and B. Yu. Analyzing bagging. *Annals of Statistics*, 30:927–961, 2003.

[61] Feng Cao, Martin Ester, Weining Qian, and Aoying Zhou. Density-based clustering over an evolving data stream with noise. In *Proceedings of the Sixth SIAM International Conference on Data Mining, April 20–22, 2006, Bethesda, MD, USA*, pages 328–339, 2006.

[62] Paris Carbone, Asterios Katsifodimos, Stephan Ewen, Volker Markl, Seif Haridi, and Kostas Tzoumas. Apache Flink^{TM}: Stream and batch processing in a single engine. *IEEE Data Eng. Bull.*, 38(4):28–38, 2015.

[63] Carlos Castillo. *Big Crisis Data: Social Media in Disasters and Time-Critical Situations*. Cambridge University Press, New York, NY, USA, 1st edition, 2016.

[64] Moses Charikar, Kevin C. Chen, and Martin Farach-Colton. Finding frequent items in data streams. *Theor. Comput. Sci.*, 312(1):3–15, 2004.

[65] Shang-Tse Chen, Hsuan-Tien Lin, and Chi-Jen Lu. An online boosting algorithm with theoretical justifications. In *Proceedings of the 29th International Conference on Machine Learning, ICML 2012, Edinburgh, Scotland, UK, June 26 – July 1, 2012*, 2012.

[66] James Cheng, Yiping Ke, and Wilfred Ng. Maintaining frequent closed itemsets over a sliding window. *J. Intell. Inf. Syst.*, 31(3):191–215, 2008.

[67] James Cheng, Yiping Ke, and Wilfred Ng. A survey on algorithms for mining frequent itemsets over data streams. *Knowl. Inf. Syst.*, 16(1):1–27, 2008.

[68] Weiwei Cheng and Eyke Hüllermeier. Combining instance-based learning and logistic regression for multilabel classification. *Machine Learning*, 76(2–3):211–225, 2009.

[69] Yun Chi, Richard R. Muntz, Siegfried Nijssen, and Joost N. Kok. Frequent subtree mining – an overview. *Fundam. Inform.*, 66(1–2):161–198, 2005.

[70] Yun Chi, Haixun Wang, Philip S. Yu, and Richard R. Muntz. Catch the moment: Maintaining closed frequent itemsets over a data stream sliding window. *Knowl. Inf. Syst.*, 10(3):265–294, 2006.

[71] Kai-Min Chung, Michael Mitzenmacher, and Salil P. Vadhan. Why simple hash functions work: Exploiting the entropy in a data stream. *Theory of Computing*, 9:897–945, 2013.

[72] Amanda Clare and Ross D. King. Knowledge discovery in multi-label phenotype data. In *Principles of Data Mining and Knowledge Discovery, 5th European Conference, PKDD 2001, Freiburg, Germany, September 3–5, 2001, Proceedings*, pages 42–53, 2001.

[73] Kenneth L. Clarkson, Petros Drineas, Malik Magdon-Ismail, Michael W. Mahoney, Xiangrui Meng, and David P. Woodruff. The Fast Cauchy Transform and faster robust linear regression. *SIAM J. Comput.*, 45(3):763–810, 2016.

[74] Edith Cohen. Size-estimation framework with applications to transitive closure and reachability. *J. Comput. Syst. Sci.*, 55(3):441–453, 1997.

[75] Edith Cohen. All-distances sketches, revisited: HIP estimators for massive graphs analysis. *IEEE Trans. Knowl. Data Eng.*, 27(9):2320–2334, 2015.

[76] Jacob Cohen. A coefficient of agreement for nominal scales. *Educational and Psychological Measurement*, 20(1):37–46, April 1960.

[77] David A. Cohn, Les E. Atlas, and Richard E. Ladner. Improving generalization with active learning. *Machine Learning*, 15(2):201–221, 1994.

[78] Giorgio Corani and Alessio Benavoli. A Bayesian approach for comparing cross-validated algorithms on multiple data sets. *Machine Learning*, 100(2–3):285–304, 2015.

[79] Graham Cormode, Minos N. Garofalakis, Peter J. Haas, and Chris Jermaine. Synopses for massive data: Samples, histograms, wavelets, sketches. *Foundations and Trends in Databases*, 4(1–3):1–294, 2012.

[80] Graham Cormode and Marios Hadjieleftheriou. Finding the frequent items in streams of data. *Commun. ACM*, 52(10):97–105, 2009.

[81] Graham Cormode and S. Muthu Muthukrishnan. Approximating data with the Count-Min sketch. *IEEE Software*, 29(1):64–69, 2012.

[82] Tamraparni Dasu, Shankar Krishnan, Dongyu Lin, Suresh Venkatasubramanian, and Kevin Yi. Change (detection) you can believe in: Finding distributional shifts in data streams. In *Advances in Intelligent Data Analysis VIII, Proceedings of the 8th International Symposium on Intelligent Data Analysis, IDA 2009*, pages 21–34, 2009.

[83] Mayur Datar, Aristides Gionis, Piotr Indyk, and Rajeev Motwani. Maintaining stream statistics over sliding windows. *SIAM J. Comput.*, 31(6):1794–1813, 2002.

[84] Jonathan de Andrade Silva, Elaine R. Faria, Rodrigo C. Barros, Eduardo R. Hruschka, André Carlos Ponce Leon Ferreira de Carvalho, and João Gama. Data stream clustering: A survey. *ACM Comput. Surv.*, 46(1):13:1–13:31, 2013.

[85] Erico N. de Souza and Stan Matwin. Improvements to Adaboost Dynamic. In *Advances in Artificial Intelligence – 25th Canadian Conference on Artificial Intelligence, Canadian AI 2012, Toronto, ON, Canada, May 28–30, 2012. Proceedings*, pages 293–298, 2012.

[86] Erik D. Demaine, Alejandro López-Ortiz, and J. Ian Munro. Frequency estimation of internet packet streams with limited space. In *Algorithms, ESA 2002, 10th Annual European Symposium, Rome, Italy, September 17–21, 2002, Proceedings*, pages 348–360, 2002.

[87] Thomas G. Dietterich and Ghulum Bakiri. Solving multiclass learning problems via error-correcting output codes. *J. Artif. Intell. Res. (JAIR)*, 2:263–286, 1995.

[88] Pedro M. Domingos and Geoff Hulten. Mining high-speed data streams. In *Proceedings of the Sixth ACM SIGKDD International Conference on Knowledge Discovery and Data Mining (KDD 00), Boston, MA, USA, August 20–23, 2000*, pages 71–80, 2000.

[89] Pedro M. Domingos and Geoff Hulten. A general method for scaling up machine learning algorithms and its application to clustering. In *Proceedings of the Eighteenth International Conference on Machine Learning (ICML 2001), Williams College, Williamstown, MA, USA, June 28 – July 1, 2001*, pages 106–113, 2001.

[90] João Duarte and João Gama. Ensembles of adaptive model rules from high-speed data streams. In *Proceedings of the 3rd International Workshop on Big Data, Streams and Heterogeneous Source Mining: Algorithms, Systems, Programming Models and Applications, BigMine 2014, New York City, USA, August 24, 2014*, pages 198–213, 2014.

[91] João Duarte and João Gama. Multi-target regression from high-speed data streams with adaptive model rules. In *2015 IEEE International Conference on Data Science and Advanced Analytics, DSAA 2015, Campus des Cordeliers, Paris, France, October 19–21, 2015*, pages 1–10, 2015.

[92] João Duarte, João Gama, and Albert Bifet. Adaptive model rules from high-speed data streams. *ACM Transactions on Knowledge Discovery from Data (TKDD)*, 10(3):30:1–30:22, 2016.

[93] Marianne Durand and Philippe Flajolet. Loglog counting of large cardinalities (extended abstract). In *Algorithms, ESA 2003, 11th Annual European Symposium, Budapest, Hungary, September 16–19, 2003, Proceedings*, pages 605–617, 2003.

[94] Benjamin Van Durme and Ashwin Lall. Probabilistic counting with randomized storage. In *IJCAI 2009, Proceedings of the 21st International Joint Conference on Artificial Intelligence, Pasadena, California, USA, July 11–17, 2009*, pages 1574–1579, 2009.

[95] B. Efron. *Large-Scale Inference: Empirical Bayes Methods for Estimation, Testing, and Prediction*. Institute of Mathematical Statistics Monographs. Cambridge University Press, 2010.

[96] Martin Ester, Hans-Peter Kriegel, Jörg Sander, and Xiaowei Xu. A density-based algorithm for discovering clusters in large spatial databases with noise. In *Proceedings of the Second International Conference on Knowledge Discovery and Data Mining (KDD 96), Portland, Oregon, USA*, pages 226–231, 1996.

[97] Min Fang, Narayanan Shivakumar, Hector Garcia-Molina, Rajeev Motwani, and Jeffrey D. Ullman. Computing iceberg queries efficiently. In *VLDB'98, Proceedings of 24th International Conference on Very Large Data Bases, August 24–27, 1998, New York City, New York, USA*, pages 299–310, 1998.

[98] Usama M. Fayyad and Keki B. Irani. Multi-interval discretization of continuous-valued attributes for classification learning. In *Proceedings of the 13th International Joint Conference on Artificial Intelligence. Chambéry, France, August 28 – September 3, 1993*, pages 1022–1029, 1993.

[99] Dan Feldman, Melanie Schmidt, and Christian Sohler. Turning big data into tiny data: Constant-size coresets for *k*-means, PCA and projective clustering. In *Proceedings of the*

Twenty-Fourth Annual ACM-SIAM Symposium on Discrete Algorithms, SODA 2013, New Orleans, Louisiana, USA, January 6-8, 2013, pages 1434–1453, 2013.

[100] Alan Fern and Robert Givan. Online ensemble learning: An empirical study. *Machine Learning*, 53(1–2):71–109, 2003.

[101] Hendrik Fichtenberger, Marc Gillé, Melanie Schmidt, Chris Schwiegelshohn, and Christian Sohler. BICO: BIRCH meets coresets for k-means clustering. In *Algorithms, ESA 2013, 21st Annual European Symposium, Sophia Antipolis, France, September 2–4, 2013. Proceedings*, pages 481–492, 2013.

[102] Douglas H. Fisher. Knowledge acquisition via incremental conceptual clustering. *Machine Learning*, 2(2):139–172, 1987.

[103] Philippe Flajolet. Approximate counting: A detailed analysis. *BIT*, 25(1):113–134, 1985.

[104] Philippe Flajolet, Éric Fusy, Olivier Gandouet, and Frédéric Meunier. Hyperloglog: The analysis of a near-optimal cardinality estimation algorithm. In Philippe Jacquet, editor, *2007 Conference on Analysis of Algorithms, AofA07*, Discrete Mathematics and Theoretical Computer Science Proceedings, pages 127–146, 2007.

[105] Philippe Flajolet and G. Nigel Martin. Probabilistic counting algorithms for data base applications. *J. Comput. Syst. Sci.*, 31(2):182–209, 1985.

[106] Philippe Fournier-Viger, Jerry Chun-Wei Lin, Antonio Gomariz, Ted Gueniche, Azadeh Soltani, Zhihong Deng, and Hoang Thanh Lam. The SPMF open-source data mining library version 2. In *Machine Learning and Knowledge Discovery in Databases – European Conference, ECML PKDD 2016, Riva del Garda, Italy, September 19–23, 2016, Proceedings, Part III*, pages 36–40, 2016.

[107] Eibe Frank, Mark A. Hall, Geoffrey Holmes, Richard Kirkby, Bernhard Pfahringer, Ian H. Witten, and Len Trigg. Weka-a machine learning workbench for data mining. In *Data Mining and Knowledge Discovery Handbook, 2nd ed.*, pages 1269–1277. Springer, 2010.

[108] Yoav Freund and Robert E. Schapire. A decision-theoretic generalization of on-line learning and an application to boosting. *J. Comput. Syst. Sci.*, 55(1):119–139, 1997.

[109] Johannes Fürnkranz, Eyke Hüllermeier, Eneldo Loza Mencía, and Klaus Brinker. Multilabel classification via calibrated label ranking. *Machine Learning*, 73(2):133–153, 2008.

[110] João Gama. *Knowledge Discovery from Data Streams*. Chapman and Hall / CRC Data Mining and Knowledge Discovery Series. CRC Press, 2010.

[111] João Gama, Ricardo Fernandes, and Ricardo Rocha. Decision trees for mining data streams. *Intell. Data Anal.*, 10(1):23–45, 2006.

[112] João Gama and Petr Kosina. Recurrent concepts in data streams classification. *Knowl. Inf. Syst.*, 40(3):489–507, 2014.

[113] João Gama and Pedro Medas. Learning decision trees from dynamic data streams. *J. UCS*, 11(8):1353–1366, 2005.

[114] João Gama, Pedro Medas, Gladys Castillo, and Pedro Pereira Rodrigues. Learning with drift detection. In *Advances in Artificial Intelligence – SBIA 2004, 17th Brazilian Symposium on Artificial Intelligence, São Luis, Maranhão, Brazil, September 29 – October 1, 2004, Proceedings*, pages 286–295, 2004.

[115] João Gama, Raquel Sebastião, and Pedro Pereira Rodrigues. Issues in evaluation of stream learning algorithms. In *Proceedings of the 15th ACM SIGKDD International Conference on Knowledge Discovery and Data Mining (KDD 09), Paris, France, June 28 – July 1, 2009*, pages 329–338, 2009.

[116] João Gama, Indrė Žliobaitė, Albert Bifet, Mykola Pechenizkiy, and Abdelhamid Bouchachia. A survey on concept drift adaptation. *ACM Comput. Surv.*, 46(4):44:1–44:37, 2014.

[117] John Gantz and David Reinsel. The digital universe in 2020: Big data, bigger digital shadows, and biggest growth in the far east, December 2012.

[118] Minos N. Garofalakis, Johannes Gehrke, and Rajeev Rastogi, editors. *Data Stream Management – Processing High-Speed Data Streams*. Data-Centric Systems and Applications. Springer, 2016.

[119] Liqiang Geng and Howard J. Hamilton. Interestingness measures for data mining: A survey. *ACM Comput. Surv.*, 38(3), 2006.

[120] Dimitrios Georgiadis, Maria Kontaki, Anastasios Gounaris, Apostolos N. Papadopoulos, Kostas Tsichlas, and Yannis Manolopoulos. Continuous outlier detection in data streams: An extensible framework and state-of-the-art algorithms. In *Proceedings of the ACM SIGMOD International Conference on Management of Data, SIGMOD 2013, New York, NY, USA, June 22–27, 2013*, pages 1061–1064, 2013.

[121] C. Giannella, J. Han, J. Pei, X. Yan, and P. Yu. Mining frequent patterns in data streams at multiple time granularities. In *Proceedings of the NSF Workshop on Next Generation Data Mining*, pages 191–212, 2002.

[122] Phillip B. Gibbons and Srikanta Tirthapura. Distributed streams algorithms for sliding windows. *Theory of Computing Systems*, 37(3):457–478, 2004.

[123] Shantanu Godbole and Sunita Sarawagi. Discriminative methods for multi-labeled classification. In *Advances in Knowledge Discovery and Data Mining, 8th Pacific-Asia Conference, PAKDD 2004, Sydney, Australia, May 26–28, 2004, Proceedings*, pages 22–30, 2004.

[124] Heitor Murilo Gomes, Jean Paul Barddal, Fabrício Enembreck, and Albert Bifet. A survey on ensemble learning for data stream classification. *ACM Comput. Surv.*, 50(2):23:1–36, 2017.

[125] Heitor Murilo Gomes, Albert Bifet, Jesse Read, Jean Paul Barddal, Fabrício Enembreck, Bernhard Pfharinger, Geoff Holmes, and Talel Abdessalem. Adaptive random forests for evolving data stream classification. *Machine Learning*, 106(9-10):1469–1495, 2017.

[126] Heitor Murilo Gomes and Fabrício Enembreck. SAE2: Advances on the social adaptive ensemble classifier for data streams. In *Symposium on Applied Computing, SAC 2014, Gyeongju, Republic of Korea, March 24–28, 2014*, pages 798–804, 2014.

[127] João Bártolo Gomes, Mohamed Medhat Gaber, Pedro A. C. Sousa, and Ernestina Menasalvas Ruiz. Mining recurring concepts in a dynamic feature space. *IEEE Trans. Neural Netw. Learning Syst.*, 25(1):95–110, 2014.

[128] Vivekanand Gopalkrishnan, David Steier, Harvey Lewis, and James Guszcza. Big data, big business: Bridging the gap. In *Proceedings of the 1st International Workshop on Big Data, Streams and Heterogeneous Source Mining: Algorithms, Systems, Programming Models and Applications (BigMine 2012). Beijing, China, August 12–12, 2012*, pages 7–11. ACM, 2012.

[129] Michael Greenwald and Sanjeev Khanna. Space-efficient online computation of quantile summaries. In *Proceedings of the 2001 ACM SIGMOD International Conference on Management of Data, Santa Barbara, CA, USA, May 21–24, 2001*, pages 58–66, 2001.

[130] Fredrik Gustafsson. *Adaptive Filtering and Change Detection*. Wiley, 2000.

[131] Jiawei Han, Jian Pei, Yiwen Yin, and Runying Mao. Mining frequent patterns without candidate generation: A frequent-pattern tree approach. *Data Min. Knowl. Discov.*, 8(1):53–87, 2004.

[132] Yang Hang and Simon Fong. Incrementally optimized decision tree for noisy big data. In *Proceedings of the 1st International Workshop on Big Data, Streams and Heterogeneous Source Mining: Algorithms, Systems, Programming Models and Applications, BigMine 2012, Beijing, China, August 12, 2012*, pages 36–44, 2012.

[133] Ahsanul Haque, Latifur Khan, and Michael Baron. SAND: semi-supervised adaptive novel class detection and classification over data stream. In *Proceedings of the Thirtieth AAAI Conference on Artificial Intelligence, February 12–17, 2016, Phoenix, Arizona, USA.*, pages 1652–1658, 2016.

[134] Stefan Heule, Marc Nunkesser, and Alexander Hall. Hyperloglog in practice: Algorithmic engineering of a state of the art cardinality estimation algorithm. In *Joint 2013 EDBT/ICDT Conferences, EDBT '13 Proceedings, Genoa, Italy, March 18–22, 2013*, pages 683–692, 2013.

[135] Geoffrey Holmes, Richard Kirkby, and Bernhard Pfahringer. Stress-testing Hoeffding trees. In *Knowledge Discovery in Databases: PKDD 2005, 9th European Conference on Principles and Practice of Knowledge Discovery in Databases, Porto, Portugal, October 3–7, 2005, Proceedings*, pages 495–502, 2005.

[136] David Tse Jung Huang, Yun Sing Koh, Gillian Dobbie, and Russel Pears. Detecting volatility shift in data streams. In *2014 IEEE International Conference on Data Mining, ICDM 2014, Shenzhen, China, December 14–17, 2014*, pages 863–868, 2014.

[137] Geoff Hulten and Pedro Domingos. VFML – a toolkit for mining high-speed time-changing data streams. http://www.cs.washington.edu/dm/vfml/, accessed May 21st, 2017, 2003.

[138] Geoff Hulten, Laurie Spencer, and Pedro M. Domingos. Mining time-changing data streams. In *Proceedings of the Seventh ACM SIGKDD International Conference on Knowledge Discovery and Data Mining (KDD 01), San Francisco, CA, USA, August 26–29, 2001*, pages 97–106, 2001.

[139] Elena Ikonomovska, João Gama, and Saso Dzeroski. Learning model trees from evolving data streams. *Data Min. Knowl. Discov.*, 23(1):128–168, 2011.

[140] Elena Ikonomovska, João Gama, Bernard Zenko, and Saso Dzeroski. Speeding-up Hoeffding-based regression trees with options. In *Proceedings of the 28th International Conference on Machine Learning, ICML 2011, Bellevue, Washington, USA, June 28 – July 2, 2011*, pages 537–544, 2011.

[141] Piotr Indyk and David P. Woodruff. Optimal approximations of the frequency moments of data streams. In *Proceedings of the 37th Annual ACM Symposium on Theory of Computing, Baltimore, MD, USA, May 22–24, 2005*, pages 202–208, 2005.

[142] Chuntao Jiang, Frans Coenen, and Michele Zito. A survey of frequent subgraph mining algorithms. *Knowledge Eng. Review*, 28(1):75–105, 2013.

[143] Paulo Mauricio Gonçalves Jr. and Roberto Souto Maior de Barros. RCD: A recurring concept drift framework. *Pattern Recognition Letters*, 34(9):1018–1025, 2013.

[144] Daniel M. Kane, Jelani Nelson, and David P. Woodruff. An optimal algorithm for the distinct elements problem. In *Proceedings of the Twenty-Ninth ACM SIGMOD-SIGACT-SIGART Symposium on Principles of Database Systems, PODS 2010, June 6–11, 2010, Indianapolis, Indiana, USA*, pages 41–52, 2010.

[145] Richard M. Karp, Scott Shenker, and Christos H. Papadimitriou. A simple algorithm for finding frequent elements in streams and bags. *ACM Trans. Database Syst.*, 28:51–55, 2003.

[146] Michael J. Kearns and Umesh V. Vazirani. *An Introduction to Computational Learning Theory*. MIT Press, 1994.

[147] Jyrki Kivinen and Manfred K. Warmuth. Exponentiated gradient versus gradient descent for linear predictors. *Inf. Comput.*, 132(1):1–63, 1997.

[148] J. Zico Kolter and Marcus A. Maloof. Dynamic weighted majority: An ensemble method for drifting concepts. *Journal of Machine Learning Research*, 8:2755–2790, 2007.

[149] Nicolas Kourtellis, Gianmarco De Francisci Morales, Albert Bifet, and Arinto Murdopo. VHT: Vertical Hoeffding tree. In *2016 IEEE International Conference on Big Data, Big-Data 2016, Washington DC, USA, December 5–8, 2016*, pages 915–922, 2016.

[150] Philipp Kranen, Ira Assent, Corinna Baldauf, and Thomas Seidl. The ClusTree: Indexing micro-clusters for anytime stream mining. *Knowl. Inf. Syst.*, 29(2):249–272, 2011.

[151] Hardy Kremer, Philipp Kranen, Timm Jansen, Thomas Seidl, Albert Bifet, Geoff Holmes, and Bernhard Pfahringer. An effective evaluation measure for clustering on evolving data streams. In *Proceedings of the 17th ACM SIGKDD International Conference on Knowledge Discovery and Data Mining (KDD 11), San Diego, CA, USA, August 21–24, 2011*, pages 868–876, 2011.

[152] Jay Kreps. Questioning the lambda architecture, 2014. `https://www.oreilly.com/ideas/questioning-the-lambda-architecture`, accessed May 21st, 2017.

[153] Ludmila I. Kuncheva. Change detection in streaming multivariate data using likelihood detectors. *IEEE Trans. Knowl. Data Eng.*, 25(5):1175–1180, 2013.

[154] Doug Laney. 3-D Data Management: Controlling Data Volume, Velocity and Variety. *META Group Research Note, february 2001*, 2001. `https://blogs.gartner.com/doug-laney/`, accessed May 21st, 2017.

[155] Herbert K. H. Lee and Merlise A. Clyde. Lossless online Bayesian bagging. *Journal of Machine Learning Research*, 5:143–151, 2004.

[156] Victor E. Lee, Ruoming Jin, and Gagan Agrawal. Frequent pattern mining in data streams. In *Frequent Pattern Mining*, pages 199–224. Springer, 2014.

[157] David D. Lewis and William A. Gale. A sequential algorithm for training text classifiers. In *Proceedings of the 17th Annual International ACM-SIGIR Conference on Research and Development in Information Retrieval. Dublin, Ireland, 3–6 July 1994 (Special Issue of the SIGIR Forum)*, pages 3–12, 1994.

[158] Hua-Fu Li, Man-Kwan Shan, and Suh-Yin Lee. Online mining of frequent query trees over XML data streams. In *Proceedings of the 15th international conference on World Wide Web, WWW 2006, Edinburgh, Scotland, UK, May 23–26, 2006*, pages 959–960, 2006.

[159] Edo Liberty. Simple and deterministic matrix sketching. In *The 19th ACM SIGKDD International Conference on Knowledge Discovery and Data Mining (KDD 2013), Chicago, IL, USA, August 11–14, 2013*, pages 581–588, 2013.

[160] Nick Littlestone and Manfred K. Warmuth. The weighted majority algorithm. *Information and Computation*, 108(2):212–261, feb 1994.

[161] Hongyan Liu, Yuan Lin, and Jiawei Han. Methods for mining frequent items in data streams: An overview. *Knowl. Inf. Syst.*, 26(1):1–30, 2011.

[162] Viktor Losing, Barbara Hammer, and Heiko Wersing. KNN classifier with self adjusting memory for heterogeneous concept drift. In *IEEE 16th International Conference on Data Mining, ICDM 2016, December 12–15, 2016, Barcelona, Spain*, pages 291–300, 2016.

[163] Qiang Ma, S. Muthukrishnan, and Mark Sandler. Frugal streaming for estimating quantiles: One (or two) memory suffices. *CoRR*, abs/1407.1121, 2014.

[164] Nishad Manerikar and Themis Palpanas. Frequent items in streaming data: An experimental evaluation of the state-of-the-art. *Data Knowl. Eng.*, 68(4):415–430, 2009.

[165] Gurmeet Singh Manku and Rajeev Motwani. Approximate frequency counts over data streams. In *VLDB 2002, Proceedings of 28th International Conference on Very Large Data Bases, August 20–23, 2002, Hong Kong, China*, pages 346–357, 2002.

[166] Gurmeet Singh Manku and Rajeev Motwani. Approximate frequency counts over data streams. *Proceedings of the VLDB Endowment*, 5(12):1699, 2012.

[167] Diego Marron, Albert Bifet, and Gianmarco De Francisci Morales. Random forests of very fast decision trees on GPU for mining evolving big data streams. In *ECAI 2014, 21st European Conference on Artificial Intelligence, 18–22 August 2014, Prague, Czech Republic*, pages 615–620, 2014.

[168] Nathan Marz. Storm: distributed and fault-tolerant realtime computation, May 2013. `http://storm-project.net/`, accessed May 21st, 2017.

[169] Nathan Marz and James Warren. *Big Data: Principles and best practices of scalable realtime data systems*. Manning Publications, 2013.

[170] Mohammad M. Masud, Qing Chen, Latifur Khan, Charu C. Aggarwal, Jing Gao, Jiawei Han, Ashok N. Srivastava, and Nikunj C. Oza. Classification and adaptive novel class detection of feature-evolving data streams. *IEEE Trans. Knowl. Data Eng.*, 25(7):1484–1497, 2013.

[171] Andrew Mccallum and Kamal Nigam. A comparison of event models for Naive Bayes text classification. In *AAAI-98 Workshop on Learning for Text Categorization*, 1998.

[172] Andrew McGregor. Graph stream algorithms: A survey. *SIGMOD Record*, 43(1):9–20, 2014.

[173] Quinn McNemar. Note on the sampling error of the difference between correlated proportions or percentages. *Psychometrika*, 12(2):153–157, June 1947.

[174] Luiz F. Mendes, Bolin Ding, and Jiawei Han. Stream sequential pattern mining with precise error bounds. In *Proceedings of the 8th IEEE International Conference on Data Mining (ICDM 2008), December 15–19, 2008, Pisa, Italy*, pages 941–946, 2008.

[175] Ahmed Metwally, Divyakant Agrawal, and Amr El Abbadi. Efficient computation of frequent and top-k elements in data streams. In *Database Theory, ICDT 2005, 10th International Conference, Edinburgh, UK, January 5–7, 2005, Proceedings*, pages 398–412, 2005.

[176] Ahmed Metwally, Divyakant Agrawal, and Amr El Abbadi. Why go logarithmic if we can go linear? Towards effective distinct counting of search traffic. In *EDBT 2008, 11th International Conference on Extending Database Technology, Nantes, France, March 25–29, 2008, Proceedings*, pages 618–629, 2008.

[177] Stanley Milgram. The small world problem. *Psychology Today*, 2:60–67, 1967.

[178] Glenn W. Milligan. A Monte Carlo study of thirty internal criterion measures for cluster analysis. *Psychometrika*, 46(2):187–199, 1981.

[179] Jayadev Misra and David Gries. Finding repeated elements. *Sci. Comput. Program.*, 2(2):143–152, 1982.

[180] Carl Mooney and John F. Roddick. Sequential pattern mining – approaches and algorithms. *ACM Comput. Surv.*, 45(2):19:1–19:39, 2013.

[181] Gianmarco De Francisci Morales and Albert Bifet. SAMOA: Scalable Advanced Massive Online Analysis. *Journal of Machine Learning Research*, 16:149–153, 2015.

[182] Jose G. Moreno-Torres, Troy Raeder, Rocío Alaíz-Rodríguez, Nitesh V. Chawla, and Francisco Herrera. A unifying view on dataset shift in classification. *Pattern Recognition*, 45(1):521–530, 2012.

[183] Robert Morris. Counting large numbers of events in small registers. *Commun. ACM*, 21(10):840–842, 1978.

[184] S. Muthukrishnan, Eric van den Berg, and Yihua Wu. Sequential change detection on data streams. In *Workshops Proceedings of the 7th IEEE International Conference on Data Mining (ICDM 2007), October 28–31, 2007, Omaha, Nebraska, USA*, pages 551–550, 2007.

[185] Hai-Long Nguyen, Yew-Kwong Woon, and Wee Keong Ng. A survey on data stream clustering and classification. *Knowl. Inf. Syst.*, 45(3):535–569, 2015.

[186] Kyosuke Nishida and Koichiro Yamauchi. Detecting concept drift using statistical testing. In *Discovery Science, 10th International Conference, DS 2007, Sendai, Japan, October 1–4, 2007, Proceedings*, pages 264–269, 2007.

[187] David W. Opitz and Richard Maclin. Popular ensemble methods: An empirical study. *J. Artif. Intell. Res. (JAIR)*, 11:169–198, 1999.

[188] Aljaz Osojnik, Pance Panov, and Saso Dzeroski. Multi-label classification via multi-target regression on data streams. *Machine Learning*, 106(6):745–770, 2017.

[189] Nikunj C. Oza and Stuart J. Russell. Experimental comparisons of online and batch versions of bagging and boosting. In *Proceedings of the Seventh ACM SIGKDD International Conference on Knowledge Discovery and Data Mining (KDD 01), San Francisco, CA, USA, August 26–29, 2001*, pages 359–364, 2001.

[190] Nikunj C. Oza and Stuart J. Russell. Online bagging and boosting. In *Proceedings of the Eighth International Workshop on Artificial Intelligence and Statistics, AISTATS 2001, Key West, Florida, US, January 4–7, 2001*, 2001.

[191] E. S. Page. Continuous inspection schemes. *Biometrika*, 41(1/2):100–115, 1954.

[192] Christopher R. Palmer, Phillip B. Gibbons, and Christos Faloutsos. ANF: a fast and scalable tool for data mining in massive graphs. In *Proceedings of the Eighth ACM SIGKDD International Conference on Knowledge Discovery and Data Mining (KDD 02), July 23–26, 2002, Edmonton, Alberta, Canada*, pages 81–90, 2002.

[193] Odysseas Papapetrou, Minos N. Garofalakis, and Antonios Deligiannakis. Sketching distributed sliding-window data streams. *The VLDB Journal*, 24(3):345–368, 2015.

[194] Pallabi Parveen, Nate McDaniel, Varun S. Hariharan, Bhavani M. Thuraisingham, and Latifur Khan. Unsupervised ensemble based learning for insider threat detection. In *2012 International Conference on Privacy, Security, Risk and Trust, PASSAT 2012, and 2012 International Confernece on Social Computing, SocialCom 2012, Amsterdam, Netherlands, September 3–5, 2012*, pages 718–727, 2012.

[195] Pallabi Parveen, Nathan McDaniel, Zackary R. Weger, Jonathan Evans, Bhavani M. Thuraisingham, Kevin W. Hamlen, and Latifur Khan. Evolving insider threat detection stream mining perspective. *International Journal on Artificial Intelligence Tools*, 22(5), 2013.

[196] Russel Pears, Sripirakas Sakthithasan, and Yun Sing Koh. Detecting concept change in dynamic data streams – A sequential approach based on reservoir sampling. *Machine Learning*, 97(3):259–293, 2014.

[197] Raphael Pelossof, Michael Jones, Ilia Vovsha, and Cynthia Rudin. Online coordinate boosting. In *On-line Learning for Computer Vision Workshop (OLCV), 2009 IEEE 12th International Conference on Computer Vision*, 2009.

[198] Bernhard Pfahringer, Geoffrey Holmes, and Richard Kirkby. New options for Hoeffding trees. In *AI 2007: Advances in Artificial Intelligence, 20th Australian Joint Conference on Artificial Intelligence, Gold Coast, Australia, December 2–6, 2007, Proceedings*, pages 90–99, 2007.

[199] Bernhard Pfahringer, Geoffrey Holmes, and Richard Kirkby. Handling numeric attributes in Hoeffding trees. In *Advances in Knowledge Discovery and Data Mining, 12th Pacific-Asia Conference, PAKDD 2008, Osaka, Japan, May 20–23, 2008 Proceedings*, pages 296–307, 2008.

[200] Daryl C. Plummer, Kurt Potter, Richard T. Matlus, Jacqueline Heng, Rolf Jester, Ed Thompson, Adam Sarner, Esteban Kolsky, French Caldwell, John Bace, Neil MacDonald, Brian Gammage, Michael A. Silver, Leslie Fiering, Monica Basso, Ken Dulaney, David Mitchell Smith, Bob Hafner, Mark Fabbi, and Michael A. Bell. Gartner's top predictions for it organizations and users, 2007 and beyond. https://www.gartner.com/doc/498768/gartners-top-predictions-it-organizations, 2006.

[201] Abdulhakim Ali Qahtan, Basma Alharbi, Suojin Wang, and Xiangliang Zhang. A PCA-based change detection framework for multidimensional data streams: Change detection in multidimensional data streams. In *Proceedings of the 21th ACM SIGKDD International Conference on Knowledge Discovery and Data Mining (KDD 15)*, pages 935–944, 2015.

[202] Massimo Quadrana, Albert Bifet, and Ricard Gavaldà. An efficient closed frequent itemset miner for the MOA stream mining system. *AI Commun.*, 28(1):143–158, 2015.

[203] Arturo Montejo Ráez, Luis Alfonso Ureña López, and Ralf Steinberger. Adaptive selection of base classifiers in one-against-all learning for large multi-labeled collections. In *Advances in Natural Language Processing, 4th International Conference, EsTAL 2004, Alicante, Spain, October 20–22, 2004, Proceedings*, pages 1–12, 2004.

[204] Chedy Raïssi, Pascal Poncelet, and Maguelonne Teisseire. Need for speed : Mining sequential patterns in data streams. In *21èmes Journées Bases de Données Avancées, BDA 2005, Saint Malo, 17–20 octobre 2005, Actes (Informal Proceedings).*, 2005.

[205] Sergio Ramírez-Gallego, Bartosz Krawczyk, Salvador García, Michal Wozniak, and Francisco Herrera. A survey on data preprocessing for data stream mining: Current status and future directions. *Neurocomputing*, 239:39–57, 2017.

[206] T. Ramraj and R. Prabhakar. Frequent subgraph mining algorithms: A survey. *Procedia Computer Science*, 47:197–204, 2015.

[207] Abhik Ray, Larry Holder, and Sutanay Choudhury. Frequent subgraph discovery in large attributed streaming graphs. In *Proceedings of the 3rd International Workshop on Big Data, Streams and Heterogeneous Source Mining: Algorithms, Systems, Programming Models and Applications, BigMine 2014, New York City, USA, August 24, 2014*, pages 166–181, 2014.

[208] Jesse Read, Albert Bifet, Geoff Holmes, and Bernhard Pfahringer. Scalable and efficient multi-label classification for evolving data streams. *Machine Learning*, 88(1–2):243–272, 2012.

[209] Jesse Read, Albert Bifet, Bernhard Pfahringer, and Geoff Holmes. Batch-incremental versus instance-incremental learning in dynamic and evolving data. In *Advances in Intelligent Data Analysis XI - 11th International Symposium, IDA 2012, Helsinki, Finland, October 25–27, 2012. Proceedings*, pages 313–323, 2012.

[210] Jesse Read, Bernhard Pfahringer, and Geoffrey Holmes. Multi-label classification using ensembles of pruned sets. In *Proceedings of the 8th IEEE International Conference on Data Mining (ICDM 2008), December 15–19, 2008, Pisa, Italy*, pages 995–1000, 2008.

[211] Jesse Read, Bernhard Pfahringer, Geoffrey Holmes, and Eibe Frank. Classifier chains for multi-label classification. In *Machine Learning and Knowledge Discovery in Databases, European Conference, ECML PKDD 2009, Bled, Slovenia, September 7–11, 2009, Proceedings, Part II*, pages 254–269, 2009.

[212] Jesse Read, Peter Reutemann, Bernhard Pfahringer, and Geoff Holmes. MEKA: A multi-label/multi-target extension to Weka. *Journal of Machine Learning Research*, 17(21):1–5, 2016.

[213] Peter Reutemann and Geoff Holmes. Big data with ADAMS. In *Proceedings of the 4th International Workshop on Big Data, Streams and Heterogeneous Source Mining: Algorithms, Systems, Programming Models and Applications, BigMine 2015, Sydney, Australia, August 10, 2015*, pages 5–8, 2015.

[214] Peter Reutemann and Joaquin Vanschoren. Scientific workflow management with ADAMS. In *Machine Learning and Knowledge Discovery in Databases – European Conference, ECML PKDD 2012, Bristol, UK, September 24–28, 2012. Proceedings, Part II*, pages 833–837, 2012.

[215] Rocco De Rosa and Nicolò Cesa-Bianchi. Splitting with confidence in decision trees with application to stream mining. In *2015 International Joint Conference on Neural Networks, IJCNN 2015, Killarney, Ireland, July 12–17, 2015*, pages 1–8, 2015.

[216] Gordon J. Ross, Niall M. Adams, Dimitris K. Tasoulis, and David J. Hand. Exponentially weighted moving average charts for detecting concept drift. *Pattern Recognition Letters*, 33(2):191–198, 2012. Erratum in Pattern Recognition Letters 33:16, 2261 (2012).

[217] Leszek Rutkowski, Maciej Jaworski, Lena Pietruczuk, and Piotr Duda. A new method for data stream mining based on the misclassification error. *IEEE Trans. Neural Netw. Learning Syst.*, 26(5):1048–1059, 2015.

[218] Leszek Rutkowski, Lena Pietruczuk, Piotr Duda, and Maciej Jaworski. Decision trees for mining data streams based on the McDiarmid's bound. *IEEE Trans. Knowl. Data Eng.*, 25(6):1272–1279, 2013.

[219] Sripirakas Sakthithasan, Russel Pears, Albert Bifet, and Bernhard Pfahringer. Use of ensembles of Fourier spectra in capturing recurrent concepts in data streams. In *2015 International Joint Conference on Neural Networks, IJCNN 2015, Killarney, Ireland, July 12–17, 2015*, pages 1–8, 2015.

[220] Sripirakas Sakthithasan, Russel Pears, and Yun Sing Koh. One pass concept change detection for data streams. In *Advances in Knowledge Discovery and Data Mining, 17th Pacific-Asia Conference, PAKDD 2013, Gold Coast, Australia, April 14–17, 2013, Proceedings, Part II*, pages 461–472, 2013.

[221] Tamás Sarlós. Improved approximation algorithms for large matrices via random projections. In *47th Annual IEEE Symposium on Foundations of Computer Science (FOCS 2006), 21–24 October 2006, Berkeley, California, USA, Proceedings*, pages 143–152, 2006.

[222] Robert E. Schapire. Using output codes to boost multiclass learning problems. In *Proceedings of the Fourteenth International Conference on Machine Learning (ICML 1997), Nashville, Tennessee, USA, July 8–12, 1997*, pages 313–321, 1997.

[223] Jeffrey C. Schlimmer and Richard H. Granger. Incremental learning from noisy data. *Machine Learning*, 1(3):317–354, 1986.

[224] B. Settles. Active learning literature survey. Computer Sciences Technical Report 1648, University of Wisconsin–Madison, 2009. https://research.cs.wisc.edu/techreports/2009/TR1648.pdf, accessed May 21st, 2017.

[225] Ammar Shaker and Eyke Hüllermeier. IBLStreams: A system for instance-based classification and regression on data streams. *Evolving Systems*, 3(4):235–249, 2012.

[226] Shai Shalev-Shwartz, Yoram Singer, Nathan Srebro, and Andrew Cotter. Pegasos: Primal estimated sub-gradient solver for SVM. *Math. Program.*, 127(1):3–30, 2011.

[227] Jin Shieh and Eamonn J. Keogh. Polishing the right apple: Anytime classification also benefits data streams with constant arrival times. In *ICDM 2010, The 10th IEEE International Conference on Data Mining, Sydney, Australia, 14–17 December 2010*, pages 461–470, 2010.

[228] R. Smolan and J. Erwitt. *The Human Face of Big Data*. Sterling Publishing Company Incorporated, 2012.

[229] Mohiuddin Solaimani, Mohammed Iftekhar, Latifur Khan, Bhavani M. Thuraisingham, Joey Burton Ingram, and Sadi Evren Seker. Online anomaly detection for multi-source vmware using a distributed streaming framework. *Softw., Pract. Exper.*, 46(11):1479–1497, 2016.

[230] Guojie Song, Dongqing Yang, Bin Cui, Baihua Zheng, Yunfeng Liu, and Kunqing Xie. CLAIM: An efficient method for relaxed frequent closed itemsets mining over stream data. In *Advances in Databases: Concepts, Systems and Applications, 12th International Conference on Database Systems for Advanced Applications, DASFAA 2007, Bangkok, Thailand, April 9–12, 2007, Proceedings*, pages 664–675, 2007.

[231] Mingzhou (Joe) Song and Lin Zhang. Comparison of cluster representations from partial second- to full fourth-order cross moments for data stream clustering. In *Proceedings of the 8th IEEE International Conference on Data Mining (ICDM 2008), December 15–19, 2008, Pisa, Italy*, pages 560–569, 2008.

[232] Ricardo Sousa and João Gama. Online semi-supervised learning for multi-target regression in data streams using AMRules. In *Advances in Intelligent Data Analysis XV – 15th International Symposium, IDA 2016, Stockholm, Sweden, October 13–15, 2016, Proceedings*, pages 123–133, 2016.

[233] W. Nick Street and YongSeog Kim. A streaming ensemble algorithm (SEA) for large-scale classification. In *Proceedings of the Seventh ACM SIGKDD International Conference on Knowledge Discovery and Data Mining (KDD 01), San Francisco, CA, USA, August 26–29, 2001*, pages 377–382, 2001.

[234] Gábor Takács, István Pilászy, Bottyán Németh, and Domonkos Tikk. Scalable collaborative filtering approaches for large recommender systems. *Journal of Machine Learning Research*, 10:623–656, 2009.

[235] Grigorios Tsoumakas and Ioannis P. Vlahavas. Random k-labelsets: An ensemble method for multilabel classification. In *Machine Learning: ECML 2007, 18th European Conference on Machine Learning, Warsaw, Poland, September 17–21, 2007, Proceedings*, pages 406–417, 2007.

[236] United Nations Global Pulse. Harnessing big data for development and humanitarian action. http://www.unglobalpulse.org, accessed May 21st, 2017.

[237] Matthijs van Leeuwen and Arno Siebes. Streamkrimp: Detecting change in data streams. In *Proceedings of the European Conference on Machine Learning and Knowledge Discovery in Databases, ECML/PKDD 2008*, pages 672–687, 2008.

[238] Joaquin Vanschoren, Jan N. van Rijn, and Bernd Bischl. Taking machine learning research online with OpenML. In *Proceedings of the 4th International Workshop on Big Data, Streams and Heterogeneous Source Mining: Algorithms, Systems, Programming Models and Applications, BigMine 2015, Sydney, Australia, August 10, 2015*, pages 1–4, 2015.

[239] Joaquin Vanschoren, Jan N. van Rijn, Bernd Bischl, and Luis Torgo. OpenML: Networked science in machine learning. *SIGKDD Explorations*, 15(2):49–60, 2013.

[240] Jeffrey Scott Vitter. Random sampling with a reservoir. *ACM Trans. Math. Softw.*, 11(1):37–57, 1985.

[241] Anh Thu Vu, Gianmarco De Francisci Morales, João Gama, and Albert Bifet. Distributed adaptive model rules for mining big data streams. In *2014 IEEE International Conference on Big Data, Big Data 2014, Washington, DC, USA, October 27–30, 2014*, pages 345–353, 2014.

[242] Kiri Wagstaff. Machine learning that matters. In *Proceedings of the 29th International Conference on Machine Learning, ICML 2012, Edinburgh, Scotland, UK, June 26 - July 1, 2012*, 2012.

[243] Boyu Wang and Joelle Pineau. Online bagging and boosting for imbalanced data streams. *IEEE Trans. Knowl. Data Eng.*, 28(12):3353–3366, 2016.

[244] Haixun Wang, Wei Fan, Philip S. Yu, and Jiawei Han. Mining concept-drifting data streams using ensemble classifiers. In *Proceedings of the Ninth ACM SIGKDD International Conference on Knowledge Discovery and Data Mining (KDD 03), Washington, DC, USA, August 24–27, 2003*, pages 226–235, 2003.

[245] Greg Welch and Gary Bishop. An introduction to the Kalman Filter, Manuscript, 1995. https://www.cs.unc.edu/~welch/media/pdf/kalman_intro.pdf, accessed May 21st, 2017.

[246] Kyu-Young Whang, Brad T. Vander Zanden, and Howard M. Taylor. A linear-time probabilistic counting algorithm for database applications. *ACM Trans. Database Syst.*, 15(2):208–229, 1990.

[247] David H. Wolpert. Stacked generalization. *Neural Networks*, 5(2):241–259, 1992.

[248] David P. Woodruff. Sketching as a tool for numerical linear algebra. *Foundations and Trends in Theoretical Computer Science*, 10(1–2):1–157, 2014.

[249] David P. Woodruff. New algorithms for heavy hitters in data streams (invited talk). In *19th International Conference on Database Theory, ICDT 2016, Bordeaux, France, March 15–18, 2016*, pages 4:1–4:12, 2016.

[250] Junjie Wu, Hui Xiong, and Jian Chen. Adapting the right measures for k-means clustering. In *Proceedings of the 15th ACM SIGKDD International Conference on Knowledge Discovery and Data Mining (KDD09), Paris, France, June 28 – July 1, 2009*, pages 877–886, 2009.

[251] Xifeng Yan and Jiawei Han. gspan: Graph-based substructure pattern mining. In *Proceedings of the 2002 IEEE International Conference on Data Mining (ICDM 2002), 9–12 December 2002, Maebashi City, Japan*, pages 721–724, 2002.

[252] Xifeng Yan and Jiawei Han. Closegraph: Mining closed frequent graph patterns. In *Proceedings of the Ninth ACM SIGKDD International Conference on Knowledge Discovery and Data Mining (KDD 03), Washington, DC, USA, August 24–27, 2003*, pages 286–295, 2003.

[253] Matei Zaharia, Reynold S. Xin, Patrick Wendell, Tathagata Das, Michael Armbrust, Ankur Dave, Xiangrui Meng, Josh Rosen, Shivaram Venkataraman, Ali Ghodsi, Joseph Gonzalez, Scott Shenker, and Ion Stoica. Apache Spark: A unified engine for big data processing. *Commun. ACM*, 59(11):56–65, 2016.

[254] Mohammed Javeed Zaki and Ching-Jiu Hsiao. CHARM: an efficient algorithm for closed itemset mining. In *Proceedings of the Second SIAM International Conference on Data Mining, Arlington, VA, USA, April 11–13, 2002*, pages 457–473, 2002.

[255] Mohammed Javeed Zaki, Nagender Parimi, Nilanjana De, Feng Gao, Benjarath Phoophakdee, Joe Urban, Vineet Chaoji, Mohammad Al Hasan, and Saeed Salem. Towards generic pattern mining. In *Formal Concept Analysis, Third International Conference, ICFCA 2005, Lens, France, February 14–18, 2005, Proceedings*, pages 1–20, 2005.

[256] Mohammed Javeed Zaki, Srinivasan Parthasarathy, Mitsunori Ogihara, and Wei Li. New algorithms for fast discovery of association rules. In *Proceedings of the Third ACM SIGKDD International Conference on Knowledge Discovery and Data Mining (KDD 97), Newport Beach, California, USA, August 14–17, 1997*, pages 283–286, 1997.

[257] Peng Zhang, Byron J. Gao, Xingquan Zhu, and Li Guo. Enabling fast lazy learning for data streams. In *11th IEEE International Conference on Data Mining, ICDM 2011, Vancouver, BC, Canada, December 11–14, 2011*, pages 932–941, 2011.

[258] Tian Zhang, Raghu Ramakrishnan, and Miron Livny. BIRCH: An efficient data clustering method for very large databases. In *Proceedings of the 1996 ACM SIGMOD International Conference on Management of Data, Montreal, Quebec, Canada, June 4–6, 1996.*, pages 103–114, 1996.

[259] Ji Zhu, Hui Zou, Saharon Rosset, and Trevor Hastie. Multi-class Adaboost. *Statistics and Its Interface*, 2:349–360, 2009.

[260] Paul Zikopoulos, Chris Eaton, Dirk deRoos, Tom Deutsch, and George Lapis. *IBM Understanding Big Data: Analytics for Enterprise Class Hadoop and Streaming Data*. McGraw-Hill Companies, Incorporated, 2011.

[261] Indrė Žliobaitė, Albert Bifet, Bernhard Pfahringer, and Geoff Holmes. Active learning with evolving streaming data. In *Machine Learning and Knowledge Discovery in Databases,*

European Conference, ECML PKDD 2011, Athens, Greece, September 5–9, 2011, Proceedings, Part III, pages 597–612, 2011.

[262] Indrė Žliobaitė, Albert Bifet, Jesse Read, Bernhard Pfahringer, and Geoff Holmes. Evaluation methods and decision theory for classification of streaming data with temporal dependence. *Machine Learning*, 98(3):455–482, 2015.

Index

Adaptive Computation and Machine Learning

Francis Bach, Editor

Christopher Bishop, David Heckerman, Michael Jordan, and Michael Kearns, Associate Editors

Bioinformatics: The Machine Learning Approach, Pierre Baldi and Søren Brunak

Reinforcement Learning: An Introduction, Richard S. Sutton and Andrew G. Barto

Graphical Models for Machine Learning and Digital Communication, Brendan J. Frey

Learning in Graphical Models, Michael I. Jordan

Causation, Prediction, and Search, second edition, Peter Spirtes, Clark Glymour, and Richard Scheines

Principles of Data Mining, David Hand, Heikki Mannila, and Padhraic Smyth

Bioinformatics: The Machine Learning Approach, second edition, Pierre Baldi and Søren Brunak

Learning Kernel Classifiers: Theory and Algorithms, Ralf Herbrich

Learning with Kernels: Support Vector Machines, Regularization, Optimization, and Beyond, Bernhard Schölkopf and Alexander J. Smola

Introduction to Machine Learning, Ethem Alpaydin

Gaussian Processes for Machine Learning, Carl Edward Rasmussen and Christopher K.I. Williams

Printed in the United States
by Baker & Taylor Publisher Services